gateway
to the world

B2

Student's Book
with Digital Student's Book

macmillan
education

David Spencer

App

Welcome to

gateway
to the world

GREAT LEARNERS
GREAT THINKERS

Learn about the world through real-world documentary video and improve your thinking skills by following Visible Thinking Routines. This section, along with the Learner Profile, also helps develop your Social and Emotional intelligence.

Collaborative projects and Virtual Classroom Exchange

Become a global citizen and build meaningful connections with students in other regions and countries by sharing your culture, via a project and a Virtual Classroom Exchange.

Real-world content

Gateway to the World is full of real-world content. You aren't only learning a language, you are also learning about real people, events and places.

David Spencer

David Spencer, best-selling author, is still teaching Secondary students. He knows what you like and what is interesting for you in the classroom, and brings this knowledge to his writing.

On-the-Go Practice

Use On-the-Go Practice to improve your English with gamified content. Win rewards in challenge mode and have fun while you learn.

Flipped classroom grammar presentation videos

All-new grammar presentation videos in four different styles help you understand English grammar, before, during or after class.

Contents

Contents 5

1 MAKE THE GRADE

Vocabulary in context

School life

Higher education

1 **SPEAKING** Read the questions and answers. What words do you think are missing?

UK SIXTH FORM CASE STUDY
Emma Johnstone (16)

Q: How many (a) .... does your academic year have?

A: Three. The first one always starts in September and finishes in December.

Q: How many (b) .... do you study and which ones?

A: Most people study three or four in the last two years of school, which we call Sixth Form in the UK. I study four. Biology, chemistry, maths and French.

Q: Do you want to go on to (c) .... when you finish school?

A: Yes, I want to study Veterinary science.

Q: What (d) .... do you usually get?

A: They're pretty high, for example A or A+.

Q: What's your (e) .... like?

A: I usually start at 9 am and finish at 4 pm, but two days a week, I finish earlier.

Q: Do you have exams or is it (f) ....?

A: Nowadays about 80% of our mark depends on exams. The rest is a question of our (g) ...., including (h) .... You need to keep all the (i) .... you make in class up to date – you know, everything you write down.

Q: Would you like to study (j) .... one day?

A: Yes. I think I'd like to spend a year studying in the US or Canada.

2 Complete the spaces in 1 with the correct form of the words in the box. One word is not used.

01 School life
abroad • assignment • break • continuous assessment • coursework • grade/mark • higher education • notes • subject • term • timetable

3 **SPEAKING** Take it in turns to ask and answer each question in 1. Give details similar to the examples in 1.

4 Read the text and check that you understand the words in bold. Use a dictionary if necessary.

Culture exchange

Getting started: Studying in the UK

UK universities organise an **induction week** to give information to new students about studying at their new uni. As part of this week, they often organise trips to show students the whole of the **campus**, especially the **lecture halls** where you **attend** your lessons, depending on the **degree** you are studying for. But they also show you all the other **facilities**, such as the library (usually open 24 hours and with a full range of digital **resources**), sports facilities, cafés, shops, fresh food markets and maybe even clubs.

In induction week, you usually meet your **personal tutor** who gives you academic and personal guidance. You also get your timetable with all the **lectures** and **tutorials** you need to attend. You may meet some of your **lecturers**, too.

Everybody who starts at uni in the UK automatically becomes a member of that uni's Student Union, which helps to organise all sorts of societies, clubs and events. Part of induction week is the freshers' fair, an event where new students can find out about all the **extra-curricular** activities that are organised.

The Student Union helps all students, both **undergraduates** and **postgraduates**. They can give you **academic support** and advice about **student finance**. Some people receive a **scholarship** to help pay for university. Most people receive **student loans** to pay for their lessons and maybe for **student accommodation**, too.

Collaborative project 1 > page 31

Use it ... don't lose it!

5 **SPEAKING** Complete the questions with words in 4. Then use them to interview your partner.

1 What special .... are there for students in your school, e.g. for studying, food and drink or sports?

2 What digital .... does your school have for students and teachers?

3 At school, do you have a personal .... who can help you with studies and other things?

Reach higher > page 136

Reading

1 **SPEAKING** 👥 Describe what you can see in the photos on this page.

2 Read the Internet forum replies (a–e) and write the name of each extra-curricular activity or club.

a .... b .... c .... d .... e ....

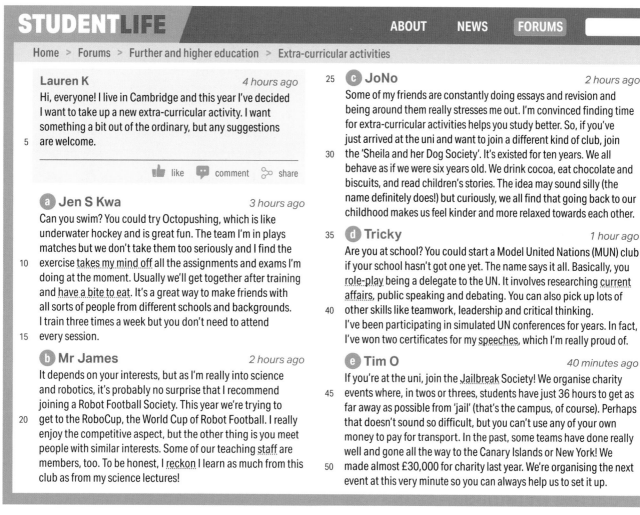

STUDENTLIFE   ABOUT   NEWS   **FORUMS**   🔍

Home > Forums > Further and higher education > Extra-curricular activities

Lauren K   *4 hours ago*
Hi, everyone! I live in Cambridge and this year I've decided I want to take up a new extra-curricular activity. I want something a bit out of the ordinary, but any suggestions
5 are welcome.

👍 like   💬 comment   ⌘ share

a Jen S Kwa   *3 hours ago*
Can you swim? You could try Octopushing, which is like underwater hockey and is great fun. The team I'm in plays matches but we don't take them too seriously and I find the
10 exercise takes my mind off all the assignments and exams I'm doing at the moment. Usually we'll get together after training and have a bite to eat. It's a great way to make friends with all sorts of people from different schools and backgrounds. I train three times a week but you don't need to attend
15 every session.

b Mr James   *2 hours ago*
It depends on your interests, but as I'm really into science and robotics, it's probably no surprise that I recommend joining a Robot Football Society. This year we're trying to
20 get to the RoboCup, the World Cup of Robot Football. I really enjoy the competitive aspect, but the other thing is you meet people with similar interests. Some of our teaching staff are members, too. To be honest, I reckon I learn as much from this club as from my science lectures!

25 **c JoNo**   *2 hours ago*
Some of my friends are constantly doing essays and revision and being around them really stresses me out. I'm convinced finding time for extra-curricular activities helps you study better. So, if you've just arrived at the uni and want to join a different kind of club, join
30 the 'Sheila and her Dog Society'. It's existed for ten years. We all behave as if we were six years old. We drink cocoa, eat chocolate and biscuits, and read children's stories. The idea may sound silly (the name definitely does!) but curiously, we all find that going back to our childhood makes us feel kinder and more relaxed towards each other.

35 **d Tricky**   *1 hour ago*
Are you at school? You could start a Model United Nations (MUN) club if your school hasn't got one yet. The name says it all. Basically, you role-play being a delegate to the UN. It involves researching current affairs, public speaking and debating. You can also pick up lots of
40 other skills like teamwork, leadership and critical thinking. I've been participating in simulated UN conferences for years. In fact, I've won two certificates for my speeches, which I'm really proud of.

e Tim O   *40 minutes ago*
If you're at the uni, join the Jailbreak Society! We organise charity
45 events where, in twos or threes, students have just 36 hours to get as far away as possible from 'jail' (that's the campus, of course). Perhaps that doesn't sound so difficult, but you can't use any of your own money to pay for transport. In the past, some teams have done really well and gone all the way to the Canary Islands or New York! We
50 made almost £30,000 for charity last year. We're organising the next event at this very minute so you can always help us to set it up.

☑ **Exam tip**

In reading activities where you match questions or statements with different texts, remember that the words in the question may not be exactly the same as those in the text.

3 📢02 Match the people (a–e) to the questions below.

Which person ...
1 thinks the name of their club clearly reflects what people in the club do? ....
2 doesn't care much about winning matches or competitions? ....
3 thinks their club can alter your personality? ....
4 talks about a club where the duration of the activity is very important? ....
5 thinks their club helps them to learn more about the subject(s) they enjoy? ....

4 **SPEAKING** 👥 Which of the extra-curricular activities would you like to do and why?

5 What do the underlined words in the text mean? Guess and then check in your dictionary.

6 ⚙ **Critical thinkers**

In your opinion, how beneficial could each of these extra-curricular activities be for you?

What makes you say that?

Use ideas from the text and/or other facts, opinions and experiences to justify your opinion. Then share your ideas.

Reach higher > page 136

Grammar in context 1

Present simple, present continuous and present habits

1a Look at the verbs in these sentences and name the tenses.

1 I **train** three times a week.
2 We**'re organising** the next event at this very minute.
3 Exercise **takes** your mind off assignments.
4 My friends **are** constantly **doing** essays and that stresses me out.
5 Usually we**'ll get** together after training.
6 The name of the club definitely **sounds** silly.

1b Read the explanations and match them to the sentences in 1a.

a We use the **present simple** for routines and habits. ....

b We use the **present simple** for things that are generally or always true. ....

c We use the **present simple**, not the present continuous, for verbs that describe states and situations, not actions. ....

d We use the **present continuous** for actions that are happening at or around the moment of speaking. ....

e We can use the **present continuous** with *always, constantly, continually* or *forever* when a habit annoys or irritates us. ....

f We can use **will** with adverbs or expressions of frequency to talk about present habits and routines. ....

☑ Check it **page 16**

2 Complete the text with the present simple or present continuous form of the verbs given.

ABOUT   LATEST NEWS   🔍

Wearing pyjamas in class

I (a) .... (have) a sister who's two years older than me. Sometimes my parents (b) .... (get) angry with her because she (c) .... (always wear) her pyjamas at home, literally all day! Anyway, she (d) .... (start) university at the moment and she's discovered a society that (e) .... (sound) perfect for her. It's called the KiguSoc. (f) .... you .... (know) what a *kigu* is? It's a Japanese word that (g) .... (describe) an animal onesie (pyjamas in just one piece). Members of the society (h) .... (believe) that any activity is better with a *kigu*. It's 10 am now and I (i) .... (think) my sister (j) .... (meet) her tutor for the first time at this very moment. I (k) .... (hope) she (l) .... (not wear) a *kigu* for that!

Flipped classroom video
Watch the Grammar Presentation video

3a Write three sentences with *will* and adverbs/ expressions of frequency to talk about some of your typical habits and routines. Then write three sentences with the present continuous and *always, constantly, forever* or *continually* to talk about other people's annoying habits.

3b SPEAKING 👥 Compare your sentences. What things do you have in common?

Present perfect simple and present perfect continuous

4a Match sentences 1–4 to the explanation of their uses (a–d).

1 The club **has existed** for ten years.
2 In the past, some teams **have done** really well.
3 You**'ve just arrived** at uni.
4 I**'ve won** two prizes, which I'm really proud of.

a An action or situation which started in the past and continues in the present
b An action that happened at an unspecified moment in the past
c A past action which has a result in the present
d An action finished very recently

4b Look at these sentences. Which is present perfect simple and which is present perfect continuous? How do we form these tenses?

1 I**'ve been participating** in conferences for years.
2 I**'ve joined** three clubs.

4c Which tense gives more importance to ...

1 the completion and result of an action?
2 the process and duration of an action?
3 quantities, e.g. how many times an action happens?
4 the fact that an action is temporary, incomplete or has finished very recently?

☑ Check it **page 16**

5 **SPEAKING** 👥 These words often go with the present perfect simple or present perfect continuous. Talk about why and how we use the words.

1	for	5	just
2	since	6	already
3	ever	7	yet
4	never		

> For *goes with periods of time, like* three hours, ten minutes, *or* a long time. *It goes just before the time period.*

6 Rewrite these sentences to correct or improve them.

1 I never have tried Octopushing.
2 Have you been switching the light off?
3 My sister has been reading six novels this month.
4 I've waited here for my friend to arrive for half an hour.
5 We've won five matches yet.
6 I've been passing six exams.
7 I've been at this school since two years.
8 We've walked for ages.
9 They've done this exam for two hours but they haven't finished yet.
10 I knew him since the summer.
11 Oh no! My phone! I lost it.
12 I haven't been finishing my essay yet.

7 Complete these questions with the present perfect simple or present perfect continuous.

1 How long have you ....?
2 How long have you been ....?
3 Have you ever ....?
4 How many times have you ....?
5 What have you just ....?
6 Have you already ....?
7 Have you .... yet?

> **Use it ... don't lose it!**
>
> **8** **SPEAKING** 👥 Interview your partner with the completed questions in 7. Tell the class one interesting thing you found out about your partner.

Reach higher 〉 page 136

Developing vocabulary

do and *make*

1 Look at these words. Do they usually go with *do* or *make*? Write two lists.

> a cake • a choice • a course • a decision • a degree • a favour • a mistake • a noise • a phone call • a plan • a promise • a suggestion • an (extra-curricular) activity • an appointment • an assignment • an effort • an essay • an exam • an excuse • an offer • business • chores • friends • homework • money • progress • sport • the dinner • the shopping • the washing • well • your best • your hair

2 Complete the sentences with *do* or *make*.

1 We usually use .... with work at school or university.
2 We usually use .... with work around the house.
3 We usually use .... with things we produce, create or construct.
4 We usually use .... when we talk about activities in general.

3 Complete the text with *do* or *make*.

> **BLOG**   About | Latest posts | Archives 🔍
>
> ## STUDYING AS YOU GET OLDER
>
> Most students who (a) .... well at secondary school (b) .... the decision to carry on into further or higher education. As you get older, you often have more options, which usually means you can choose to (c) .... the course or subjects that you enjoy and are good at. Of course, you'll probably still have to (d) .... lots of assignments and exams if you want to (e) .... your best and (f) .... good progress. The main difference as you get older is that now you generally need to (g) .... your own plans, because your teachers won't always be telling you what to (h) .... and when. And your parents may give you more freedom, too. Imagine what it's like in the UK, where university students often live away from home. That means they need to (i) .... chores themselves. They need to (j) .... the shopping and washing and probably (k) .... their own meals. With so much studying and other work, it's good to stay fit and (l) .... sport and physical exercise. This can also help you to meet other people and (m) .... friends with them. If you (n) .... a little effort, these can be the best years of your life!

4 Choose three expressions with *do* and three with *make*. Use the expressions to write questions to ask other people in your class.

Have you made any decisions about your future?
Which chores do you usually do at home?
How many phone calls do you make every day?

> **Use it ... don't lose it!**
>
> **5** **SPEAKING** 👥 Interview your partner and then as many other people as possible with your questions in 4.

Reach higher 〉 page 136

GREAT LEARNERS
GREAT THINKERS

STUDY CHOICES

Lesson aim: To think about how to make good decisions and study choices

Video: A day in the life of a forensic science student

SEL **Social and emotional learning:** Making balanced decisions

1 **SPEAKING** **Ask and answer these questions.**

1 Have you decided yet where you would like to go when you finish studying at school? If so, do you know what you would like to study/do there?

2 What do you know about the subject of 'forensic science'? Would you be interested in studying this subject? Why/Why not?

3 What do you imagine a forensic science student does on a typical school day?

2 **VIDEO** Watch a video of a forensic science student called Angela talking about a typical day in her life. Were any of your predictions in 1 right?

3 **VIDEO** Watch again and complete the sentences with between one and three words.

1 It's important for Angela to investigate the .... that people commit their crimes. That can change the way you do ....

2 She has lunch in ....

3 After lunch she worked on her .... where she had to .... a pair of trousers.

4 It would be good to find the same fibres on the trousers as at the ....

GREAT THINKERS

Compass points (N-S-E-W)

4 **SPEAKING** With a partner, talk about the next time you will need to make decisions about your studies, for example choosing different subject options or passing from one stage of education to another (e.g. from school to vocational training or university).

1 What would you **need** to know that could help you to prepare for the situation?

2 What **steps** could you take to deal with the situation in a positive way?

3 What could be **exciting** about being in this situation? What positives are there?

4 What **worries** would you have in this situation? What could be negative about it?

5 Read this text about making decisions. What do you think of the advice?

Making the RIGHT choice

When you have a difficult choice to make, remember to do it the **RIGHT** way.

1 Take time to research and list all the **Real info** from reliable sources that could help you decide intelligently.

2 Think about what you can do **Instead**. Measure the pros and cons of the different choices you have.

3 Get the opinions of parents, teachers, friends and experts you trust and pay attention to them. What do you **Gain or lose** from their ideas?

4 With all of this advice, decide what will work best and make things **Happen**.

5 After a while, you should revisit your choice and **Test** its impact. Did you make the right decision or not? Think about how happy you are now with your decision, but remember not to expect perfection.

6 **SPEAKING** Think about your next study decisions and answer these questions.

1 Where or how could you find out the facts that you need to know in order to make an intelligent decision?

2 Apart from facts, how important do you think feelings are when you make your choices?

3 Who will you ask for advice? Who do you think will be most helpful and why?

GREAT LEARNERS SEL

Great learners are good decision makers.

How important is it to make sensible, balanced decisions as you get older? Why?

Learner profile > page 142

Listening

1 **SPEAKING** 👥 What do you think are the advantages and disadvantages of studying abroad in a secondary school for a year? Make two lists.

2 🔊 03 Listen to two students, Poppy and Harry, talking about their experiences of studying abroad. Which of your ideas in 1 do they mention?

3 🔊 03 Who says these statements? Write *Poppy*, *Harry* or *Both*. Don't worry about the words or phrases in bold. Listen again to check.

1 **Studying** abroad is expensive. ....

2 It's hard **to make** friends when you don't speak the language. ....

3 I love **experiencing** new things. ....

4 Go to classes **to learn** the language before studying abroad. ....

5 I've always been interested in **learning** languages. ....

6 I went **swimming** in the middle of the week. ....

7 It wasn't too far **to come** and go from England. ....

8 I suggest **reading** about the country before you go. ....

9 I needed **to study** a lot of things when I came back to the UK. ....

4 ⚙️ **Critical thinkers**

> In your opinion, are there more advantages or disadvantages to studying abroad for a year?
>
> What makes you say that?
>
> Use ideas from the listening and/or other facts, opinions and experiences to justify your opinion. Then share your ideas.

Grammar in context 2

Gerunds and infinitives 1

1 **Match statements 1–9 in Listening exercise 3 to these rules.**

We use the **gerund** ...

a as the subject/object of a sentence. ...1...

b with *go* to talk about physical activities. ....

c after prepositions. ....

d after verbs of liking or disliking (except when the verb goes with *would*, e.g. *would like, would prefer*). ....

e after certain verbs like *admit, avoid, consider, involve, recommend, risk, suggest*. ....

We use the **infinitive** ...

f to explain why somebody does something. ....

g immediately after adjectives. ....

h after *too, enough, the first, the last*. ....

i after certain verbs like *agree, appear, arrange, ask, decide, expect, help, learn, manage, need, promise, seem, try, want*. ....

☑ Check it **page 16**

2 **Is the gerund or infinitive used correctly in each sentence? If not, rewrite it.**

1 I managed to learn Portuguese after six months in Brazil.

2 My friend seems finding German easy.

3 I usually avoid to do the housework.

4 I decided not to study abroad next year.

5 I was the first British student studying in the school.

6 The exams seem easy here so I expect passing them all.

7 My American friend suggested go to school in the US.

8 You risk to feel lonely if you can't speak the language.

9 Have you ever considered to live in another country?

10 My friend promised helping me to learn the language.

3a Choose the correct alternative.

Grammar | **Vocabulary** | Reading | Writing | Listening

LANGUAGE FOCUS

LEARNING A NEW LANGUAGE?
LEARN VOCABULARY!

(a) *Learning/To learn* vocabulary is an essential part of learning any language because, after all, it's very difficult (b) *communicating/to communicate* much without words. Some experts believe there must be at least a million words in English. It's clearly impossible (c) *learning/to learn* all the words in a language. And it's important (d) *remembering/to remember* that when we don't know a word for something, we can always paraphrase it, or explain it by (e) *using/to use* other simpler words. But it's always useful (f) *learning/to learn* lots of new words, too.

When we come across an important new word, most people use a dictionary (g) *looking/to look* up the meaning. But avoid only (h) *looking/to look* at the first definition you see – you risk (i) *making/to make* a big mistake, because many words in English have more than one meaning. And if you use a translation app or website (j) *finding/to find* the meaning of a new word, be aware that they don't always manage (k) *giving/to give* you the right word, so check somewhere else, too.

If you want (l) *remembering/to remember* new vocabulary, most people suggest (m) *writing/to write* the words down in a list (in a notebook, for example, or with an app if you prefer). Of course, (n) *memorising/to memorise* new words involves (o) *revising/to revise* them from time to time. It helps (p) *revising/to revise* frequently for shorter periods than for a long time just before a vocabulary test. If you can't stand (q) *sitting/to sit* on your own with your vocabulary list, find a study buddy and get some exercise. Go (r) *to run/running* together and test each other!

3b SPEAKING Ask and answer the questions.

1 How and when do you use a dictionary?
2 What do you think are good ways to learn vocabulary?

4a Complete the text with the gerund or infinitive form of the verbs given.

New kid at school?
ADVICE FROM PAST STUDENTS

1 'I was worried about .... (make) friends but you just need .... (remember) lots of other people are probably in the same position as you.'

2 'I was afraid of .... (get) lost in my new school, but now it's funny .... (think) that I met the person who has become my best friend when we both got lost and asked each other for help.'

3 'You need .... (pay) attention to what your teachers say because, if not, you risk .... (make) a bad impression on the first day.'

4 'I suggest .... (join) a club. Why? .... (meet) people who enjoy .... (do) the same things as you. .... (make) new friends is much easier that way.'

5 'I recommend .... (speak) to other students and teachers if you have any problems. It always helps .... (talk) to someone because .... (share) a problem makes you feel much better.'

4b SPEAKING What do you think of the advice? Can you think of any other advice for someone starting at a new school or a new stage of their academic life?

5 Continue these sentences with a verb in the gerund or infinitive form. Make the sentences true for you.

1 This year I would like ....
2 Generally I don't mind ....
3 Last year I managed ....
4 I often go ....
5 I think it's essential ....
6 I relax in the evening by ....
7 I'm really interested in ....
8 To learn English well, I suggest ....
9 This year at school I really want ....
10 I think I'm old enough ....

> **Use it ... don't lose it!**
>
> **6** SPEAKING Compare your completed sentences in 5. Are any of them similar?

Reach higher ⟩ page 136

Developing speaking

Giving personal information – preferences

Speaking bank
Expressing preferences

prefer
1 I **prefer (not) to go** out.
2 They **prefer me to spend** more time with them.
3 I **prefer revising** alone.
4 I **prefer doing** homework on Saturday **to doing** it on Sunday.

would prefer
5 I**'d prefer (not) to study** at the weekend.
6 I**'d prefer to study** in the US **than to do** it here.
7 They**'d prefer me (not) to go** out with my friends.

would rather
8 I**'d rather (not) live** in a big city.
9 I**'d rather study** abroad **than study** here.
10 My parents **would rather I didn't study** abroad.

1 Read questions 1–5 and match them to categories a–d. Some questions can go in more than one category.

1 Are there many interesting things to do in your town at the weekend?
2 Do you usually have a lot of homework at the weekend?
3 What would you like to do when you leave school?
4 What sports or games do you enjoy playing?
5 Do you prefer spending time with your family or with your friends at the weekend?

a your home and family
b your interests
c your studies/work
d your plans for the future

2 🔊 **04** Listen to five students answering the questions in 1. Match each student to one of the questions.

Student A ....
Student B ....
Student C ....
Student D ....
Student E ....

3 🔊 **04** Listen again. Does each student give a reason, or any personal details or examples to support their answer? Why is it a good idea to do this?

4 **SPEAKING** 👥 Take it in turns to ask and answer the questions in 1. Remember to give reasons and personal details.

5 Look at the different ways of expressing preferences in the Speaking bank. Write the structure for each one as in this example.

1 subject + 'prefer' + infinitive with 'to'

6 Put the verbs in the correct form.

1 She'd prefer .... (not go) to university.
2 She prefers .... (speak) English.
3 He'd rather .... (have) continuous assessment than .... (do) exams.
4 I'd prefer .... (learn) languages than .... (study) science.
5 They'd prefer me .... (not leave) home yet.
6 I prefer .... (do) sport to .... (do) homework.
7 I'd rather we .... (go) cycling.

Practice makes perfect

7a **SPEAKING** 👥 Ask and answer the questions. When you answer, remember to give reasons and personal details and to use expressions from the Speaking bank.

Student A: Ask these questions.

1 Would you rather do physical or mental work?
2 Would you rather study at home or in a library?
3 Would you like to have an end-of-year school trip this year or would you prefer to go somewhere with your family?

Student B: Ask these questions.

1 Would you prefer to study in a big school or a small school?
2 Do you prefer studying alone or with other people?
3 Would you rather have a school uniform or wear what you like?

7b **SPEAKING** 👥 Change partners and repeat.

Developing writing

An informal email 1

1 What do you think are some good reasons for studying history? And biology? Write two lists with your ideas.

2 Read this email from an English friend called Freya. What help does she need and why?

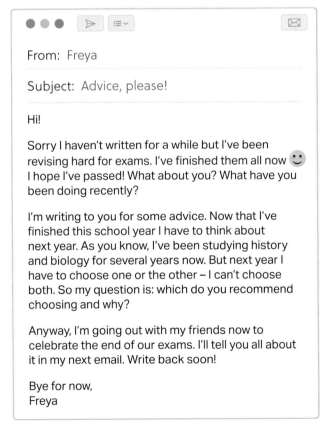

From: Freya

Subject: Advice, please!

Hi!

Sorry I haven't written for a while but I've been revising hard for exams. I've finished them all now 😊 I hope I've passed! What about you? What have you been doing recently?

I'm writing to you for some advice. Now that I've finished this school year I have to think about next year. As you know, I've been studying history and biology for several years now. But next year I have to choose one or the other – I can't choose both. So my question is: which do you recommend choosing and why?

Anyway, I'm going out with my friends now to celebrate the end of our exams. I'll tell you all about it in my next email. Write back soon!

Bye for now,
Freya

3 Look at the style of the email in 2. What things in the email are typical of informal emails?

4 Look at the Writing bank. What are the five different categories? Write titles.

Writing bank
Useful expressions in informal emails

1 ....
   Hi, Dear (Mary/John) ..., Hey

2 ....
   Thanks for your last email, It was great to hear from you, Sorry I haven't written for a while, I'm writing to tell you about ..., I have some exciting news

3 ....
   How are you?, How are things?, Are you doing exams/on holiday at the moment?, What have you been doing? What have you been up to?

4 ....
   By the way, Anyway, That reminds me

5 ....
   Write back soon, That's all for now, Bye for now, See you soon, All the best, Lots of love

5a SPEAKING 👥 Imagine that you have received Freya's email. Discuss the advice you would give her.

5b Make a paragraph plan for your reply to Freya. Decide what information to include in each paragraph.

   Paragraph 1 – Thank her for her email. Tell her what you've been doing.

   ┌─ **Practice makes perfect** ─
   6a Write your reply to Freya. Use your ideas in 1 and 5a and your paragraph plan in 5b to help you.

   6b When you finish your email, use the Writing checklist on page 141 to check it.

   ☑ **Exam tip**

   In this type of writing exercise, follow the instructions carefully. You lose marks if your reply does not include all the necessary information, if it is not in the correct style or if it is not the correct number of words.

Grammar reference

Present habits

- We use the present simple to talk about current routines and habits.
  I often listen to music.
- We use the present continuous with *always, constantly, forever, continually* for habits that annoy or irritate us.
  My brother and sister are <u>always</u> fighting.
- We can use *will* for repeated or habitual behaviour.
  They'll sit there for hours.

Present perfect simple

We use the present perfect simple to talk about:

1 an action that happened at an unspecified moment in the past. What is significant is the experience, not exactly when it happened.
  I've been to Egypt.

2 recent events which have a result in the present.
  She's lost her bag. (= She hasn't got it now.)

3 actions or situations that began in the past but continue in the present.
  Mark's lived here for ten years. (= Mark started to live here ten years ago and he still lives here now.)

4 actions that finished very recently.
  They've just had an accident.

Present perfect continuous

The present perfect continuous has a similar meaning to the present perfect simple. However, we use the continuous when we want to emphasise the process and duration of an action.
I've been studying in this school for more than five months.

For that reason, if an action is very short, we cannot use the continuous form.
NOT I've been breaking the window.

We also use the continuous to emphasise that an action finished very recently or is incomplete.
I've been working on my project ... I'm going to eat now and finish it after dinner.

If we want to emphasise the completion and result of an action, or how many times an action happens, we must use the present perfect simple.
I've painted my bedroom. (It's finished).
I've seen that film three times.
NOT I've been seeing that film three times.

Gerunds and infinitives

We use the gerund:	We use the infinitive with *to*:
as the subject/object of a sentence. *Studying is hard but interesting.*	to explain why somebody does something. *Why did he go to university? To study languages.*
with *go* to talk about physical activities. *go running, swimming, cycling, shopping, swimming, fishing*	immediately after adjectives. *It's good to revise with other people.*
after prepositions. *I'm interested in studying history.*	after *too, enough, the first, the last.* *It's too cold to go out.*
after verbs of liking or disliking, e.g. *like, love, enjoy, can't stand, don't mind, hate.* *I enjoy watching TV.*	after certain verbs like *want, learn, agree, decide, expect, hope, seem, would like, appear, arrange, ask, manage, help, need, promise.* *I want to work for a newspaper.*
after certain verbs like *admit, avoid, consider, risk, suggest.* *I suggest studying this book.*	

Vocabulary

1 School life

abroad (adj) • continuous assignment (n) • break (n) • assessment (n) • coursework (n) • grade/mark (n) • higher education (n) • notes (n) • subject (n) • term (n) • timetable (n)

2 Higher education

academic support (n) • attend (v) • campus (n) • degree (n) • extra-curricular activity/club/society (n) • facilities (n) • induction week (n) • lecture (n) • lecture hall (n) • lecturer (n) • postgraduate (n) • resource (n) • scholarship (n) • student accommodation (n) • student finance (n) • student loan (n) • (personal) tutor (n) • tutorial (n) • undergraduate (n)

3 *do* and *make*

do: an (extra-curricular) activity • an assignment • an essay • an exam • a course • a degree • homework • the shopping • the washing • chores • well • your best • a favour • business • sport • your hair
make: the dinner • a cake • a decision • a noise • friends • a mistake • an appointment • an effort • an excuse • money • progress • a phone call • a plan • a promise • an offer • a suggestion • a choice

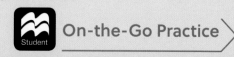

On-the-Go Practice

Grammar test

Present simple, present continuous and present habits

1 Complete each sentence with an appropriate word.

1 Normally I .... like classical music, but this song is beautiful.

2 This year my best friend and his brother .... studying abroad.

3 In some schools, they'll .... the first term with special activities for new students.

4 My parents .... constantly telling me to get my hair cut. It's so annoying.

5 My little brother is .... shouting! It drives me mad.

6 Why are you always .... me for help with your homework?

/ 6 points

Present perfect simple and continuous

2 Choose the correct alternative.

1 Have you *switched/been switching* the TV off?

2 We've been here *for/since* two hours.

3 My feet are tired. I've *stood/been standing* here for hours.

4 We've *seen/been seeing* this film twice.

5 My Indian friend's *stayed/been staying* in my house but she goes back home today.

6 My eyes are tired. I've *read/been reading* without the light on.

7 OK! I've *finished/been finishing* my exam.

/ 7 points

Gerunds and infinitives

3 Complete the second sentence so that it has a similar meaning to the first sentence, using the word given. Do not change the word given. Use between two and five words.

1 Don't do that because there's a chance you'll fail. (risk)

Don't do that because you

....

2 He loves to ride his bike at the weekend. (go)

He loves to .... at the weekend.

3 I think it's terrible to get up early. (stand)

I .... early.

4 I think it's essential to have a valid passport. (have)

I think .... is essential.

5 Please think about joining our club. (consider)

Please .... our club.

6 Nobody finished the exam before Sarah. (first)

Sarah was .... the exam.

7 It would be great to see him in concert next week. (love)

I .... him in concert next week.

/ 7 points

Vocabulary test

School life

1 Complete the sentences with the correct form of these words.

abroad · continuous assessment · higher education · subject · term · timetable

1 I'd like to study .... instead of studying in my own country.

2 Maths is my favourite ....

3 Our school year has three ....

4 After school, I want to continue in .... and go to university.

5 I can't remember my .... What do we have after English on Tuesday morning?

6 I like .... because it means not everything depends on exams.

/ 6 points

Higher education

2 Write simple definitions of these words and phrases.

1 lecture hall

2 resources

3 student loan

4 lecturer

5 campus

6 undergraduate

7 tutorial

/ 7 points

do and make

3 Do these words go with *do* or *make*?

an assignment · a decision · a favour · a plan · progress · the lunch · the shopping

/ 7 points

Total: / 40 points

2 A JOB WELL DONE

Vocabulary in context
Work conditions and responsibilities
Working life, hours and pay

1a SPEAKING 👥 Think of one job for each letter of the alphabet. Leave out any difficult letters.

A – analyst, B – businessman/woman, …

1b Which of your jobs in 1a are related to science or new technologies?

2 Read the text and complete it with the correct form of the words in the box. Check that you understand all the words.

(◀))) 05 Work conditions and responsibilities
career • colleague • deal with (the public) • earn a salary • employee • employer • experience • high-pressure • in charge of • indoors • in good/bad/dangerous conditions • internship • manual • outdoors • permanent • promotion • qualifications • responsible for • secure • self-employed • skilled • temporary • training

Unusual jobs explained:
THE FLAVOURIST

My name is Kim and I'm a flavourist. You need special
(a) .... to do my job – most of us have degrees in microbiology and/or chemistry.
Basically, a flavourist is (b) .... creating new and amazing flavours for all sorts of food products like yoghurts, sweets and drinks. It's a very (c) .... job because you need to know the science and be able to distinguish between a thousand different ingredients just by tasting them. In fact, I had over three years of special (d) .... with experts to learn to do the job well. And, of course, the more you work, the more (e) .... you get, and that helps you to become better at the job. I began my professional (f) .... working in a small department with three other
(g) .... But then I got a (h) .... and now I'm (i) .... my own department, which specialises in fruit flavours. The money isn't bad at all – I (j) .... quite a good .... because I've become an expert in my field.
I'm an (k) .... of a very big international company. I usually work (l) ...., in a laboratory or office, but sometimes we visit farms to taste fruit fresh off the tree. It's a comfortable job and we definitely work (m) ....
I sometimes (n) .... because we meet and talk to customers and people who try our new flavours, to see if they like them or not.
So, if you're interested in trying this job, I suggest applying for an (o) .... with a company like ours.

3 Look at the words and phrases in the box and separate them into the four lists below.

(◀))) 06 Working life, hours and pay
apply for a job • be made redundant • be offered a job • be sacked/fired • be well/badly paid • become unemployed • do shift work • go job hunting • look for a job • on flexitime • on the minimum wage • out of work • resign • retire • sign a contract • work from nine to five • work full-time • work long hours • work overtime • work nights • work part-time

Getting a job	Leaving or not having a job	Working hours	Pay
apply for a job			

4 SPEAKING 👥 Explain the difference between these words and expressions. If there is no difference, say so.

1 resign/retire
2 be made redundant/be sacked
3 go job hunting/look for a job
4 apply for a job/sign a contract
5 work part-time/on flexitime
6 do shift work/work nights

5 Think of three examples for each category.

1 nine to five jobs
2 manual jobs
3 jobs where you deal with the public
4 jobs that often receive the minimum wage
5 jobs where you need special training
6 reasons why people can be fired
7 reasons why people resign
8 jobs where you need science qualifications

> **Use it … don't lose it!**
>
> **6** SPEAKING 👥 Imagine your dream job. Use words on this page to talk about the conditions, responsibilities, working hours and pay.
>
> Reach higher > page 136

Reading

1 **SPEAKING** Look at the photos on this page. Describe what you can see. What do you think is the story behind each photo?

2 Read these two articles. Were your ideas in 1 right?

CLIMBING, NOT COOKING

Doing the same job year after year can become very <u>dull</u>, but when Lidia Huayllas Estrada and a group of her colleagues changed careers, it was quite a radical move.

Lidia and her friends are <u>indigenous</u> Aymara women from Bolivia. Life used to be very different for them. They would cook for rich mountaineers from all over the world and look after their needs as they prepared to reach the top of different <u>peaks</u> in the Andes. One day, as Lidia was preparing a meal for the mountaineers, she stopped and noticed the excitement on their faces as they prepared to climb the <u>summit</u>. She wondered what it felt like to get to the top of a mountain. When she asked her mountain-guide husband, he suggested trying it herself, which is exactly what she did.

When Lidia's group of 11 women climbed their first peak (at a height of just over 6,000 metres), they had no training. They learned to climb by watching experienced mountaineers in camp and by talking to the mountain guides. But of the 11 women who set out to climb that day, all of them kept at it and reached the summit. For future climbs, they decided to take mountaineering safety lessons to improve their knowledge and skills.

This <u>intrepid</u> group of women called themselves the 'Climbing Cholitas', proudly asserting their Aymara origin, and wearing their traditional long, colourful skirts, although they are not very practical for climbing. Even though they wear their traditional dresses rather than professional climbing gear, they do wear protective helmets and use proper climbing equipment. Cooks are not exactly well paid, so the women <u>pool</u> their money to pay for all of this <u>gear</u>.

On 23rd January 2019, a group of five Cholitas achieved their dream and reached the highest peak in the Andes, Aconcagua (6,962 metres). Despite some of the women being over 50, there's already talk of the Cholitas next attempting Everest.

MAKING GAMES, not just playing them

Laila Shabir didn't use to take video games too seriously when she was growing up. Now she's in charge of an organisation called 'Girls Make Games'. So, how did that happen?

After school, Laila received a grant to study at the world-famous Massachusetts Institute of Technology (MIT) and eventually got a degree in economics. Thanks to her qualifications, she was quickly offered a job in finance but, after a year, decided it wasn't for her. She then decided to do a PhD and become a professor, although that plan suddenly changed too when Laila met someone who <u>opened her eyes to</u> the serious educational potential in video games.

Excited by the educational power of video games, Laila set up her own company. She was looking for somebody to work in her development team and was surprised when almost no women applied. She was disappointed to see that not many women were working in the games industry in general. The statistics point to the same problem. A 2017 report by Statista claimed that women make up 46% of the gaming population, but only 22% of the video games industry.

The games industry is bigger than films and music combined and so if women are not employed to make games, their perspective and <u>insights</u> are <u>left out</u> of a whole area of entertainment which influences millions of people around the world. What's more, women are <u>missing out on</u> important job opportunities as creators, designers, producers, musicians, artists and engineers.

That's why, in 2014, Laila created 'Girls Make Games', which has already reached more than 6,000 girls in over 60 cities around the world. She aims to encourage more women to work in the games industry by organising workshops where teams of girls compete against each other to make the best game. Laila is optimistic about how girls are going to influence the video games industry in the future, one pixel at a time.

3 **07** Read the text again. Answer the questions in your own words.

1 Why did Lidia start to climb high peaks in the Andes?

2 How did Lidia and her colleagues pick up all the skills and knowledge needed to climb?

3 How did Laila end up working in the video games industry?

4 What are two consequences of so few women working in the video games industry?

5 What is the aim of the 'Girls Make Games' workshops?

6 What similarities, if any, exist between the two articles?

4 What do the <u>underlined</u> words in the text mean? Guess and then check in your dictionary.

5 **Critical thinkers**

In your opinion, how important, useful or necessary is an organisation like 'Girls Make Games'?

What makes you say that?

Reach higher > page 136

Past simple and past continuous

1a Match sentences 1–5 to the rules a–e.
Is each rule for the past simple (PS), the past
continuous (PC), or both (B)?

1 In 2014, Laila **created** 'Girls Make Games'.

2 She **was looking** for somebody to work in her
team.

3 She **finished** school, **received** a grant to study
at MIT and finally **got** a degree in economics.

4 One day, as Lidia **was preparing** a meal, she
stopped and **noticed** their excited faces.

5 They **were wearing** long colourful skirts while
they **were climbing**.

a We use it to say that one thing
happened after another.   *PS/PC/B*

b We use it to talk about an activity in
progress at a moment in the past. *PS/PC/B*

c We use it for descriptions or to describe
scenes in a story.   *PS/PC/B*

d We use it to talk about finished actions
or situations in the past.   *PS/PC/B*

e We use it to talk about an activity in
progress in the past that was
interrupted by another action.   *PS/PC/B*

1b Is it more common to use the words *while*
and *as* with the past simple or the past
continuous?

☑ **Check it page 28**

2 Choose the correct alternative.

1 Jordan Romero was just 14 when he *got/was getting*
to the top of Everest on 22nd May 2010.

2 My friends and I *played/were playing* a video game
when we suddenly had an idea to create our own.

3 She was just 17 when she *decided/was deciding* to
compose music for video games.

4 They put their boots on, walked out of their tent and
started/were starting to climb.

5 He decided he wanted to be a musician when he
heard/was hearing that song for the first time.

6 Atari® *created/was creating* one of the first ever video
games. It was called *Pong*.

7 I *chatted/was chatting* with my friends on social
media at 8.30 last night.

8 When they got back from the top of the mountain,
they *called/were calling* their friends to celebrate.

Flipped classroom video

Watch the Grammar Presentation video

3 Complete the text with the past simple or past
continuous form of the verbs given.

Culture exchange

Dangerous work in South Africa

A few years ago, Collet Ngobeni
(a) .... (sit) at her home in South
Africa. She **(b)** .... (not work). But
that day she suddenly **(c)** .... (hear)
some news on the radio. They **(d)** ....
(talk) about a group of poachers who at that
time **(e)** .... (kill) rhinos in the nearby
nature reserve. She **(f)** .... (find)
out about a group of women called the Black
Mambas who **(g)** .... (try) to protect
wildlife in the area. She **(h)** .... (apply)
for a job with them and **(i)** .... (got)
it. She **(j)** .... (do) some intensive
training, including living wild for seven
weeks and learning about elephants, lions,
leopards and rhinos. One day, Collet and some
colleagues **(k)** .... (patrol) the fences
of the nature reserve when they **(l)** ....
(come) across some poachers. Even though the
Black Mambas are always completely unarmed,
the poachers **(m)** .... (turn) away and
(n) .... (leave). It looks like the Black
Mambas are finally putting an end to poaching
in the nature reserves of South Africa.

Past habits and states: *used to, would*

4 Look at sentences 1–4 and answer questions
a–e.

1 They **used to** be cooks, not mountaineers.

2 She **didn't use to** take video games too
seriously.

3 They **would** cook for rich mountaineers.

4 On 23rd January, they **reached** the highest
peak in the Andes.

a Which activities in 1–4 are things that
happened regularly?

b Which happened just once?

c We can replace *would* with *used to* in 3 but
we cannot replace *used to* with *would* in 1.
Why not?

d Can we make *would* negative in 3 to talk
about past habits?

e Can we use periods of time with *used to*?
(Try adding a period of time to sentence 1.)

☑ **Check it page 28**

5 Is the underlined part of the sentence correct to talk about past habits and states? If not, rewrite it correctly.

1 When my dad was young, he says he would play in the street for hours.

2 My sister wouldn't enjoy playing video games, but now she does.

3 At primary school, I would eat lots of sweets.

4 We used to live in the mountains for a year.

5 In the past, people didn't use to use phones so much.

6 Complete this text. When both *used to* and *would* are possible, use *would*. When neither *used to* nor *would* are possible, use the past simple.

TERRIBLE JOBS

Working conditions (a) .... (not be) great in the 1800s in Victorian England. Here are just two terrible jobs that people had to do.

Chimney sweeps
In Victorian England they (b) .... (employ) children as young as four to clean chimneys. The poor boys (c) .... (climb) up the dark and dirty chimney, breathing in dust and smoke as they went. Some people say that when a boy couldn't (or refused to) move in the chimney, their boss (d) .... (light) a fire underneath them to 'encourage' them to keep moving. Finally, in 1840, a law (e) .... (make) it illegal for anybody under 21 to climb and clean a chimney.

Rat catchers
In the 1800s, London (f) .... (not be) a very clean place to live. To keep their houses clean, people (g) .... (pay) 'ratters' to catch and kill rats. Generally, rat catchers (h) .... (use) dogs to do this work. Apart from being filthy and unpleasant, it (i) .... (be) a very dangerous job because a bite from a rat could lead to terrible infections. A man called Jack Black (j) .... (become) famous because he (k) .... (catch) rats on a regular basis for Queen Victoria herself.

7 Complete these sentences. Make some of them true for you, and some false. Make your false sentences believable.

1 I used to .... at school but now I don't.

2 I used to .... at the weekend.

3 I didn't use to like ...., but now I do.

4 When I was five, I would ....

Use it ... don't lose it!

8 SPEAKING 👥 Read out your sentences. Can your partner say which sentences are true and which are false?

Reach higher > page 136

Developing vocabulary

Phrasal verbs connected with work

1 Read the text and match the phrasal verbs in bold with their meanings (a–j).

A COMPANY BOSS **AT 16**

When David Eisman was just 16 and still at high school, he **set up** his own video game company. He always wanted to work in the video game industry. He **filled in** applications for different companies to do an internship but they **turned** him **down** because they said he had no experience. He **kept at** it but always faced the same problem. That didn't **put** him **off**, though. He decided to do something radical. He couldn't **take over** an existing company because he didn't have any money. So he started his own company by getting people to work for him for free, by offering to share the company's profits with them. He and his team began to **work on** an educational game. Being the boss of a company is hard work and it's difficult to **keep up with** all the elements of game production. But if you want to **get ahead** in the world of work, don't **put** things **off** until tomorrow if you can do them today!

a spend time producing or improving something

b start (a business, organisation, etc.)

c continue working at something even if you want to stop

d be more successful, or progress faster than other people

e go at the same speed as something or someone

f add information such as your name or address on a document

g not accept an offer, request or application

h take control of something

i (with a person) make someone not want to do something

j (with a thing) postpone, make something happen later than originally planned

2 Complete the questions with the correct form of the phrasal verbs in 1.

1 When something is difficult, do you quickly stop trying or do you .... it?

2 Are you ambitious? Do you want to .... and reach the top of a company?

3 Do you usually .... doing your homework or do you usually do it straight away?

4 Have you ever applied for something and not got it because they .... you .... ?

5 Would you prefer to .... your own company or work for somebody else?

6 Do you find it easy to .... all your assignments or do you sometimes go a bit slow?

7 Have you ever .... an application form with all your personal details? If so, what was it for?

8 When you're revising, what can .... you .... and make you want to stop?

Use it ... don't lose it!

3 SPEAKING 👥 Take it in turns to ask and answer the completed questions in 2.

Reach higher > page 136

GREAT LEARNERS
GREAT THINKERS

TRANSFERABLE SKILLS

Lesson aim: To assess your own transferable skills

Video: Working at sea

SEL Social and emotional learning: Recognising strengths and weaknesses

1 **SPEAKING** Answer these questions about the three jobs below.

> Firefighting · Deep-sea fishing · Construction

1 How dangerous do you think each job is?
2 What dangers does each one involve?
3 What qualities or skills do you think you need to be able to do the jobs?
4 What are the positive aspects of doing the jobs?

2 **VIDEO** Watch a video about a younger fisher with the sound off and answer the questions.

1 What dangers, or potential dangers, can you see?
2 What positive aspects to the job can you find?

3 **VIDEO** Watch the video again and answer the questions.

1 What do people want the young woman to do and why?
2 What is the attitude of some men towards what she does?
3 How does she feel about their attitude and what effect does it have on her?
4 What aspects of nature does she mention?
5 How does her job help her to relax?

4 Read this text about 'transferable skills'. The words in bold are things we can use in almost any job. How important do you think each skill is for the young fisher in the video and why? Give examples.

TRANSFERABLE SKILLS

Your personal qualities are very important, for instance being **patient**, **well-organised** and **responsible**. Most teachers will also look for people who are **ambitious** and **inquiring** (wanting to continue learning and improving). **Problem-solving** is another important transferable skill, being able to react to difficult situations in a positive way and find solutions. There are other general skills that can be important, for example **mathematical** and **IT skills**, and **dexterity** (being good with your hands) can be useful in many subjects. Meanwhile, very few people work completely alone, so in order to be successful you need interpersonal skills such as **communication skills**, **leadership** and **teamwork**.

GREAT THINKERS

Diamond Ranking

5 **SPEAKING** **Follow the instructions.**

1 Separate the different transferable skills in the text in 4 into two groups: the six skills you think are the most important and the six least important ones for the job of a research scientist.

2 Look at the **diamond** diagram and **rank** your group of most important skills. Choose the most important one and put it in the top position. Then put the next two most important skills in the second line and the last three in the third line. Then do the same for the ideas that were not so important in the bottom half of the diamond.

3 Work with a partner and compare your **diamonds**.

6 Make a list of the transferable skills mentioned in the text in 4 and give yourself a mark from 5 (brilliant) to 1 (weak) for each one. Add any other skills you have which are not in the list.

When you score a 3 or more, think of an example to justify your answer, based on the things you do at school, in your free time or at home.

When you have less than a 3, what could you do to improve that skill?

GREAT LEARNERS SEL

Great learners are reflective.

How easy or difficult did you find it to reflect on your own strengths and weaknesses? Why is it important to be able to reflect on these things?

Learner profile > page 142

Listening

1 SPEAKING 👥 **Answer these questions about people who worked as human computers.**

1 What do you think a human computer did in their job?

2 What qualifications do you imagine were necessary to become a human computer?

2 SPEAKING 👥 **Look at the gaps in this text. Predict what words or types of word could fill each one.**

Gillian Conway is an expert in the
(a) .... She talks about a place called
Langley (b) ...., where they employed
many human computers. They worked in a thing
they called the 'computer (c) ....'.
Many women worked there during the Second
World War because a lot of men were
(d) .... A number of the women used
to be (e) .... before they worked at
Langley.
After 1950, a lot of the work at Langley was for
NASA because of the (f) .... The
human computers learned to (g) ....
the first digital computers. They also
(h) .... the answers that digital
computers gave them.
Astronaut John Glenn wanted Katherine Johnson
to personally calculate where his spaceship was
going to (i) .... She also prepared
manual calculations for astronauts in case there
were problems with the (j) .... She
contributed to a (k) .... about space
travel. Apart from medals and awards, Katherine
Johnson was glad to receive (l) ....
from young students.

> ☑ **Exam tip**
>
> Always read the incomplete notes *before* you
> listen. Look carefully at the words that come
> just before or after each space and think about
> the meaning and *type* of word that is missing.

3 🔊 08 **Listen to a podcast about human computers and check your answers in 1 and 2.**

4 ✳ **Critical thinkers**

> In your opinion, why didn't people
> recognise the work of the human
> computers who worked for NASA?
>
> What makes you say that?

Grammar in context 2

Past perfect simple and continuous

1a Look at the sentences and then decide which actions happened first.

1 The astronaut only **took off** when Katherine Johnson **had checked** the calculations.

2 She **received** a medal for the work she **had done**.

3 Digital computers **began** to do a lot of the work that human computers **had been doing** for years.

4 A group of women **had been working** there for five years before the war **started**.

1b Choose the correct alternative.

1 We use the past perfect simple and continuous to talk about actions that happened *after/before* another action in the past.

2 We use the past perfect *simple/continuous* to give more importance to the duration of an action.

3 We use the past perfect *simple/continuous* to give more importance to the completion of an action.

1c Look again at the sentences. How do we make the past perfect simple? How do we make the past perfect continuous?

— ☑ **Check it page 28**

2 Complete the sentences with the past simple or past perfect simple form of the verbs given.

1 I didn't want to watch the documentary because I .... (see) it twice already.

2 We were tired because we .... (not sleep) the night before.

3 When I .... (write) my essay, I handed it in.

4 He opened the bottle of water and .... (drink).

5 She didn't see the start of the film because when she arrived at the cinema it .... (begin).

6 I .... (not hear) about human computers until yesterday's lesson.

7 We were surprised when we .... (see) her walk into the room.

3 Complete the sentences in a logical way using a verb in the past perfect simple and the words in bold.

1 I got 10/10 in my last exam because .... **revision**

2 She couldn't get into her locker .... **key**

3 The teacher wasn't happy .... **late**

4 They gave him the job because .... **interview**

5 They took him to hospital because .... **accident**

6 We weren't hungry because .... **lunch**

7 He knew all the words because .... **song**

8 She was happy because .... **promotion**

4 Choose the best alternative.

1 She had *directed/been directing* three films by the time she was 25.

2 He couldn't call because he had *lost/been losing* his phone.

3 I was tired because I'd *played/been playing* for a long time.

4 She lost her voice because she had *sung/been singing* throughout the concert.

5 We'd *waited/been waiting* for the bus for half an hour when it eventually came.

6 Last week I finally had enough money to buy the game. I *have/had* been saving for months to buy it.

7 Luckily, by the end of the exam, I'd *answered/been answering* all the questions.

8 My eyes were tired. I'd *worked/been working* all day on the computer.

5 Write sentences in the past perfect simple or continuous to explain the situations.

1 Why was Laura upset?

lose her job

She had lost her job.

2 Why was the boss angry with Harry?

not concentrate on his work

....

3 Why were Chris and Mark tired?

work overtime all week

....

4 Why did Sarah celebrate?

pass all her exams

....

5 Why didn't Emma and Jack want to see the film?

see it three times already

....

6 Why didn't Oliver have his bike?

his friend take it

....

7 Why was Silvia tired?

work out in the gym all afternoon

....

8 Why were they hungry?

not eat since 6 am

....

6 Complete the text with one word in each gap. Sometimes more than one answer is possible.

KARINA'S (IM)PERFECT JOB

Karina Sudenyte (a) .... to live in Lithuania but moved to Wales when she was 14. After secondary school, she (b) .... studying travel and tourism when she decided to start her own company. She discovered that for the last 12 months British farmers had (c) .... throwing away 4.4 million apples every day. They (d) .... not done this because the apples were bad. It was because they looked ugly or were the wrong size or shape. Supermarkets don't usually want to buy those apples because they say their appearance (e) .... customers off and they can't sell them. However, despite their appearance, many of the apples are still perfectly fine to eat. So, Karina and a partner (f) .... the idea to make juice from these apples that nobody wanted. She set (g) .... a company with her partner and called the product 'Flawsome!' (It used to (h) .... called 'Wonky'). Their idea was that although the fruit they (i) .... using was imperfect and had flaws, the flavour of the juice was awesome. By 2019, they calculated they (j) .... saved 7,500,000 pieces of fruit. They're now working (k) .... lots of other products with different fruit and vegetables, not just apples. In the past, nearly all fruit juice used to come in plastic bottles, but since plastic is responsible (l) .... so much pollution every year, Karina's company uses recyclable glass bottles or cardboard boxes. Karina's proud to be (m) .... charge of such an eco-friendly company.

7 Individually, think about these things and make notes.

1 something you had learnt to do by the age of five

2 something interesting/surprising/unusual you had done before you started secondary school

3 something you had planned to do but didn't

4 something you had already been doing for a long time before the start of this school year

5 something you had been doing for a while before you went to bed last night

Use it ... don't lose it!

8 SPEAKING 👥 Discuss your notes in 7.

Reach higher ⟩ page 136

Developing speaking

Negotiating and collaborating 1

1 **SPEAKING** 👥 **Ask and answer the questions.**

1 Have you ever done any type of part-time or weekend job? If so, what was it? If not, would you like to?

2 What do you think are the good and bad things about teenagers doing weekend jobs?

2 🔊 **09** **Look at the diagram. Listen to two students doing a speaking task involving the diagram and then answer these questions.**

1 What does the examiner ask them to talk about first?

2 What is the second question the examiner asks them?

3 What is the students' final answer to that question?

4 Do you agree with their answer? Why/Why not?

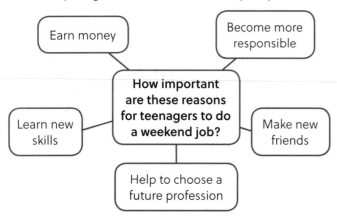

Earn money

Become more responsible

Learn new skills

How important are these reasons for teenagers to do a weekend job?

Make new friends

Help to choose a future profession

3 🔊 **09** **Listen again and answer these questions.**

1 Do the two students ask each other's opinions?

2 Do they talk about all of the reasons?

3 Do they come to a decision at the end of the conversation?

4 Do they listen to each other and respond to each other's comments?

5 Do they both speak the same amount, more or less?

> ### ☑ Exam tip
>
> In the second part of the task, the best strategy is to agree partially with your partner's first idea but then suggest alternative ideas. It is better not to agree completely straight away because otherwise the conversation will end too quickly.

4 **Look at the expressions in the Speaking bank. What are the different categories? Write titles.**

> ### Speaking bank
> Useful expressions for negotiating and collaborating 1
>
> **1** ....
>
> What do you think?
> What do you think about (money/earning money)?
> What about you?
> What about (making new friends/learning new skills)?
> Do you agree?
> Don't you think so?
>
> **2** ....
>
> Yes, I agree.
> Yes, you're right.
> I think you're right.
> That's true.
> I agree with you.
> I see what you mean.
> That's a good idea.
> Sure.
>
> **3** ....
>
> I see what you mean, but …
> I suppose so, but …
> I'm not sure.
> Maybe, but …
> I agree up to a point, but …
> Yes, but I think it depends on …

5 **SPEAKING** 👥 **Practise doing the task in 2, giving your own opinions about the reasons in the diagram. Then say which you think is the most important.**

> ### Practice makes perfect
>
> **6** **SPEAKING** 👥 **Work with a partner and do this task. Remember to use expressions from the Speaking bank.**
>
> 1 Here are some different factors to think about when you choose a job. Talk to each other about how important you think the factors are.
>
> 2 When you finish 1, you have a minute to decide which factor you think is the most important.
>
>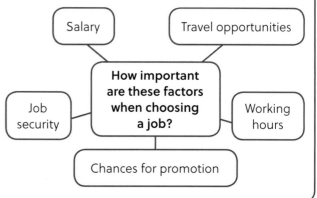
>
> Salary
>
> Travel opportunities
>
> Job security
>
> **How important are these factors when choosing a job?**
>
> Working hours
>
> Chances for promotion

Developing writing

A story 1

1 Look at the two photos. What do you think the connection between them is?

2 **SPEAKING** 👥 Read the task. What do you think happens in the story in 3?

HOME   SUBMISSIONS   YOUR STORIES   ABOUT   🔍

STORIES NEEDED!

We want stories for our new international magazine for teenagers. Your story must begin with this sentence:
Sam got the job that he had always wanted.
Your story must include:
▸ a trip
▸ an accident

3 Read this story. What similarities are there between your ideas in 2 and the story?

HOME   SUBMISSIONS   YOUR STORIES   ABOUT   🔍

YOUR STORIES ✒

Sam got the job that he had always wanted. He had been studying hard to be a doctor for years and years. He used to imagine how it would feel to finally qualify. After finishing his degree and his training, he applied for a place in a famous hospital in Edinburgh and was amazed to get it.

That weekend, he wanted to go out with some friends to celebrate. His favourite band were playing in Edinburgh so they decided to eat out first and then go to the concert. Everybody was incredibly excited to see the band because it was their first ever trip to Scotland.

At 8.30 pm the concert began. Sam and his friends were standing right at the front. After just five minutes, there was an awful accident. The singer hadn't seen the edge of the stage and had fallen off it. Having seen the accident, Sam quickly explained he was a doctor and offered to help. He went backstage with the singer and told him that it was really dangerous to move his ankle. However, the singer refused to stop the concert because thousands of people were waiting to see the band perform.

Ten minutes later, the singer went back on stage to finish the concert, sitting in a chair. Unbelievably, Sam was right there on stage too, trying to keep the singer's ankle safe. Watching his favourite band from up on the stage, Sam couldn't believe what a week it had been!

4a Put these events in the story in order.

a The singer sang in a chair. ☐
b The singer had an accident. ☐
c Sam went on stage at a concert. ☐
d Sam was offered his dream job. ☐
e Sam went to see a concert. ☐
f Sam spoke to the singer. ☐
g Sam ate out with his friends. ☐
h Sam did special training. ☐

4b Most stories have a beginning, a middle and an end. What would you say is the beginning, the middle and the end in this story?

5 Find examples in the story in 3 for each different piece of advice in the Writing bank.
Variety of past tenses – past continuous: Sam and his friends were standing right at the front.

Writing bank
Useful language and linkers for writing stories

- Use a variety of past tenses: past simple, past continuous, past perfect simple and continuous, and *used to/would*.
- Use participle clauses:
  Looking up, he saw …, After looking up, he saw …, Having looked up, he saw …
- Use time expressions and sequence linkers:
  Last weekend, Three years ago, On Friday …
  At first, Next, Then, After that, Finally, In the end …
- Use adjectives and adverbs to make the story more descriptive.

Practice makes perfect

6a Look at the task in 2. Think of some ideas for a story, then plan it. Think about the main events, the background and any important scenes.

6b Individually, write your story. Remember to follow the advice in the Writing bank.

6c When you finish your story, use the Writing checklist on page 141 to check it.

Grammar reference

Past simple

We use the past simple to:

1 describe finished actions or situations in the past.
I went to Ireland last year.

2 say that one thing happened after another.
When the teacher came in, we took out our books.

Past continuous

We use the past continuous to:

1 talk about activities in progress at a moment in the past.
At four o'clock this afternoon, I was watching TV.

2 describe scenes in a story or description.
They were all wearing long coats because the cold wind was blowing hard.

3 talk about an activity in progress when another, shorter activity happened or interrupted it. It tells us that an action was in progress, but not that the activity was finished.
I was listening to music when my father suddenly ran into the room.

Past habits and states

used to

My grandfather <u>used to</u> work as a postman.
He <u>didn't use to</u> have much free time.
<u>Did</u> your grandmother <u>use to</u> work?
Yes, she did./No, she didn't.

would

They <u>would</u> work eight hours a day.

- We use *used to* and *would* to talk about past habits – things we did regularly in the past but don't do now.
- We cannot use *used to* and *would* to talk about single events in the past. In this case, we use the past simple.

We use *would* with past actions but not past states.
He would come and visit us on Sundays.
NOT He would have a bike.

- We do not usually use *wouldn't* to talk about past habits.
He didn't use to give us presents.
NOT He wouldn't give us presents.

- When we give a period of time, we use the past simple, not *used to*.
She used to work in a factory. She worked there for five years.
NOT She used to work in a factory for five years.

Past perfect simple

To make the past perfect simple, we use *had* + past participle.

We use the past perfect simple to talk about actions that happened before another action or actions in the past. It gives importance to the completion of an activity.
When the interview had finished, I left.

Past perfect continuous

To make the past perfect continuous, we use *had* + *been* + verb-*ing*

We use the past perfect continuous to talk about actions that happened before another action or actions in the past. It gives importance to the duration of an activity.
I was tired because I had been studying all night.

Vocabulary

1 Work conditions and responsibilities

career (n) • colleague (n) • deal with (the public) (v) • earn a salary (v) • employee (n) • employer (n) • experience (n) • high-pressure (adj) • in charge of (adj) • indoors (adj) • in good/bad/dangerous conditions (adv) • internship (n) • manual (adj) • outdoors (adv) • permanent (adj) • promotion (n) • qualifications (n) • responsable for (adj) • secure (adj) • self-employed (adj) • skilled (adj) • temporary (adj) • training (n)

2 Working life, hours and pay

apply for a job (v) • be made redundant (v) • be offered a job (v) • be sacked/fired (v) • be well/badly paid (v) • become unemployed (v) • do shift work (v) • go job hunting (v) • look for a job (phrasal verb) • on flexitime (adj) • on the minimum wage (adj) • out of work (adj) • resign (v) • retire (v) • sign a contract (v) • work from nine to five (v) • work full-time (v) • work long hours (v) • work overtime (v) • work nights (v) • work part-time (v)

3 Phrasal verbs connected with work

fill in • get ahead • keep at • keep up with • put somebody off • put something off • set up • take over • turn down • work on

On-the-Go Practice

Grammar test

Past simple and past continuous

1 Complete the text with the past simple or past continuous form of the verbs given.

She (a) _____ (get) up and (b) _____ (look) out of the window. It (c) _____ (rain). As she (d) _____ (look) out of the window, she (e) _____ (hear) her phone ring. Who (f) _____ (call) her so early in the morning?

/ 6 points

Past habits

2 Choose the correct alternative. In one sentence, both alternatives are correct. Which one?

1 When he was small, he *used to/would* be shy.

2 I *used to study/studied* in Ireland last year.

3 I *used to/usually* go to the cinema at the weekend before it was closed.

4 Last year I *had/used to have* a big party to welcome my American friend.

5 Did you *use/used* to have a pet?

6 Children *used to/would* work in factories in Britain in the 19th century.

7 They *didn't use to/wouldn't* go out on Friday evenings, but now they do.

/ 7 points

Past perfect simple and continuous

3 Is the underlined part of the sentence correct? If not, rewrite it.

1 I <u>have been waiting</u> for an hour when the film finally started.

2 He was tired and decided to rest because he <u>had studied</u> all day.

3 She <u>had been writing</u> seven text messages.

4 Everything was white because it <u>had been snowing</u> all night.

5 When they <u>ate</u> their dinner, they washed the dishes.

6 They heard a loud noise and thought that somebody <u>had been falling</u> over.

7 When they <u>had been finishing</u> their homework, they played a video game.

/ 7 points

Vocabulary test

Work conditions and responsibilities

1 Write simple definitions of these words and phrases.

1 self-employed

2 manual

3 promotion

4 salary

5 training

6 qualifications

/ 6 points

Working life, hours and pay

2 Complete each sentence with one word.

1 He was _____ because he arrived late every day and never did what his boss told him.

2 He's on _____. He chooses the times he works.

3 She _____ from the company when she was 30 because she didn't enjoy her job.

4 He only receives the minimum _____.

5 Kevin lost his job and he is now _____.

6 They work _____, just from 9 to 12.30.

7 She's signing the _____ for her new job tomorrow.

/ 7 points

Phrasal verbs connected with work

3 Match the parts of the phrasal verb and the meaning.

	Verb	Particle		Meaning
1	set	ahead	a	not accept an offer, request or application
2	get	off	b	start a new business, office, etc.
3	turn	up	c	progress faster than other people
4	work	in	d	add information on a document
5	fill	over	e	spend time working or improving something
6	take	down	f	take control of something
7	put something	on	g	postpone to do at a later time

/ 7 points

Total: / 40 points

Reading

1 Read the text. Who do you think it is written for? What is the main point in the text?

2 Choose the best answer (A–D) to complete the text.

PLAYING FOR THE TEAM

Most of us will have to work as part of a team when we start work. Even at university students have to do projects and experiments in teams and this is good (1) .... for the real world. Teams need to be (2) .... up of different types of workers in order to function well. So it's (3) .... considering what kind of team player you might be. There are four main types of worker in a team. First, there is the contributor, who is the person who comes (4) .... with lots of ideas and suggestions. Then we have the collaborator, who prefers working things out with someone else and (5) .... ideas together. Another type of worker is the communicator. This is someone who (6) .... to make sure that the process runs smoothly and that the task is completed. And finally, we have the challenger, who will ask difficult questions but who can help the rest of the team think things through so the (7) .... result is better. Everybody has a (8) .... to play.

1	A	rehearsal	B	repetition	C	practice	D	routine
2	A	got	B	made	C	fitted	D	done
3	A	use	B	merit	C	value	D	worth
4	A	up	B	out	C	down	D	by
5	A	building	B	making	C	hoping	D	setting
6	A	keeps	B	tends	C	leans	D	minds
7	A	concluded	B	finished	C	closed	D	final
8	A	portion	B	section	C	part	D	piece

3 SPEAKING 👤 What kind of team player do you think you are? Why? How could you help a team be successful?

Speaking

4 SPEAKING 👤 Ask and answer these questions.

People you know

What is your best friend like?

Tell us about someone in your family whose job you admire.

Things you like

What kind of things do you like doing in your free time? Why?

Tell us about what you enjoy most in school.

Places you go

What's your favourite kind of holiday? Why?

Tell us about where you like to spend time in your town or city. Why?

5 SPEAKING 👤 Tell your partner how well they did with these speaking points. Did they:

- use correct grammar and vocabulary?
- speak clearly so you could understand?
- give the right information in answer to the questions?
- give explanations for their answers?

6 SPEAKING 👤 What do you need to do in order to do well in this part of the speaking exam?

Exam success
Listening and Writing > page 144

Studying in your country

Virtual Classroom Exchange

 1 SPEAKING 👥 **Starting point**

How much do you remember about the Culture exchange text on page 6 about studying in the UK? What are Student Unions and what do they do? What happens at a freshers' fair?

2 SPEAKING 👥 **Project task**

You want to inform students from other countries about an aspect of studying in your country. Use your own knowledge and search the Internet for interesting information and facts about anything connected with studying in your country. You can focus on Secondary school, vocational studies, professional training, university life or the education system in general. Prepare one of these:

A poster   C video message

B presentation   D information leaflet

Research areas

- terms and timetables
- typical, popular, obligatory or unusual subjects
- usual and unusual extra-curricular activities
- exams and assessment, including university entrance exams
- English language teaching
- famous or local universities
- different options students have at different stages of education

 3 **Think about ...**

Digital skills

You may find that many texts about studying in your country are in your own language. Be careful using online translation tools to translate the texts. They are not always 100% correct!

Academic skills

On any assignment, it's important to manage your time carefully. Find out when you have to finish the project and how much time you have. Then decide how long each stage (e.g. research, writing, checking) will take. Make sure everybody in the team knows when they have to finish their part.

Collaboration

When you work in a team, decide the best way to divide the work equally and fairly. You could all search for different information, for example. Or some people could look for information while others are responsible for preparing artwork or writing the final version or giving the presentation. Make sure that everyone is happy with the distribution of work.

Useful language

Who wants to ...?, Are you happy doing ...?, Can I ...?, I'd like to ..., Can I volunteer for ...?, Why don't I/you/we ...?

Intercultural awareness

Think about any elements in your presentation that would be new or unusual for somebody not from your country. Check also for any words or expressions in your language that you think are difficult to translate. Then decide how to explain those elements, words and expressions.

4 SPEAKING 👥 **Project time**

Do the project. Then present it to the class.

5 **Evaluation**

Give each project a mark from 1 to 5 (5 = very good) for these categories.

Content	☐	Design	☐
Presentation	☐	Language	☐

Vocabulary in context
Words connected with transport and travel

1 SPEAKING 👥 How many different types of transport can you write down in three minutes?

2 Look at the words in the box. Name one or two types of transport you associate with each one.

> 🔊 10 **Words connected with transport and travel 1**
> carbon emission • catch • commute • crew •
> cruise • departure lounge • driver • flight • gate •
> get in/out • get on/off • give somebody a lift •
> land • launch • miss • motorway • overtake •
> platform • port • rail • road sign • seat belt •
> steering wheel • take off • traffic jam • tyre •
> vehicle • waiting room • wheel

3 Complete the text with the correct form of the words in the box.

> 🔊 11 **Words connected with transport and travel 2**
> arrival • board • cancellation • contactless • delay •
> destination • fare • fine • lost property • network •
> off-peak • passenger • route • ticket inspector •
> travel update • zone

4 SPEAKING 👥 Ask and answer the questions.

1 How important is travel for you? Why?
2 Do you ever travel abroad in the holidays? What are your favourite destinations?
3 What types of transport do you prefer for short trips? And for long journeys? Why?
4 How often do you use public transport? Which types and why?
5 Where are some good places to go on a day trip from your town or city? Give reasons.

Use it ... don't lose it!

5 Choose the correct alternative. If necessary, use the definitions on page 137.

1 I enjoy going on camping *journeys/trips* with my friends.
2 One day astronauts will go on a *trip/voyage* to Mars.
3 Some people are against spending money on space *journey/travel*.
4 They're organising a school *journey/excursion* to see a Shakespeare play.
5 Crossing the Atlantic is a long *excursion/voyage* by boat.
6 *Journey/Travel* helps you to see the world with different eyes.
7 We went on an amazing train *journey/travel*.
8 The *trip/excursion* to school is quite short.

Reach higher > page 137

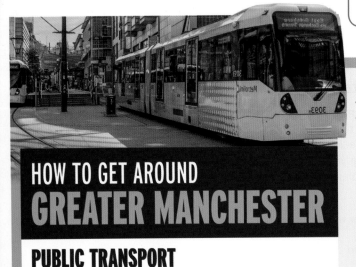

HOW TO GET AROUND GREATER MANCHESTER

PUBLIC TRANSPORT
Travel by tram

There's an official website where you can check the times of departures and (a) .... at the main tram stops. It includes live (b) .... with the latest news about any (c) .... to their service. But don't worry – if your tram is significantly late, or if there is no tram because of (d) ...., you can see your rights as a (e) .... here.

PRACTICAL INFORMATION 🛈

Ticket (f) .... View the map here.
1 = the city centre.
4 = the area furthest from the centre.

Ticket prices. The (g) .... you pay depends on the distance you travel. See here.

Weekend and (h) .... **prices.** There are special price offers for less busy times of the day or week. See here.

(i) .... **map.** See how the trams link up with bus (j) .... and trains here.

(k) .... **payment.** To pay on a tram, simply touch your credit card in at the start of your journey, just before you (l) .... the tram, and again when you get off at your (m) .... Be warned: if you can't show the (n) .... a valid ticket, expect to pay a (o) .... of £100.

(p) .... **office.** Find out what to do if you forget any objects on a tram here.

Reading

1 **SPEAKING** 🗣 How do you think cars will change in the future? Do you think they will look like the cars in the photos? Why/Why not?

2 Read this article quickly. What are the four main predictions it makes about cars in the future? Did you make any of the same predictions in 1?

> ☑ **Exam tip**
>
> In tasks where sentences are missing from a text, read the text carefully looking at the information before and after each gap. Then read the sentences and look for words and phrases which connect with information in the text. When you finish, read the text again to check that your answers make logical sense.

3 🔊12 Read the text again. Put the sentences into the correct places in the text (a–g). There is one extra sentence that you do not need to use.

1 This problem won't disappear with electric cars.

2 You won't need a driver, remember?

3 Or perhaps cars will simply disappear completely.

4 But it will certainly be less than from fossil fuels.

5 It takes a lot of energy, electrical or otherwise, to power so many cars for so few people.

6 In these cases, the car can take full control from the driver.

7 The technology is getting there.

8 In the UK's case, this will happen by the year 2040 at the latest.

4 What do the <u>underlined</u> words and phrases in the text mean? Guess and then check in your dictionary.

5 🧠 **Critical thinkers**

> In your opinion, how important or necessary are (a) fully electric cars? (b) driverless cars? (c) ideas for car sharing? (d) flying cars?
>
> What makes you say that?
>
> Use ideas from the reading and other information to justify your opinion. Then share your ideas.

DRIVING – THE FUTURE

In the next twenty or thirty years, cars will change dramatically. In fact, several of the biggest changes have already begun. Firstly, instead of being a luxury for a relatively limited group of car-owners, fully electric cars will become <u>the norm</u>. According to the International Energy Agency, by 2040 there will be nearly one billion completely electric vehicles on the road. Many countries have decided that they are going to stop the sale of petrol or diesel cars. (a) .... Right now, in the UK alone, there are approximately 31 million cars on the road, making cars and lorries a major <u>source</u> of carbon dioxide, the gas most responsible for global warming.

Will electric cars solve the problem of pollution completely? It's clear that all these new cars are going to need lots of electricity and this will still cause some pollution. (b) .... Unfortunately, however, much of the pollution caused by driving comes from cars <u>braking</u>, releasing microplastics from tyres and the road surface into the air. (c) .... As for noise pollution, electric cars are almost silent. But that could lead to accidents with cyclists and pedestrians who are unable to hear cars approaching. So a new European law says that electric cars will have to start producing noises so that people know they are there.

Meanwhile, another major change to cars has also already begun thanks to self-driving, driverless or autonomous cars. There are officially five levels of autonomy. Today, most cars that we call self-driving are only partially autonomous (between levels 2 and 3) – the car <u>handles</u> some aspects of driving and the driver can occasionally <u>take their eyes off</u> the road, very briefly. Despite the <u>misleading</u> things we hear in the press, it will still be a while before we sit inside a vehicle with no steering wheel and fall asleep as it drives us away (level 5). (d) .... But we shouldn't underestimate the need for significant improvements to roads and road signs to avoid accidents with autonomous vehicles. Talking of accidents, one major question is to decide who will be legally responsible when you have an accident in a self-driving car – you or the car manufacturer?

It seems then that cars of the future will be electric, driverless ... and possibly shared. At the moment most commuters drive to work alone. (e) .... It also takes a lot of space for parking. According to one calculation in a study by the Journal of the American Planning Association, 14% of the county of Los Angeles is used exclusively for parking. Owning a car is expensive and cars spend 96% of their time not moving. So maybe people will just take a taxi (driverless, electric) to work. Most of these vehicles only need to be big enough for one person. (f) .... On the other hand, the people who do decide to own a car will probably have much bigger vehicles that will also serve as an office space, bedroom and living room.

Looking further to the future, our driverless, electric cars will one day be able to <u>take to the sky</u>. In a few years a company called Terrafugia says it will have a vehicle that will be able to take off, fly and land autonomously. When you find yourself in a traffic jam, you'll be able to get up and away to escape the motorway. (g) .... Next summer, a Chinese company is testing a large drone that they hope will be capable of carrying a single passenger 23 minutes, <u>cruising</u> at an average speed of nearly 100 kph at a maximum height of over 3,000 metres. The passenger will simply enter their destination into a smartphone app and the drone will do the rest. It seems that, in the long term, the future of driving will have no need for cars, drivers ... or even roads.

Reach higher > page 137

Grammar in context 1
Future forms

1a Look at the sentences. What future form is the verb in bold in each sentence?

1 Many countries have decided that they **are going to** stop the sale of petrol cars.

2 Experts believe there **will** be nearly one billion completely electric vehicles.

3 When you **find** yourself in a traffic jam, you'll be able to get up and away.

4 It's clear that a billion electric cars **are going to** need lots of electricity.

5 Next summer a Chinese company **is testing** a large passenger drone.

1b Complete the rules for when we use *will, be going to*, the present simple or the present continuous.

a .... for predictions based on evidence.

b .... for plans and intentions.

c .... for predictions based on thoughts, opinions and expectations.

d .... for confirmed plans and arrangements.

e .... after expressions of time like *when, before, after, by the time, until, as soon as.*

1c Look at the sentences and complete rules a–c with *will* or the present simple.

1 2033 **will** be the 120th anniversary of the first mass-produced car, the Ford Model T.

2 I've just missed the bus. I know! I**'ll** get a taxi.

3 Their flight **leaves** tomorrow morning.

a We use .... for decisions made at the moment of speaking.

b We use .... for future facts.

c We use .... for events that are part of a timetable or routine.

☑ **Check it page 42**

2 SPEAKING 👥 Look at the sentences. Name the <u>underlined</u> future form and explain why it is being used.

1 I'm going to finish my homework before my dad <u>gets</u> home.

2 Tomorrow <u>will</u> be Friday the 13th.

3 We<u>'re seeing</u> the exhibition tomorrow.

4 My parents <u>are going to</u> buy a new car next year.

5 Take an umbrella. It looks like it<u>'s going to</u> rain.

6 Somebody's knocking on the door. I<u>'ll</u> get it.

7 Scientists expect they <u>will</u> solve the problem soon.

8 What time <u>do</u> you <u>start</u> school tomorrow?

Flipped classroom video
Watch the Grammar Presentation video ⟳

3 Read the text. Are the <u>underlined</u> sections of the text correct? If not, rewrite them correctly.

GRETA'S VOYAGE TO THE US

24th August 2019

Next week climate activist Greta Thunberg **(a)** <u>is setting off</u> on her first journey to the US. She **(b)** <u>isn't flying</u> because she is against the environmental impact of planes. She **(c)** <u>sails</u> across the Atlantic in a high-tech racing yacht which **(d)** <u>will not</u> harm the environment because it only uses solar panels to generate electricity. Weather experts predict that the crossing **(e)** <u>is</u> quite difficult because the winds **(f)** <u>are being</u> strong next week.

When Greta **(g)** <u>will arrive</u> in the US, she **(h)** <u>attends</u> the United Nations Climate Action Summit. The meetings **(i)** <u>start</u> on 23rd September. António Guterres, Secretary-General of the United Nations, **(j)** <u>is speaking</u> there. He hopes that, at the meetings, world leaders **(k)** <u>are listening</u> to the voices of young people like Greta Thunberg who are worried about the future of the planet.

Meanwhile, not everybody is impressed with Greta's travel plans. Some critics point out that various members of her ship's crew **(l)** <u>will need</u> to fly back to the UK as soon as they **(m)** <u>will arrive</u> in the US, and other crew members have already flown out to the US to sail the yacht back to the UK. The evidence suggests that Greta's journey **(n)** <u>isn't going to be</u> carbon zero after all.

4 Choose the best alternative.

1 The weather forecast says it's *snowing/going to snow* next week.

2 My family and I *are going/will go* to London next weekend. We've already booked our tickets.

3 What are your plans? What *do you do/are you doing* next weekend?

4 I won't start dinner until you *arrive/will arrive*.

5 Don't worry. I'*m going to/'ll* answer the door.

6 I've already decided. Next year I'm *working/going to work* harder.

7 Next year, February *is having/will have* 29 days.

8 Look at that car! It *isn't going to/won't* stop at the traffic lights.

5 Complete the sentences with an appropriate future form of the verbs given.

1 I think we _____ (have) flying cars before I _____ (be) 50 years old.

2 A: This bag is too heavy for me to carry.
   B: Don't worry. I _____ (help) you.

3 When I _____ (finish) school, I _____ (go) to university in a different city.

4 I _____ (see) the dentist tomorrow. I've got an appointment.

5 The next train _____ (leave) at 11.05 according to this timetable.

6 Wear your coat. It looks like it _____ (rain) later.

7 Next Saturday, it _____ (be) my parents' wedding anniversary.

8 Annie is pregnant. She _____ (have) twins.

6a Complete the questions about the future with your own ideas.

1 What do you think will happen when _____?

2 Are you going to _____ tonight?

3 _____ next weekend?

4 Is your favourite sports team _____?

5 _____ in 2040?

6 After you leave school, _____?

7 _____ when you're 25 years old?

6b Predict your partner's answer for each of your questions. Write down your predictions.

┌─ **Use it ... don't lose it!** ─┐

7 SPEAKING Ask your partner your questions in 6a. How many of your predictions in 6b were right?

Reach higher ⟩ page 137

Developing vocabulary

Prefixes

1 Make the negative form of these words. Use the prefixes *dis-*, *il-*, *im-*, *in-*, *ir-* or *un-*.

advantage • agree • believable • capable • comfort • complete • correct • employed • expected • experienced • inspiring • legal • likely • logical • mature • necessary • obey • patient • possible • practical • predictable • probable • regular • relevant • reliable • responsible • secure • successful • usual

2 SPEAKING Underline the prefix in each word. What is the meaning of the prefix?

cooperate • interactive • miscalculate • overpopulated • postgraduate • prefix • reinvent • semicircular • subway • supersonic • underestimate

3 Complete the text by adding the correct prefix to the words given.

NEWS   BLOG   **FEATURED ARTICLE**   MORE ▾

FRANKY FLIES INTO THE FUTURE

French inventor Franky Zapata became the first person to cross the English Channel on a jet-powered flyboard. The flyboard is a (a) _____ (production) between Franky and the French army, who think his invention could have military uses in the future. (b) _____ (flight), Franky was a little nervous because he hadn't had time to do all the tests he wanted to do, but once he began flying, he felt fine. The flyboard only has enough kerosene for ten minutes of flight so he had to (c) _____ (fuel) on a ship in the middle of the trip. Unfortunately, the first time he tried to do this he (d) _____ (calculated) his landing and fell into the sea. He went under the waves for a second. His team were glad to see him when he (e) _____ (appeared). However, there was a lot of (f) _____ (comfort) for Franky because his helmet filled with seawater and he had to drink it to be able to continue breathing. He realised he had (g) _____ (estimated) the size of the ship he would need to land on and used a bigger one for his second attempt. He travelled a total distance of 22 miles and reached a maximum speed of approximately 160 kph. That isn't exactly (h) _____ (sonic) but it's not bad for a small flyboard. Flying without wings, he looked like a (i) _____ (hero). Next, he says he's going to build a flying car. Some people think he's (j) _____ (confident) when he says that the car will fly at a speed of 400 kph!

4 Add a prefix to the words in bold and then complete the sentences to make them true for you.

1 I _____ **agree** with the idea that ...

2 I'm _____ **capable** of ...

3 I think people _____ **estimate** ...

4 As a _____ **hero**, I would like to be able to ...

5 I think a lot of people _____ **understand** ...

6 In my opinion, it's _____ **responsible** to ...

┌─ **Use it ... don't lose it!** ─┐

5 SPEAKING Compare and discuss your answers in 4.

Reach higher ⟩ page 137

GREAT LEARNERS
GREAT THINKERS

NEW TRAFFIC SOLUTIONS

Lesson aim: To think about better ways of moving around the city

Video: Bionic boots

SEL Social and Emotional Learning: Listening to others

1 **SPEAKING** 👥 Discuss the advantages and disadvantages of these different types of transport in the city.

   1 cars   2 trams   3 the underground   4 bicycles

2 **VIDEO** ▷ Watch the video and answer these two questions.

   1 Which of the types of transport (1–4) in 1 is the only one NOT to appear in the video?

   2 Which is faster in the video – a bicycle or the bionic boots?

3 **VIDEO** ▷ Watch again and complete the sentences with between one and three words for each gap.

   1 Justin, the presenter, says that thanks to scientists we can have ....

   2 Justin has gone to .... to meet Keahi, the inventor of bionic boots.

   3 Justin describes Keahi's workshop as a .... of mad science.

   4 It was always Keahi's ambition to run like a .... or an ....

   5 Keahi's next aim is to .... of the boots so that he can travel very ....

   6 Keahi thinks the boots are easy to ....

   7 Keahi thinks that the ability to move easily between lanes is a real .... compared with bikes.

   8 The narrator thinks it's quite .... to use the boots.

4 Do you think that Keahi's bionic boots will be the way we move around cities in the future? Individually, make notes with your ideas.

GREAT THINKERS

Share-Wait-Think-Discuss

5 **SPEAKING** 👥 Work in groups of three and follow this procedure.

   1 **Share**. The first person uses their notes from 4 to share their ideas. The others listen.

   2 **Wait** in silence. Don't interrupt! **Think** about what the first person said.

   3 Repeat this procedure for the second and third person.

   4 **Discuss** all the ideas that you have shared. Make comments and ask questions about what other people said.

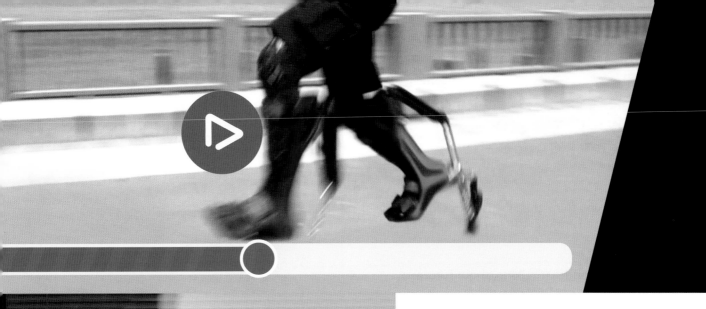

6 Read the text about traffic congestion in big cities. Which do you think are the most important arguments in the text?

ELECTRIC SCOOTERS: THE SOLUTION?

YES

- They're easy to ride.
- You can move faster than in a car at busy times of the day.
- You don't get hot and sweaty like when you ride a bike.
- They're cheap and don't pollute as much as cars.

NO

- They aren't very safe for people riding them and have already led to many injuries, some serious.
- They're dangerous for pedestrians, too.
- People park them on pavements, making walking difficult for pedestrians.
- There's a lack of control over scooters and their riders. For example, in many cases you don't need a license, insurance or a helmet.

7 **SPEAKING** Imagine that you are responsible for transport and traffic in your city. Do you allow electric scooters to move freely in the city centre, do you ban them, or do you set some controls and limitations to their use? Use the ideas in 6 and add your own. Come to a satisfactory decision as a whole group.

GREAT LEARNERS **SEL**

Great learners are good at problem-solving.

Was it easy to find a solution to the problem in 7? How did you come to a solution that you were all happy with?

Learner profile page 142

Listening

1 SPEAKING 👥 **Do you think that it will be possible to travel from New York to London in 30 minutes one day? If so, how?**

2 🔊13 **Listen to a podcast talking about future transport. Choose the best answer.**

1 Entrepreneur and engineer Elon Musk …
   a got the idea for an electric plane from an *Iron Man* film.
   b is more interested in creating a fast plane than an eco-friendly plane.
   c needs a special advance in technology in order to create his electric plane.

2 The company SpaceX®'s biggest contribution to space travel has been …
   a creating rockets that can go into space again and again.
   b helping to take important material to the International Space Station.
   c taking heavy cargo into space in a very powerful rocket.

3 Musk's biggest interest is …
   a promoting space tourism and making it a reality.
   b getting humans to live on another planet.
   c making it possible to get to anywhere on Earth in less than sixty minutes.

4 Tyler, the guest, is most impressed by what quality in top engineers and entrepreneurs?
   a imagination
   b ambition
   c determination

5 The Hyperloop is an example of …
   a an ambitious and successfully completed project.
   b a project that could solve several problems that exist today.
   c a project that is designed above all to revolutionise flying.

3 SPEAKING 👥 🔊13 **Listen again. Why do they mention these things, names or numbers?**

1 carbon dioxide emissions   4 100
2 vertical take-off and landing   5 2013
3 the Dragon spacecraft   6 470 kph

4 🧠 **Critical thinkers**

> **In your opinion, how useful is it to spend money on space travel?**
>
> What makes you say that?

Grammar in context 2

Future continuous, future perfect simple and future perfect continuous

1a Look at these sentences. What tense are the verbs in bold? Explain how we form the tenses.

1 Companies **will be developing** electric planes in the next few years.

2 In a few years, people **will be flying** from New York to London in about thirty minutes.

3 By 2030, the time of the journey **will have gone** down to just half an hour.

4 He expects astronauts **will have landed** on Mars by 2030 or before.

5 By 2030, they**'ll have been working** on the Hyperloop for over 15 years.

1b Complete the rules with *future continuous, future perfect* or *future perfect continuous*.

a We use the .... to talk about activities that will be finished before a particular time in the future.

b We use the .... to talk about activities in progress at a particular moment in the future.

c We use the .... to talk about how long an activity has been in progress before a particular moment in the future.

d We often use *by* with the .... and the ....

☑ Check it **page 42**

2a Complete each prediction with one word.

1 Nobody will .... driving in 2040 because all cars will be autonomous.

2 Carbon emissions from transport will .... disappeared by 2050 because all transport will be carbon zero.

3 By 2050, passengers will have .... using the Hyperloop for at least ten years already.

4 By 2030, astronauts .... have landed on the Moon again.

5 In 2030 nobody will be .... their holidays on the Moon as there won't be any buildings there.

6 In 2030, we will all be .... in electric planes.

7 By 2050, astronauts will .... been living in special camps on Mars for at least five years.

8 The time it takes to travel between Europe and America will have .... much shorter thanks to supersonic planes.

2b What do you think of these predictions? Which do you think will come true?

3a Read about Mark's trip to work. Would you like to do what he does each morning? Why/Why not?

Morning commuters

'Hi, I'm Mark. I live in Brighton and work in London. Every day I get up at 6.50. I don't live near the train station, so I cycle there. I leave home at 7.15 and get to the station at 7.30. I leave my bike there and catch the 7.44 train to London Victoria. I always have my breakfast on the train – just some juice and a cake. At 8.54, I arrive at London Victoria. Then I take the underground from London Victoria to Kings Cross. I usually get the 9.03 which arrives at Kings Cross at 9.11. Then it takes me exactly ten minutes to walk to my office. I'm usually completely exhausted before I begin work!'

3b Complete the sentences to talk about Mark's commute tomorrow. Use the future continuous, future perfect simple or future perfect continuous.

1   By 7.10, he .... (get up).
2   At 7.25 he .... (cycle) to the train station.
3   He .... (cycle) for exactly 15 minutes by 7.30.
4   He .... (get on) the Victoria train at 7.44.
5   By 8.54, he .... (have) his breakfast.
6   At 9.05 he .... (travel) on the London Underground.
7   He .... (not arrive) at his office by 9.11.
8   At 9.15 he .... (walk) to work.
9   By 9.21, he .... (travel) for about two hours!

3c Write four questions about Mark's commute to work tomorrow, two using the future continuous and two using the future perfect simple.

What will he be doing at 7.50?

3d SPEAKING 👥 Ask and answer your questions. Try to answer without looking at the book!

4 Put the verbs in the correct form of the future continuous or future perfect simple.

LIFE AT
30

'There's something I often wonder. What (a) .... I .... (do) when I'm 30? Will I be unemployed or (b) .... I .... (work)? I know that I (c) .... (finish) school, and I imagine I (d) .... (leave) university because not many people continue studying at the age of 30. One thing I do know is that I (e) .... (not live) in this town because I want to leave here when I go to university. I'm not sure if I (f) .... (get) married by the time I'm 30. It just depends on meeting the right person. I don't think I (g) .... (buy) a house or car because they'll still be really expensive, but I imagine I (h) .... (save) up my money each month hoping to buy them one day. Anyway, I'm really looking forward to seeing what's going to happen!'

5 Write predictions about yourself when you are 30. Use the ideas below and the future continuous, future perfect simple or future perfect continuous.

1   live abroad
2   buy a motorbike
3   see my old school friends regularly
4   speak English every day
5   stop playing video games
6   become famous on social media
7   get married
8   work in a big multinational company
9   do lots of sport
10 make lots of money

Use it ... don't lose it!

6 SPEAKING 👥 Compare your sentences and ask questions to find out what your partners have written. Are any answers particularly common?

Reach higher > page 137

Developing speaking

Talking about photos 1

a

b

1a **SPEAKING** 🗣 Look at the photos. Write down similarities and differences between the two photos.

Similarities	Differences

1b The people in the photos look secure. What reasons can you give for this?

2a 🔊 **14** Listen to a student doing this task and answer the questions.

> Compare the photographs and say why you think the people are feeling happy.

1 Does the student mention any of your ideas in 1?
2 Does she describe each photo in great detail?
3 Does she do both parts of the task?

2b **SPEAKING** 🗣 Would you like to try to do either of the activities in the photos? Why/Why not?

3 🔊 **14** Listen again and complete the expressions in the Speaking bank.

Speaking bank
Useful expressions to compare and contrast photos

Comparing
- (1) .... photographs show ...
- In (2) .... photos,
- In the second photograph, they're also ...
- One/Another (3) .... is that ...

Contrasting
- One big (4) .... between the photos is that ...
- Another important (5) .... is that ...
- The first photograph shows ... whereas/while the second shows ...
- In the first photo ... but in the second photo ...
- (6) .... the one hand, ...
- (7) .... the other hand, ...

4 **SPEAKING** 🗣 Use the phrases in the Speaking bank to talk about the similarities and differences between the photos that you wrote down in 1.

Practice makes perfect

5a Student A, look at the photos below. Student B, look at the photos on page 149. Think about similarities and differences between your two photos.

5b **SPEAKING** 🗣 Student A, do the task below. Student B, listen to your partner.

> Compare the photographs and say why the people are travelling in these different ways.

a

b

5c **SPEAKING** 🗣 Now change roles. Student B, your task is on page 149.

Developing writing

An opinion essay 1

1 [SPEAKING] **Read the text about UK school runs. What do you think about them and why?**

Culture exchange

The UK school run

The 'school run' is what happens when parents drive their kids to school. They park in the school car park (or anywhere else they can find) and drop their children off. Many parents are worried that something could happen to their children if they walk or cycle to school. Others just want to save their kids' time or protect them from bad weather. But apart from the negative effect on traffic and the environment, others worry that young people are just not getting enough exercise.

2 [SPEAKING] **Read this writing task. What is your opinion? Make a list of arguments to support it.**

> In your English class, you have been talking about how students get to school. Now your teacher has asked you to write an essay for homework.
>
> 'Do you think it's OK for parents to drive their kids to and from school each day?'
>
> Notes
>
> Write about:
> 1   traffic and the environment
> 2   independence
> 3   .... (your own idea)

3 **Read this essay. Is the opinion of the writer similar to yours? Don't worry about the gaps at this stage.**

Many parents give their kids a lift to school in the morning, instead of letting them walk, cycle or take public transport. (a) ...., this is a terrible idea.

(b) ...., just think how many cars make the journey to school each day. This creates terrible traffic jams because everybody is going to the same place at the same time. (c) ...., these traffic jams are responsible for much more pollution than school buses or public transport. An even better solution is walking or cycling, which causes zero carbon emissions.

(d) ...., some people say that walking or cycling to school can be dangerous. (e) .... if we are talking about very young children. (f) ...., teenagers need to learn to become independent and to look after themselves.

(g) ...., students spend a long time sitting and studying or playing video games. Cycling or walking to work or school would help us to be more healthy.

(h) ...., I believe that by driving their kids to school, parents are causing problems for the roads, the environment and for their own children. It's time to change this bad habit.

4 [SPEAKING] **Answer the questions.**

1   How many paragraphs are there in the essay in 3?
2   What is the function or topic of each paragraph?
3   What is the writer's own idea in the fourth paragraph? Is it a completely new idea from notes 1 and 2 in the writing task?

5 **Complete the essay with these phrases.**

> As far as I'm concerned · Furthermore · However · I agree up to a point · Lastly · On the other hand · To begin with · To sum up

6 **Put the words and expressions in 5 in the correct place in the Writing bank.**

Writing bank
Useful linkers and expressions in opinion essays

Expressing opinions
- Personally, I think …
- ....
- In my opinion,
- I believe that …
- ....

Adding opinions and putting them in order
- Firstly, ...
- Secondly, In addition, ...,
  What is more,
- Finally, ...

Contrasting opinions
- ...., Nevertheless
- On the one hand, ...

Concluding
- In conclusion, ..., All things considered,

☑ Exam tip

When you write opinion essays, there is no right or wrong opinion, but you must give different reasons and examples to defend your opinions in a logical way. You can use linkers to help you do this.

Practice makes perfect

7a **Look at this task. Write notes with your ideas. Then write your essay using linkers and expressions from the Writing bank.**

> 'What can we do to cut down the pollution caused by transport and travel?'
>
> Write notes about:
> 1   cars
> 2   long-distance travel
> 3   .... (your own idea)

7a **When you finish your essay, use the Writing checklist on page 141 to check it.**

Grammar reference

be going to, will, present continuous and present simple for future

1 We use *be going to* to talk about plans and intentions for the future. We use it for things that we have already decided to do in the future.

They've decided that they're going to fly to Dublin.

2 We can also use *be going to* to make predictions about the future, particularly when we have evidence for the prediction.

The Sun is up already. I think it's going to be hot today.

3 We use *will* and *won't* to make general predictions about the future. We often use *think, hope, expect, imagine,* etc. with *will* and *won't* to show that our prediction is based on thoughts, opinions or expectations.

I think humans will land on Mars one day.

4 We also use *will* and *won't* when we decide to do something at the moment of speaking, for example when we suddenly offer to do something for someone.

A: I can't answer the phone. My hands are wet.
B: I'll get it for you.

5 We use *will* and *won't* to talk about the future when we consider it to be an objective truth.

Next week it will be my birthday.

6 We use the present continuous to talk about future arrangements and plans that have been confirmed.

Tomorrow I'm having my first job interview. They called me for the interview last week.

7 We use the present simple with time expressions like *when, as soon as, until, after* and *before*. We cannot use *will* with these time expressions.

When I go to university, I'll study chemistry.

8 We can also use the present simple to talk about the future when the action is part of a timetable or routine.

Tomorrow I have my English class at two o'clock.

Future continuous

We form the future continuous with *will/won't* + *be* + verb-*ing*.

We use the future continuous to talk about activities in progress at a particular time in the future. The activities are in progress and so they are unfinished.

At this time tomorrow, he'll be flying to the US.

Future perfect simple

We form the future perfect simple with *will/won't* + *have* + past participle.

We use the future perfect simple to talk about activities that will be finished by a certain time in the future. We often use the preposition *by* with the future perfect. It means 'some time before'.

I will have gone to bed by midnight.

Future perfect continuous

We form the future perfect continuous with *will/won't* + *have been* + verb-*ing*.

We use the future perfect continuous to talk about how long an activity has been in progress before a particular moment in the future. We often use the preposition *by* with the future perfect. It means 'some time before'.

By 8pm, I'll have been revising history for five hours!

Vocabulary

1 Words connected with transport and travel

arrival (n) • board (v) • cancellation (n) • carbon emission (n) • catch (v) • commute (n, v) • contactless (adj) • crew (n) • cruise (n) • delay (n) • departure lounge (n) • destination (n) • driver (n) • excursion (n) • fare (n) • fine (n) • flight (n) • gate (n) • get in/out (phrasal verb) • get on/off (phrasal verb) • give somebody a lift (v) • journey (n) • land (v) • launch (n, v) • lost property (n) • miss (v) • motorway (n) • network (n) • off-peak (adj) • overtake (n) • passenger (n) • platform (n) • port (n) • rail (n) • road sign (n) • route (n) • seat belt (n) • steering wheel (n) • take off (phrasal verb) • ticket inspector (n) • traffic jam (n) • travel (n, v) • travel update (n) • trip (n) • tyre (n) • vehicle (n) • voyage (n) • waiting room (n) • wheel (n) • zone (n)

2 Prefixes

cooperate (v) • disadvantage (n) • disagree (v) • discomfort (n) • disobey (v) • illegal (adj) • illogical (adj) • immature (adj) • impatient (adj) • impossible (adj) • impractical (adj) • improbable (adj) • incapable (adj) • incomplete (adj) • incorrect (adj) • inexperienced (adj) • insecure (adj) • interactive (adj) • irregular (adj) • irrelevant (adj) • irresponsible (adj) • miscalculate (v) • overpopulated (adj) • postgraduate (n) • prefix (n) • reinvent (v) • semicircular (adj) • subway (n) • supersonic (adj) • unbelievable (adj) • underestimate (v) • unemployed (adj) • unexpected (adj) • uninspiring (adj) • unlikely (adj) • unnecessary (adj) • unpredictable (adj) • unreliable (adj) • unsuccessful (adj) • unusual (adj)

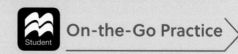

On-the-Go Practice

Grammar test

Future forms 1

1 Complete the sentences with the correct future form of the verbs given. Use *will*, *be going to*, the present simple or the present continuous.

1 I'll change places when the teacher .... (come).

2 **A:** I can't do this exercise.
   B: I .... (help) you.

3 Last week I made a decision. Next year I .... (do) more exercise.

4 Mark and Jenny .... (get) married next Saturday.

5 I think robots .... (take) over the world one day.

6 The coach .... (leave) at 8.25 tomorrow.

/ 6 points

Future forms 2

2 Which sentence in 1 …

a is a confirmed plan or arrangement? ....

b is a prediction based on a thought, opinion or expectation? ....

c is an event that is part of a timetable or routine? ....

d is a plan or intention? ....

e is a decision taken at the moment of speaking? ....

f needs a special tense after an expression of time? ....

/ 6 points

Future continuous, future perfect simple and future perfect continuous

3 Tick the correct sentences and rewrite the incorrect ones.

1 I can't go out at seven o'clock because I'll have done my homework then.

2 She started driving home at 3 pm. By 6 pm, she'll have been driving for three hours.

3 Don't call me at nine o'clock because I'll be watching a film with Lara in the cinema.

4 I can write a summary of the book tomorrow because I'll be reading it by then.

5 At five o'clock next Saturday I'll have been playing basketball.

6 I can't give you my assignment tomorrow because I won't be finishing it.

7 I'll be wearing my new jacket when I go to Sam's party tomorrow.

8 When I'm 20, I'll have finished school.

/ 8 points

Vocabulary test

Words connected with transport and travel

1 Write simple definitions of these words.

1 platform   3 vehicle   5 gate   7 off-peak

2 crew   4 delay   6 lift   8 launch

/ 8 points

excursion, journey, travel, trip, voyage

2 Complete the sentences with *excursion*, *travel*, *trip*, *journey* or *voyage*.

1 When we were in London, we went on a special .... in a tourist boat on the River Thames.

2 I think .... is the best way to learn about life.

3 It will be difficult for humans to make the long .... to Mars.

4 We were tired when we arrived because the .... by plane and coach had lasted 18 hours!

5 Last week we went on a day .... to Liverpool.

/ 5 points

Prefixes

3 Complete the sentences with prefixes added to the words given.

1 Please don't .... me – it was just a joke. (understand)

2 They're going to .... the film and do a new version. (make)

3 I can't do it. I'm totally .... (capable)

4 There's no space on this flight. It's already .... (booked)

5 I don't know why you did that. In my opinion, it was .... (necessary)

6 Do what she says. Don't .... her. (obey)

7 She already has a degree in architecture. Now she's doing a .... course. (graduate)

/ 7 points

Total: / 40 points

4 OUR STRENGTHS

Vocabulary in context

Personality adjectives
Idioms connected with personality

1 Complete sections O, C and E in the text with the words in the box. Check that you also understand the words in bold in those sections. Use a dictionary if necessary.

> 🔊 **15** Personality adjectives 1
> broad-minded · down-to-earth · impetuous · laid-back · outgoing · reserved · resourceful

The Big Five is a well-known system used by psychologists to describe personality. A popular acronym for the Big Five is OCEAN.

O penness to experience

People who have high scores in this factor are usually **curious** and (a) .... so they like new, interesting experiences. They are also **creative** and clever. People with low scores tend to be **practical** and (b) ...., preferring to be **sensible** rather than **imaginative**.

C onscientiousness

People with a high score in this factor are usually very (c) .... and good at finding ways to deal with problems. They are also usually **reliable** and **hard-working**. People with low scores are often (d) ...., doing things without thinking of the consequences, and also very **relaxed** and (e) ....

E xtroversion

Extroverted people tend to be (f) .... and **talkative**, generally enjoying interacting with others. Introverts tend to be **quiet** and (g) ...., preferring reading a book alone to going out partying.

A greeableness

People with a high score in agreeableness are usually (h) .... and **diplomatic**. They are also **kind** and (i) ...., thinking of others' feelings. They often tend to be **modest**, too. People with a low score are often (j) ...., thinking more about themselves. They can also be (k) .... and difficult to rely on.

N euroticism

This is a question of not feeling (l) ...., not believing that you can do things well. People with a high score may well be (m) .... and become **serious** or angry for no reason. They may also be (n) ...., needing more confidence in themselves. On the other hand, a low score suggests that a person is **calm** and (o) ...., able to come back strong after a problem.

2 Now do the same with sections A and N and the words in this box.

> 🔊 **16** Personality adjectives 2
> considerate · insecure · moody · resilient · self-confident · selfish · tactful · untrustworthy

3 **SPEAKING** 👥 Look at these words. Discuss what you think they mean. Find any related or opposite adjectives in the vocabulary boxes in 1 and 2 or the text.

> 🔊 **17** Personality adjectives 3
> big-headed · cheerful · easy-going · energetic · humble · introverted · loud · loyal · narrow-minded · sensitive · shy · sociable · tactless

4 Match the idiomatic expressions in the box to their explanations (1–8).

> 🔊 **18** Idioms connected with personality
> a big mouth · a bright spark · a great laugh · a live wire · a pain in the neck · a party animal · a social butterfly · a wallflower

1 someone who enjoys going to lots of parties

2 someone who is very annoying or irritating

3 someone who is very funny

4 someone at a social event who has no one to talk to or dance with because they are shy

5 someone who says things they shouldn't

6 someone who is clever or has a clever idea (but often used to mean just the opposite!)

7 someone who has a lot of energy and is interesting to be with

8 someone who is very sociable and goes to lots of different social events with lots of different people

> ### Use it ... don't lose it!
>
> **5** **SPEAKING** 👥 What type of personality do you think the people in 1–4 below typically have? Use adjectives or idiomatic expressions from this page and give reasons for your answers.
>
> **1** a film star · **3** the president
> **2** a top scientist · **4** a novelist
>
> Reach higher ⟩ page 137

Reading

1 **SPEAKING** Do the informal personality test on page 149. Do you agree with what it says about you? Why/Why not?

2 Read the text quickly. What are its main messages?

 LUCY'S REFLECTIONS *Random thoughts about my life*

HOME / ABOUT ME / **BLOG** / CONTACT

Let me tell you about something that happened to me recently: I went to a party. 'What's so special about that?', you're wondering. Well, I hardly ever go to parties because, get ready for this – I don't like them much. I guess I'm the typical wallflower. As teenagers, it seems we almost have to feel guilty about that because people assume we should all be party animals. Anyway, I've just discovered something that's made me realise that it's okay to prefer quiet chats to loud crowds. So, I thought I'd share some of the ideas I learned from a book I've just read.

It's called *Quiet Power*, by Susan Cain. She suggests that being introverted isn't necessarily the same as being shy. When you're shy, you're quiet because you're afraid of what other people will think of you. Being introverted, on the other hand, is more a question of preferring situations that are quieter and stimulating. I don't know about you, but I could relate to that immediately. Some of my friends like to fill their weekends with countless things to do and people to see. Me, I'm happy to spend the weekend painting, reading, and taking my dog for a walk.

Here's the important message, though. It's OK to prefer quiet situations. It's true that society seems to pay more attention to extroverts. We're often given the idea that we should all be trying to be the life and soul of the party. But as Susan Cain points out in her book, it's about time society paid more attention to what quiet people bring to the table, too. They have special skills and qualities that extroverts just don't have. For example, most of us would agree that introverts tend to be more reflective and think things through more slowly and deliberately, whereas extroverts are more impetuous. In fact, some of the most creative people in history, like Bill Gates for example, have been introverts.

Think about when you do collaborative assignments at school. The loudest students tend to dominate and make quicker decisions. But it's usually the quieter people who see the bigger picture and are more focused on the task itself. After all, the quieter you are, the better you listen to everyone else. Now, don't get me wrong here. It's always better to have a mix of all different kinds of people working together. I just wonder whether the talents of the quieter members of the group are taken less seriously than they should be.

It's important to remember that, even if you are quiet, that doesn't mean that you can't do things like stand up and give a presentation that's just as good as anyone else's. You can rise to the occasion when you need to and push yourself to take centre-stage. Afterwards, it's perfectly okay to recognise that on the whole you feel happier and more comfortable behind the scenes rather than in the spotlight. As I get older, I feel more and more confident that it's fine not to be a social butterfly. And I feel inspired enough after reading the book to give a presentation on this topic at school next week. I know I'll be nervous, but I think it's time to shout out loud that 'quiet is all right'!

3 **19** Read the text again and choose the best answers.

1 Lucy is writing this blog post because …
   a something unusual happened to her recently.
   b she's just done something that people consider out of the ordinary.
   c she wants other people to know about something she recently found out.

2 Lucy suggests …
   a society doesn't really like people who spend a long time thinking.
   b society has never fully recognised the talents of people like Bill Gates.
   c there is some social pressure on people to be more extroverted.

3 Lucy's problem with group work at school is that she feels that …
   a extroverts never listen to the ideas of quiet people.
   b introverts don't get enough recognition for their contributions.
   c the groups don't have a proper balance of personality types.

4 Lucy's last message is that …
   a quiet people have a preference for quiet situations but that doesn't mean they are limited to those situations.
   b as they get older, quiet people start to feel more confident about public speaking.
   c now that she's more mature, she enjoys telling people all about the hidden skills of quiet people.

4 **What do the underlined words in the text mean? Guess and then check in your dictionary.**

5 🧠 **Critical thinkers**

   In your opinion, is the blog post true and/or fair?

   What makes you say that?

Reach higher > page 137

Grammar in context 1

Comparatives and superlatives

1 Look at the sentences and answer the questions.

1 They make **quicker** decisions.
2 They tend to see the **bigger** picture.
3 You feel **happier** being behind the scenes.
4 They feel **more comfortable** out of the spotlight.
5 It's **better** to have a mix of people.
6 The **loudest** students tend to dominate.
7 Some of the **most creative** people in history have been introverts.
8 They often work **more slowly** and **deliberately**.
9 They tend to work **faster**.

a Sentences 1 to 4 all contain comparative adjectives. What rule explains the form of each comparative adjective?

b Sentence 5 contains an irregular comparative adjective. What are the two other common irregular comparative adjectives?

c Sentences 6 and 7 contain superlative adjectives. What are the rules for making superlative adjectives?

d Sentence 8 contains regular comparative adverbs. How do we make regular comparative adverbs? How do you think we make regular superlative adverbs?

e Sentence 9 contains an irregular comparative adverb. What are the irregular comparative and superlative adverbs for these words? *hard, early, late, long, soon, good/well, bad/badly, far*

f In sentence 4, *a lot* is used with a comparative adjective to talk about a big difference. Do these words talk about big or small differences? *a bit, far, a little, a lot, much, significantly, slightly, way* (informal)

☑ Check it **page 54**

2 Find and correct the mistakes.

1 I'm going to try more hard to listen to others in group discussions.
2 Einstein was one of the more famous introverts in the world of science.
3 Mexico is slightly biggest than Indonesia.
4 She's the friendlier person of this class.
5 I think Jack is more laid-back that Sam.
6 She's the most moody person I know.
7 Try to do the exercise quicklier.
8 You need to get here much more soon.
9 She did far more well than me in the test.
10 Poland is more further from England than Germany.

3 Complete the text with the correct comparative or superlative adjective or adverb form of the word given. Sometimes more than one answer is possible.

HAPPINESS IS A PENCIL!

It's one of **(a)** .... (unusual) psychology experiments ever done. In the 1980s, Fritz Strack and his colleagues asked two groups of people to look at a cartoon and say how funny they found it and how happy it made them feel. They wanted to know if one group would find it **(b)** .... (funny) than the other. While looking at the cartoon, one group had to hold a pencil between their teeth, without it touching their lips. The other group held a pencil with their lips but not their teeth. The first group felt much **(c)** .... (good) than the second. They laughed **(d)** .... (quick) and **(e)** .... (long). Why? It wasn't because they looked **(f)** .... (close) at the cartoon than the second group. It was because holding the pencil between their teeth forced their mouth into a smile. It seems that people smile more when they are happy, but they also feel **(g)** .... (happy) when they smile! So if you want to be one of **(h)** .... (cheerful) people in your social group, all you need to do is try **(i)** .... (hard) to behave like you're happy. We could go **(j)** .... (far) than that. Think of some of **(k)** .... (happy) people you know. They probably walk **(l)** .... (dynamic) than most other people, speak slightly **(m)** .... (fast), wear **(n)** .... (colourful) clothes, and have a **(o)** .... (firm) handshake. Copying their behaviour could make you feel **(p)** .... (positive) about life. Try it! After all, what could be **(q)** .... (easy) than just putting a pencil between your teeth to feel happy?

4 🔊 SPEAKING 👥 Decide who in your class ...

1 shouts the loudest.
2 speaks the quietest.
3 draws the best.
4 is the best laugh.
5 talks the fastest.
6 is the brightest spark.
7 arrives the earliest.
8 writes the neatest.
9 is the biggest live wire.
10 laughs the most often.

5 🔊 SPEAKING 👥 Say one of the names you chose in 4. Can your classmates guess the description?

6 Look at the sentences and answer the questions a–c.

1 Some people don't take introverts **as** seriously **as** extroverts.

2 Introverts are **not as/so** talkative **as** extroverts.

3 They are taken **less** seriously **than** they should be.

4 As people get **older and older**, they feel **more and more confident**.

5 **The longer** you think about a task, **the smarter** your decisions are.

6 **The quieter** you are, **the better** you listen.

a When do we use *as ... as*?

b When do we use *not as ... as*, *not so ... as* or *less ... than*?

c How do you translate 4–6 into your language?

☑ Check it **page 54**

7 Complete the second sentence so that it has a similar meaning to the first sentence, using the word given. Do not change the word given. Use between two and five words.

1 When you run far, you become healthier.
(the)
The .... you become.

2 Public speaking becomes easier depending on your age.
(older)
The .... public speaking becomes.

3 Our goal seems increasingly far away from us.
(and)
Our goal seems .... from us.

4 My exam results were good, but Mark's were better.
(so)
I didn't do .... Mark in my exams.

5 Ben thinks books are better than parties.
(not)
For Ben, parties .... books.

8 Complete the expressions with the words in the box.

better • done • merrier • never • safe • worse

1 Better late than ....

2 Easier said than ....

3 The sooner, the ....

4 Better to be .... than sorry.

5 The more, the ....

6 This is going from bad to ....

Use it ... don't lose it!

9 SPEAKING 🗣 Prepare three mini-dialogues. Each one must include an expression in 8.

Reach higher ⟩ page 137

Developing vocabulary

Noun suffixes

1 Make nouns for people with these words and a suffix. You may need to change the spelling.

invent • lead • psychology • assist • history

inventor

2 Make abstract nouns from these words and a suffix. You may need to change the spelling.

sensitive • shy • free • prefer • appear • involve • connect • relate (three possibilities)

sensitivity

3 Read the text below. Use the words given to form a word that fits in the gap.

☑ Exam tip

In this type of exercise, you sometimes need to add a prefix or a suffix, or both. Sometimes, the word also needs to be plural. Look at the context carefully to decide.

DO NOTHING!

It may sound strange, but many people today think that (a) .... (bored) is good for you and helps to build your personality. They say that today's world is full of too many (b) .... (distract) like smartphones and the Internet. They are worried about the (c) .... (appear) of periods of quiet, peace and (d) .... (relax) in our daily lives. Some (e) .... (research) claim that nowadays we cannot maintain (f) .... (concentrate) for as long as before. A famous (g) .... (write) called Lauren Child, author of the *Ruby Redfort* series, believes that doing nothing, being quiet and (h) .... (active) can lead to greater (i) .... (creative), because it's only when you're bored that you have time to think and form ideas. Great (j) .... (science) and (k) .... (music) need time and (l) .... (free) to be able to come up with new works. However, there are other people who argue that having nothing to do just leads to (m) .... (lazy) and maybe even (n) .... (depress). What do *you* think?

Use it ... don't lose it!

4 SPEAKING 🗣 Discuss the ideas in the text in 3 and answer the final question. Try to use as many of the words you formed in the text as possible in your discussion.

Reach higher ⟩ page 137

GREAT LEARNERS
GREAT THINKERS

PERSONALITY AND STEREOTYPES

Lesson Aim: To think about regional and national personalities and stereotypes

Video: British personality types

SEL Social and Emotional Learning: Keeping an open mind

1 **SPEAKING** What stereotypical ideas do you have about the personality of people from Scotland, Wales or England? Think in terms of the five categories (Openness to experience, Conscientiousness, Extroversion, Agreeableness, Neuroticism) in the text on page 44. Explain your ideas to the class.

2 **VIDEO** Watch the video. What are the general ideas about people from Scotland, Wales and England (specifically, Cambridge)? Are they similar to your ideas?

3 **VIDEO** Watch the video again and choose the correct alternative. In one case, both alternatives are correct.

1 The idea that people from different parts of Britain have specific personalities is a relatively *recent/old* concept.

2 Almost 400,000 people answered the questions *in person/on the Internet*.

3 The *BBC/University of Cambridge* organised the research to discover if there is any real basis for these stereotypes.

4 The expert believes *the results from this research/other factors* should help you to decide where to live.

5 The expert thinks the results *prove/disprove* regional stereotypes.

6 The Scottish woman interviewed *agrees/disagrees* that Scottish people are often sociable.

7 The Welsh woman suggests that Welsh people *immediately trust/don't immediately trust* strangers.

8 The video says the results of the survey *prove regional differences/might help you to choose which area you should live in*.

4 Read the text. What does it say about national stereotypes?

NATIONAL STEREOTYPES

Whether it's the caricature of the introverted English, the loud Americans or the industrious Japanese, national stereotypes are extremely common. However, is it true to say that people from different countries are actually different? Well, when the same psychology tests have been done with massive numbers of people from different countries, the average results do, in fact, vary from one country to the next. So, it's fair to say that, in terms of personality, the average Norwegian, for example, is *not* the same as the average Spaniard. Interestingly, however, these average differences in personality between nations are not the same as the stereotypes we hold. Although we tend to agree with each other about what the typical personality type is in a given country, including our own, the research suggests that our ideas are often quite inaccurate.

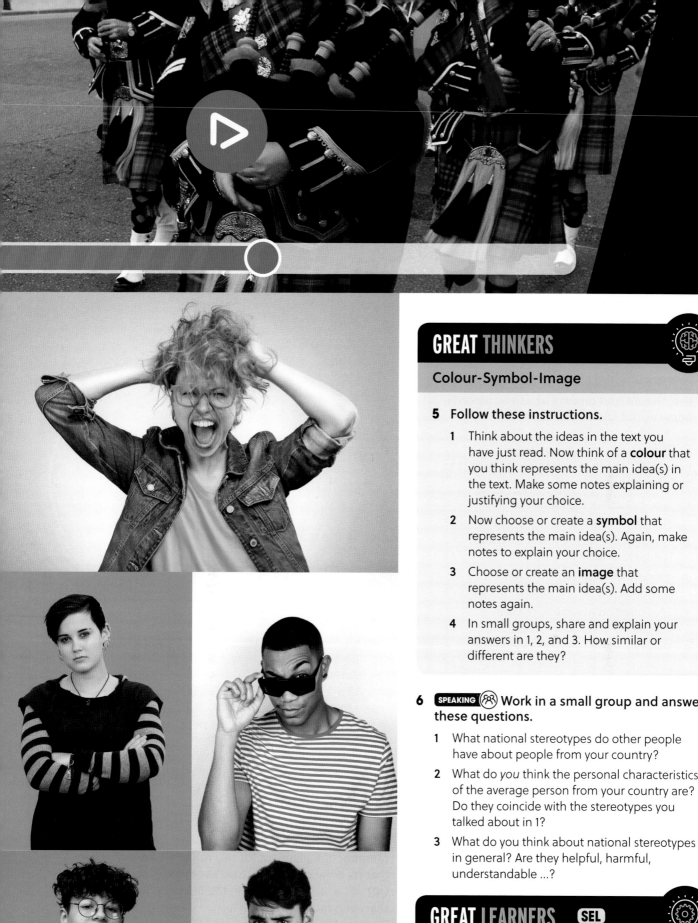

GREAT THINKERS

Colour-Symbol-Image

5 Follow these instructions.

1 Think about the ideas in the text you have just read. Now think of a **colour** that you think represents the main idea(s) in the text. Make some notes explaining or justifying your choice.

2 Now choose or create a **symbol** that represents the main idea(s). Again, make notes to explain your choice.

3 Choose or create an **image** that represents the main idea(s). Add some notes again.

4 In small groups, share and explain your answers in 1, 2, and 3. How similar or different are they?

6 **SPEAKING** Work in a small group and answer these questions.

1 What national stereotypes do other people have about people from your country?

2 What do *you* think the personal characteristics of the average person from your country are? Do they coincide with the stereotypes you talked about in 1?

3 What do you think about national stereotypes in general? Are they helpful, harmful, understandable ...?

GREAT LEARNERS SEL

Great learners are open-minded and positive towards others.

Why is it important to be aware of and question stereotypes?

Learner profile page 142

Listening

A page from one of Leonardo da Vinci's notebooks

1 **SPEAKING** 👥 **Describe what you can see in the picture and discuss what you already know about Leonardo da Vinci.**

2 🔊 20 **Listen to a podcast about Leonardo. Are these statements True (T) or False (F)?**

1 They talk about the *Mona Lisa* in detail.   T / F

2 They describe an important map that Leonardo drew.   T / F

3 They explain how Leonardo wrote in his notebooks.   T / F

4 They mention where you can see Leonardo's notebooks today.   T / F

5 They talk about some of the journeys Leonardo made in his lifetime.   T / F

6 They mention the length of Leonardo's notebooks.   T / F

3 🔊 20 **Listen again and answer the questions.**

1 What were Leonardo's 'To Do' lists?

2 Name one of the things on his 'To Do' lists.

3 What was special about the way Leonardo wrote in his notebooks?

4 Why did Leonardo write and draw so much on every page of his notebooks?

5 How is Leonardo's work helping Stanford University to create a mechanical bird?

6 What was Leonardo's attitude to art, science and engineering?

4 ⚙️ **Critical thinkers**

In your opinion, which of the many things that Leonardo da Vinci did in his lifetime is the most interesting or impressive?

What makes you say that?

Grammar in context 2

Articles

1 **Read these sentences. Then complete rules a–f with *a/an*, *the* or *no article*. Match each rule to a sentence (1–6).**

1 He was probably **the** greatest genius of all.

2 [–]Scientists, [–]doctors and [–]engineers are still examining his notes today.

3 He designed **a** statue of **a** horse.

4 They built **the** statue 500 years later.

5 He was passionate about **the** world.

6 He didn't separate [–]art and [–]science.

a We use .... to talk about a singular countable person or thing for the first time, or to say that the person or thing is one of a number of people or things.

b We use .... to talk about a specific person or thing or a person or thing mentioned before.

c We use .... to make general statements about uncountable nouns.

d We use .... to make general statements about plural countable nouns.

e We use .... to talk about someone or something that is unique.

f We use .... with superlative adjectives and adverbs, and *first* and *last*.

☑ **Check it page 54**

2 **Complete the text with *a*, *an*, *the* or [–].**

Culture exchange

An English genius

Sir Isaac Newton was **(a)** .... famous English mathematician, astronomer and physicist. He is considered to be one of **(b)** .... most important scientists of all time. He provided **(c)** .... new mathematical description of **(d)** .... universe in his book, the *Principia*. Many people consider his work to be the beginning of **(e)** .... physics as a modern subject of study. Newton said that he came up with **(f)** .... theory of gravity after watching **(g)** .... apple fall from **(h)** .... tree. But **(i)** .... people now think this is just **(j)** .... myth. It seems Newton was **(k)** .... introvert. He was **(l)** .... Member of Parliament for two years but was so quiet that he only spoke once, to ask somebody to close **(m)** .... window in the building. But it's clear that even today, **(n)** .... scientists owe a lot to Sir Isaac Newton. Einstein kept **(o)** .... picture of him on his study wall. Today there is **(p)** .... statue of Newton at **(q)** .... National Library in London.

Collaborative project 2   **page 57**

Ability in the past, present and future

3 **Look at these sentences and complete rules a–g with the words or expressions in bold.**

1 By **being able to** make connections, it's easier to innovate.

2 They think that one day they **will be able to** make a mechanical bird.

3 Leonardo **couldn't** build the statue himself.

4 He **could** write with both hands.

5 They **were able to** build/**managed to** build/**succeeded in** building the statue 500 years later.

6 We **can** learn a lot from Leonardo.

7 You need a mirror **to be able to** read the writing.

8 In the exhibition we visited yesterday, we **could** see some pages from Leonardo's notebooks.

a We generally use .... to talk about ability in the present.

b We usually use .... to talk about ability in the future.

c When we need an infinitive or gerund to talk about ability, we use .... or ....

d To talk about general ability in the past, we use ....

e To talk about the ability to do something on one specific occasion in the past, we use ...., ..., or ....

f We can use the negative form .... to talk about both general ability or one specific occasion in the past.

g In the past, we can use .... with verbs of the senses (*see, hear, feel, smell, taste*) to talk about general ability or one specific occasion.

☑ **Check it page 54**

4 **Choose the best alternative.**

1 Last week I *could/was able to* finish the book I'd been reading for months.

2 Yesterday my parents *succeeded/managed* to buy tickets for the concert.

3 One day I'd like to *be able to/can* visit Egypt.

4 The exam was difficult but he *could/was able to* get a good mark.

5 My dad *could/couldn't* finish the marathon yesterday because he had a cramp.

6 I'm sure that one day I *can/will be able to* speak Russian.

7 Last week I *managed to/could* give a good presentation even though I felt quite nervous.

8 When I was about four or five, I *could swim/succeeded in swimming* quite well.

9 I wasn't wearing glasses, so I *didn't manage to read/couldn't read* the book.

5 **Complete the text with an appropriate word from sentences 1–8 in 4 to talk about ability.**

FROM CIRCUS STRONGMAN TO ANCIENT EGYPTIAN ARCHAEOLOGIST

Amongst the personal strengths of Giovanni Battista Belzoni (1778–1823) was precisely that: his physical strength. At a height of over two metres, the Italian was so strong that he (a) .... carry a human pyramid of twelve adults, which he often did! He was known as The Great Belzoni when he joined a circus in Britain. Over ten years later, he was (b) .... to find a very different job. He travelled to Egypt and became an archaeologist and explorer. He managed (c) .... transport a massive statue called *The Younger Memnon* over three kilometres to the River Nile, get it on to a boat, and send it off to London. It weighed over 7,000 kilos! You (d) .... still see the statue at the British Museum today. Belzoni also succeeded (e) .... uncovering the temple at Abu Simbel after spending months clearing away a mountain of sand that covered it. He found amazing hieroglyphics on the walls there but (f) .... understand them since it was only later that a Frenchman called Jean-François Champollion (g) .... able to crack the code of Egyptian writing. Belzoni was also the first person in modern times to (h) .... able to get inside the Pyramid of Khafre in 1818. If you go inside the tomb there today, you (i) .... be able to read Belzoni's graffiti in Italian celebrating his discovery.

6 **Complete the sentences to make them true for you.**

1 I think that one day I'll be able to ....

2 One day I managed to .... even though it was difficult.

3 Last week I succeeded in ....

4 I couldn't .... because it was too difficult.

5 I could .... on my own when I was at primary school.

6 I'd love to be able to .... one day.

Use it ... don't lose it!

7 **SPEAKING** 🗣 **Compare your sentences in 6. Are any of your answers similar?**

Reach higher ⟩ page 137

Developing speaking

Presentations 1

a | Rosa Parks

b | Alexander Fleming

c | Amelia Earhart

d | William Shakespeare

1 SPEAKING 👥 Talk about the people in the images. What did they do to become famous?

2 SPEAKING 👥 Look at this presentation topic. Who in history would you choose to talk about and why?

> Give a presentation about somebody who you think was an inspirational and influential figure in history. Explain in what way(s) the person was inspirational or influential.

3 🔊 21 Listen to a student giving a presentation on this topic and answer the questions.

1 Who did they choose and why?

2 What do you think of their choice?

4 🔊 21 Listen again. Which expressions in the Speaking bank do you hear?

Speaking bank
Useful expressions to structure a presentation

Beginning your presentation
- I'd like to begin by saying …
- To start with …
- The first thing I'd like to say is …
- I'm going to talk about …

Structuring arguments and events
- First of all,
- Firstly,
- Secondly,
- Another thing is that,
- Furthermore,
- What's more,
- It's important to remember that …
- It's also true that …

Concluding your presentation
- In conclusion,
- Finally,
- To sum up,
- Last but not least,
- The point I'm trying to make is …
- In short,

5a Look back at your answer in 2. Make notes about the person you chose. Do some research about them if necessary.

5b Organise your notes from 5a in a logical order, with an introduction and a conclusion.

Practice makes perfect

6a SPEAKING 👥 Read the advice in the Exam tip box and then take it in turns to give your presentation using your notes from 5b. Remember to use expressions from the Speaking bank.

6b SPEAKING 👥 When you finish, discuss how well you did your presentations.

☑ Exam tip

When you give a presentation, remember that you can look at your notes, but don't just read them aloud. Don't forget to look at your audience to see if they understand you and are interested.

Developing writing

An article 1

1 SPEAKING 👥 Read this announcement and discuss possible people that you could write about and why you think they would be a great choice.

Articles wanted!
The best guest!

If you could invite a famous person to your school for the day, who would you choose?

Write an article explaining who the famous person is, why you think they would be a great guest and what you would like the person to do at your school.

Send us your articles today!

---

2 Read a student's answer to this writing task. Would you like this person to visit your school? Why/Why not?

A Have you ever heard of the football manager Jürgen Klopp? Whether you like football or not, I think this live wire is the best person to invite to our school. Let me explain why.

B Klopp is a very cheerful, friendly, outgoing person and is famous for being a great laugh. He's very knowledgeable about football but what I like most about him is that he's absolutely brilliant at motivating and inspiring people and building their self-confidence. Just imagine how somebody like that could inspire all of us to do well at school and in life afterwards!

C At school, I'd like him first to give a talk to all of us to explain the secrets of his success. Then I think it would be great for students to be able to ask him questions about some of his most interesting experiences. In the afternoon, he could watch our sports classes and maybe give us advice about how to do better. After all, he has won the FIFA® Football Manager of the Year award.

D Personally speaking, I think Jürgen Klopp is one of the most inspiring people I know. The world of sport can be very competitive and aggressive but Jürgen Klopp is a great example of fair play and respect. What's more, he also gives away 1% of his salary to help people who are less well-off than him. Can you think of a better role model for students like us today?

3 Match the paragraphs A–D to these topics.

1 A conclusion with one or two further reasons to justify your choice ....
2 A brief introduction to the person chosen ....
3 Reasons why you chose this person ....
4 What you would like the person to do at your school ....

4 Look at the Writing bank. Which of the techniques does the student in 2 use? Give examples.

Writing bank
Useful ways to involve the reader in articles

- Use *you, your, we, our.*
- Use direct questions like: *Have you ever ...?, Are you like me?, Can you think of ...?*
- Use expressions that make a connection with the reader: *Imagine ..., Just think ...*
- Use colourful, descriptive language: *He/She is very/ really/extremely/quite/rather* + 'normal' adjectives (*inspiring, talkative ...*), *He/She is completely/ totally/absolutely/really* + 'extreme' adjectives (*fantastic, amazing ...*)
- Use expressions to make your opinion clear: *What I like (most) about him/her is ..., In my experience ..., Personally speaking ..., To be honest ..., Let me explain why ...*

Practice makes perfect

5a Choose a famous person and write your article for the task in 1. Follow the paragraph plan in 3 and use expressions from the Writing bank.

5b When you finish your article, use the Writing checklist on page 141 to check it.

5c Read other people's articles. Vote for the best guest!

Grammar reference

Making comparisons

- *Less* is the opposite of *more*.
  Animals are less intelligent than humans.
  (= Humans are more intelligent than animals.)
- We use *as ... as* to say two things are the same.
  Dogs are as clever as cats.
- We use *not as ... as* or *not so ... as* to say that the second person or thing is more ... than the first one.
  Animals aren't as intelligent as humans.
  (= Humans are more intelligent than animals.)
- We use *The + comparative, the + comparative* to talk about two things that happen together.
  The faster I run, the more tired I feel.
  The harder you study, the better your results.
- We use *comparative and comparative* to talk about situations that are increasing.
  Things are getting better and better.

Articles

a/an

- We use *a/an* with singular countable nouns. We use it when we mention something for the first time, or to say that the person or thing is one of a number of things or people.
  I've got a computer. It's a laptop.
- We use *a/an* to say what somebody's profession is.
  He's a scientist.

the

We use *the* with countable (singular and plural) and uncountable nouns. We use it to refer to something or somebody previously mentioned.
I've got a computer. The computer's really fast.

- We also use *the* to talk about specific things or people.
  The computer I bought was quite cheap.
- We use *the* to talk about something unique, something that there is only one of.
  the Sun, the government (in a particular country), the floor
- We use *the* with superlative adjectives and adverbs, and with *first* and *last*.
  He was the first person to arrive.

No article

We do not use an article with plural countable nouns or uncountable nouns when we are talking about people or things in general.
Scientists say that animals have complex brains.

Ability in the past, present and future

- We generally use *can* and *can't (cannot)* to talk about ability in the present. We use *be able to* in its present form to suggest we can do something special, that is not easy.
  I can swim quite well.
  I'm able to swim for an hour without stopping.
- We generally use *will/won't be able to* to talk about ability in the future.
  With more training, I'll be able to run a marathon.
- We can also use *can* to talk about future plans and arrangements.
  I can finish the project tomorrow if I plan my time carefully.
- When we need an infinitive or gerund to talk about ability, we use *to be able to* or *being able to*. We cannot use *can*.
  I'd love to be able to draw well.
  I love being able to walk to the gym.
- To talk about general ability in the past, we use *could*.
  I could speak English when I was just five years old.
- To talk about the ability to do something on one specific occasion in the past, we use *was/were able to, managed to + infinitive* or *succeeded in + gerund*. We can use their negative forms to talk about inability.
  Last week he was able to break/managed to break/succeeded in breaking the world record.
- We can use the negative form *couldn't* to talk about both general ability or one specific occasion.
  I couldn't speak English when I was just five years old.
  Last week he couldn't break the world record.
- In the past, we use *could* with verbs of the senses (e.g. *see, hear, feel, smell, taste*) to talk about general ability or one specific occasion.
  It was very dark but I could see something moving.

Vocabulary

1 Personality adjectives

big-headed • broad-minded • calm • cheerful • clever • considerate • creative • curious • diplomatic • down-to-earth • easy-going • energetic • hard-working • humble • imaginative • impetuous • insecure • introverted • kind • laid-back • loud • loyal • modest • moody • narrow-minded • outgoing • practical • quiet • relaxed • reliable • reserved • resilient • resourceful • self-confident • selfish • sensible • sensitive • serious • shy • sociable • tactful • tactless • talkative • untrustworthy

2 Idioms connected with personality

a big mouth • a bright spark • a great laugh • a live wire • a pain in the neck • a party animal • a social butterfly • a wallflower

3 Noun suffixes

People: assistant • historian • inventor • leader • musician • psychologist • researcher • scientist • writer
Abstract/concrete: activity • appearance • boredom • concentration • connection • creativity • depression • distraction • freedom • involvement • laziness • preference • relation • relationship • relaxation • sensitivity • shyness

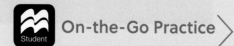

Student On-the-Go Practice

Grammar test

Making comparisons

1 Choose the correct alternative.

1 She doesn't work *as hard/hardly* as me.

2 My classmates are a lot less hard-working *than/as* me.

3 The sunnier it is, *it gets hotter/the hotter it gets*.

4 She speaks *faster/more fast* than anybody else I know.

5 The Theory of Relativity is not so difficult *as/that* people imagine.

6 They're the *most/more* confident people that I know.

7 The sooner she finishes her work, the *earlier/earliest* she can get home.

8 When you write your composition, do it more *careful/carefully* than the last one you did.

/ 8 points

Articles

2 There are no articles in these sentences. Add five articles in the correct places.

1 I met friend yesterday in city centre.

2 Most important thing in life is having friends.

3 Experts say government is having problems.

4 I like listening to actors and things they say about life in Hollywood.

/ 5 points

Ability in the past, present and future

3 Find and correct the mistakes in the sentences.

1 Yesterday the firefighters managed rescuing five people from a burning house.

2 They succeeded to climb the mountain.

3 I can to speak English.

4 I've got tickets so I'll able to see the match next week.

5 I had to go through the window because I could open the door.

6 I'd really like to be able play a musical instrument.

7 Yesterday I could buy tickets for the concert!

/ 7 points

Vocabulary test

Personality adjectives

1 Look at the adjectives and write the opposites.

1 humble ....

2 introverted ....

3 reliable ....

4 broad-minded ....

5 self-confident ....

6 talkative ....

7 diplomatic ....

/ 7 points

Idioms connected with personality

2 Complete these sentences with an appropriate word.

1 He's so irritating. He's a real .... in the neck.

2 She's a great .... She tells some really funny stories!

3 He's a real party .... He always goes to every party there is.

4 Don't be such a big ...., telling everybody our secrets!

5 Who's the bright .... who answered all the exercises before the teacher asked us to?

/ 5 points

Noun suffixes

3 Put the words in the correct noun form.

1 One day she'd like to become a professional .... (music).

2 What an .... (improve)! Your work is much better now.

3 Giving a presentation is often a question of .... (confident).

4 They're spending more and more money on health and .... (educate).

5 There was no light, just .... (dark) everywhere.

6 Who was the .... (create) of Facebook®?

7 The lights aren't working. We need to call an .... (electric).

8 Her .... (lazy) is having a negative effect on her marks.

/ 8 points

Total: / 40 points

Reading

Reading exam tip

In activities where you have to transform a sentence, remember ...

You must use the key word in your answer. You will probably have to change other words and re-order the sentence.

1 SPEAKING Complete the second sentence so that it has a similar meaning to the first sentence, using the word given. Discuss the questions.

> It's been over a year since I last flew to Italy. (flown)
>
> I .... over a year.

1 Which words are the same in the second sentence?

2 Which part of the first sentence comes first in the second sentence?

2 Complete the second sentence so that it has a similar meaning to the first sentence, using the word given. Use between two and five words.

1 The weather this winter has been much colder than last year.

   COLD

   Last winter the weather was .... this year.

2 The beach was so lovely that we went every day.

   SUCH

   It was .... that we went every day.

3 I am not as good at science as you.

   BETTER

   You .... me.

4 Do you think you should study another language?

   LEARN

   Have you ever considered .... another language?

5 Do what she says. You must obey her.

   OBEY

   Do what she says. Don't .... her.

3 SPEAKING Which sentences in 2 did you find the hardest? Why?

Speaking

Speaking exam tip

In speaking exams where you have to speak about some photographs, remember ...

You need to compare your photographs rather than just describe them. Make sure you listen to and read the instructions so you understand exactly what you need to talk about.

4 SPEAKING You are each going to compare a set of two photos and talk about them for about one minute. At the end of your partner's turn, comment on their photos.

Student A, look at photos a and b showing people on holiday. Compare the photos and say what you think the benefits are of each holiday.

Student B, say which holiday you think is the most enjoyable.

a

b

Student B, your task is on page 150.

Student A, say which person you would like to know.

5 SPEAKING Discuss the situations in your photos. Talk to each other about things your partner could have compared but didn't.

Exam success
Listening and Writing > **page 145**

A genius from your country

Virtual Classroom Exchange

 1 SPEAKING **Starting point**

What do you remember from the Culture exchange text on page 50 about the English genius Sir Isaac Newton? What type of person was he? Why was/is he so famous?

 2 SPEAKING **Project task**

You want to help more people from other countries to know about a genius from your country, somebody who was particularly skilful in any area of science or the arts. You are going to search the Internet for interesting information and facts about the person. Prepare one of these:

A poster   **C** video message

B presentation   **D** information leaflet

Research areas

- the life of the person
- their personality and personal strengths
- their works, masterpieces, discoveries, inventions, theories, publications, etc.
- any prizes or awards that they won
- any films, series, books or works inspired by, or dedicated to, them
- their importance and relevance today

3 **Think about ...**

Digital skills

Always copy and keep a record of links to the sources of information that you want to use in your project so that you can find that information again quickly and easily when you need it.

Academic skills

Don't just copy and paste information and say it's yours. That is called plagiarism. Read the information and then write a simple summary of what you remember and think is important, *in your own words*. Remember to say where you found the information.

Collaboration

When you work on a collaborative task like this, the main objective should be to produce an excellent piece of work. That's why it's important, as a team, to give and accept constructive criticism.

Useful language

I think we should ..., I think it would be better to ..., Maybe we ought to ... instead of ..., Yes, that's a good idea, Okay, let's try ..., Let's see if it's better to ...

Intercultural awareness

Look at sources <u>in English</u> to find out how famous the genius you have chosen is <u>outside</u> your country. Is the fame and reputation of the person similar to their reputation inside your country, or are there any differences? What could explain any differences?

4 SPEAKING **Project time**

Do the project. Then present it to the class.

5 **Evaluation**

Give each project a mark from 1 to 5 (5 = very good) for these categories.

Content   ☐   Design   ☐

Presentation   ☐   Language   ☐

5 FINANCIAL ADVICE

Vocabulary in context

Spending and saving money
Idioms connected with money

1 **SPEAKING** **How many different types of shop can you name in two minutes?**

2 **SPEAKING** **Look at the photo on the right. Describe it using the words in the box. Use a dictionary if necessary.**

22 Spending and saving money 1

ATM/cashpoint • bank charge/fee • bargain • change • credit/debit card • discount • (bank)note • receipt • refund • sale • save • take out (money) • waste (money)

3 **Complete the text with the correct form of the words in the box. Use a dictionary if necessary.**

23 Spending and saving money 2

account • afford • allowance • budget • cash • coin • get into debt • payment • purchase • spend on • spending habits • swipe • tax • value

Culture exchange

US teens and money

An American bank called Piper Jaffray has recently conducted its 37th Annual Taking Stock with Teens® Survey amongst 8,000 US teens of an average age of 16 to discover more about their **(a)** .... – what they usually do with their money. They discovered that on average they **(b)** .... $2,600 a year .... food and clothes.

US teenagers can clearly **(c)** .... to spend a lot! They spent more than $75 billion in 2018. Favourite **(d)** .... are food (24%) and clothing (19%). **(e)** .... for money is important for them – they don't mind paying for good quality. In general, US teens get their money from gifts (64%), an **(f)** ...., for doing chores (32%), and jobs (22%).

Many US teens no longer use **(g)** .... to buy things – they shop directly by making electronic **(h)** .... They are more likely to **(i)** .... a debit card than search for banknotes or **(j)** ....

However, another survey by Junior Achievement USA and Citizens Bank discovered that the biggest financial worry of 34% of US teenagers is to **(k)** .... by spending too much with the credit card attached to their bank **(l)** .... 43% are worried about paying **(m)** .... to the government when they start work. Only 33% of teens have ever calculated a financial **(n)** .... to really know how much they can spend.

4 **SPEAKING** **Ask and answer the questions.**

1 What type of things do you usually spend your money on?
2 How do you usually pay for the things that you buy?
3 Are you saving money at the moment? If so, what for?

5 **Guess the meanings of the idioms connected with money in bold. Use a dictionary if necessary.**

1 When there are sales, do you try to quickly **snap up a bargain**?
2 Have your parents ever bought something that **cost an arm and a leg**?
3 Have you ever **spent a fortune** on an electronic gadget?
4 Do you find it difficult to **tighten your belt** when you don't have much money left?
5 Do you know anybody who simply **throws money down the drain**?

Use it ... don't lose it!

6 **SPEAKING** **Ask and answer the questions in 5.**

Reach higher page 138

Reading

1 **SPEAKING** 👥 Each photo on this page illustrates a different article from a money website. What do you think they will be about?

2 Read the articles. Explain what each photo in 1 shows exactly.

3 🔊 24 Answer the questions with information from the text.

1 Why is it strange or unusual that Sweden in particular will probably be the first country to stop using cash?

2 How is it possible that 97% of all Swedish people can use debit or credit cards?

3 What is Swish and how is it helping Sweden to become cashless?

4 Why is small change not necessary in Sweden?

5 What are two advantages and two disadvantages of the disappearance of cash from daily life?

6 What two main types of tax are mentioned at the beginning of the second article?

7 Why and how did Peter the Great implement his Beard Tax?

8 What effect did King Henry VIII's beard tax have and why?

9 In the past, what different things have English people done to their houses to avoid paying special taxes?

10 In the UK, what are television licences and why do they exist?

4 What do the <u>underlined</u> words in the text mean? Guess and then check in your dictionary.

5 🧠 **Critical thinkers**

> In your opinion, is it better to use cash or to pay for things with a phone?
>
> What makes you say that?

The Money Manager – Helping teens to understand money ✕ 🔍

WITHOUT A PENNY IN THEIR POCKETS

It was the first country in Europe to <u>adopt</u> banknotes, back in 1661. However, now it seems that in a few years Sweden will become the world's first country to <u>do away with</u> cash completely. In fact, they are nearly there already. Only 13% of the population rely on notes and coins and over 80% of all purchases are cashless. To make sure nobody is excluded, anyone over seven is allowed to have a debit card, <u>as long as</u> they have their parents' permission. That means that 97% of the population have a card. It's curious to think that most young people growing up in Sweden today will probably never see or use cash.

One reason why this is happening in Sweden is because it is one of the world's most technologically advanced nations. In 2012, the six biggest banks there joined together to create a mobile payment platform that made electronic payments easier. The application, called Swish ®, is so widely used now that people generally don't have to carry cash and needn't worry about having the correct change. When tourists come to Sweden, they realise they needn't have changed their dollars or euros for local currency because you just can't use it anywhere, not even on public transport.

There are fewer bank robberies now in Sweden because banks don't keep cash. There are no problems with theft near cashpoints. The staff in shops and restaurants all feel safer too because they no longer worry about protecting cash. A cashless society may not be perfect, though. When all payments are made through your phone, if your battery <u>runs out</u>, so does your money. Many people are worried about hackers too, not to mention what companies can do with all the information they get about our spending habits. And you'd better <u>keep track of</u> your money because it's easy to get into debt when all you need to do to buy things is swipe your phone or card, without counting out those hard-earned notes and coins.

updated 1 hour ago

UNUSUAL TAX FACTS

Tax is a way to raise money to pay for all sorts of things that a country needs, from roads to health care. Everybody who works has to pay it and we also pay it on a wide range of goods. In the UK, a tax of 20% is added to the price of chocolate bars, for example.

Historically, there have been some highly unusual taxes. At the end of the 17th century, Tsar Peter the Great put a tax on beards. This was a clever way to encourage people to shave as he wanted them to adopt the Western style, and also to show loyalty towards him. Most people didn't have to do anything but people with beards weren't allowed to keep them unless they paid. They then received a <u>copper</u> coin with a moustache and beard to prove they had paid. In England, King Henry VIII did something similar but with different results. With his law, the longer your beard, the more you paid. The elite grew longer beards just to prove their <u>stature</u>.

In England, there has been a long tradition of trying to tax homes, and of trying to <u>dodge</u> these taxes. In 1660, there was a tax on fireplaces. People bricked them up to hide them. In 1696, they introduced a tax where you paid more according to the number of windows you had. People built houses with very few windows, leading to health problems. Next, there was a tax on bricks. Builders began to use bigger (and therefore fewer) bricks to save money.

One UK tax that has lasted longer is a kind of tax on televisions. Traditionally, if you own a television, you must pay an annual fee called a television licence. This money finances the BBC and keeps it advert-free. The penalty for not having a licence is a large fine. Last year, 240,000 people were caught. If you get a fine you ought to pay it fast or you could go to prison.

posted 3 hours ago

Reach higher → **page 138**

Modal verbs of obligation, prohibition and advice – present

1a Look at the sentences and answer the questions below.

1 You **ought to** pay the fine fast.
2 You **should** be careful with contactless payment.
3 You **don't have to** carry change.
4 You **must** pay an annual fee.
5 Everybody who works **has to** pay tax.
6 You **mustn't** watch TV without a licence in the UK.
7 You**'d better** keep track of your money.
8 People under seven **aren't allowed to** have a card.
9 You **need to** pay by card.
10 You **needn't** worry about having change.
11 They **don't need to** protect cash anymore.
12 You **can't** use cash on public transport in Sweden.

Which grammatical structure(s) do we use to:

a express obligation or necessity?
b say there is no obligation or necessity?
c say something is prohibited or not possible?
d give advice or recommendations?

1b Answer these questions.

a Which structures need *to* + infinitive? Which need the infinitive without *to*?
b How do you make sentence 5 into a question?
c How do you make sentences 2 and 7 negative?
d How do you make sentence 10 affirmative?
e Is *'d* an abbreviation of *had* or *would* in sentence 7?

☑ **Check it page 68**

2 Find and correct the mistakes in these sentences. One of the sentences is correct.

1 You would better pay online because it isn't safe to carry all that cash.
2 We ought ask if we can pay in cash.
3 You don't have to be an adult to open a bank account.
4 Have you to be British to open an account in the UK?
5 You needn't to carry cash if you have a card.
6 You use somebody else's ID to open a bank account.

3 Complete each space with one word to talk about obligation, prohibition or advice. Sometimes there may be more than one possibility.

BANK ACCOUNTS FOR **TEENAGERS**

❶ You (a) .... have to be over 16 to open your own bank account in most UK banks, you can be younger. But usually you (b) .... be at least 11. That is generally the minimum age. You (c) .... better explain your age clearly when you go to the bank because there are normally different types of accounts for ages 11 to 15, and 16 to 19. In any case, when you are under 18, you (d) .... use your bank account to borrow money – no bank will let you do that.

❷ To open your account, you (e) .... to show two types of identification, for example a passport is usually essential, and something to show where you live. If you're under 16, our advice is that your parents (f) .... to go to the bank with you because it makes it easier to open the account.

❸ Many accounts are free, so you don't (g) .... to pay any fees. You often get a debit card, too. Some banks even let you design your own card using your favourite photo!

❹ Eventually, when you become 18 or 19, you (h) .... continue to use a young person's bank account. That's not permitted since these accounts have special conditions exclusively for young people. But you (i) .... worry because your bank (j) .... remind you to change your account to make it an adult bank account. It's not their obligation, but it's a good idea for them to do this.

4 SPEAKING 🗣 **You have an American friend who is coming to visit you. Think of useful information and advice to give them about spending and looking after money in your country. Use these words and expressions.**

are/aren't allowed to • can't • don't have to • had better not • must • mustn't • needn't • ought to

Modal verbs of obligation, prohibition and advice – past

5a Look at the sentences and answer the questions on page 61.

1 People with beards **had to** pay the tax.
2 Those without beards **didn't have to** pay.
3 They **needn't have** changed their dollars for local currency.
4 They **weren't allowed to** keep their beards unless they paid.
5 They **needed to** pay more if their beard was long.
6 They **should/ought to have** thought of that before.
7 They **shouldn't have** introduced that tax.
8 They **didn't need to** pay tax if they didn't have any windows.
9 He **couldn't** pay with cash because they only accepted card payments.

Which grammatical structure(s) do we use to:

a express obligation and necessity in the past?

b say that something happened but it was not necessary?

c say that something was not necessary (maybe it happened or maybe it didn't)?

d say something was prohibited or not possible?

e criticise a past action or say that it was a mistake?

5b For sentences 3, 6 and 7, complete the structure.

should/shouldn't/ought to/needn't +

.... + ...

☑ Check it **page 68**

---

6 Add one word to correct each sentence.

1 We ought have gone to a cheaper restaurant.

2 I allowed to open an account in that bank so I went to another.

3 They thought I was too young so I had show my ID.

4 You have paid for my sandwich because I had enough to pay for it, but thanks!

5 We have to go to the bank to open the account yesterday because we could do it online.

6 We didn't need buy bread because we already had some.

7 Anne shouldn't had such a big lunch because she wasn't really very hungry.

7 Look at each situation and then write a sentence using a word or expression from sentences 1–9 in 5a.

1 She didn't open a bank account and that was a mistake.
  She ....

2 You bought me a present but it wasn't necessary.
  You ....

3 It was obligatory for me to show my student ID.
  I ....

4 We didn't have permission to speak to the director.
  We ....

5 It wasn't necessary to pay a fee so he didn't do it.
  He ....

6 Paying the waiter a tip was optional for us last night.
  We ....

8 Write six sentences about yourself using three expressions from 1a and three from 5a. Make two of your sentences false but believable.

Use it ... don't lose it!

9 SPEAKING 👥 **Tell your partner your sentences. Can they identify which sentences are false?**

Reach higher ▷ page 138

Developing vocabulary

Phrasal verbs connected with money and shopping

1 SPEAKING 👥 **Look at the phrasal verbs in bold in these sentences and discuss their meaning. Use a dictionary to check your ideas.**

Money *rights* and *wrongs*

1 It's a good idea to **set** money **aside** each week so you have money for emergencies.

2 Even when there's little money, governments shouldn't **cut down on** health care or education.

3 When a friend lends you money, you should **pay** it **back** as quickly as possible.

4 It's okay to **splash out** and buy yourself some luxury items from time to time.

5 It's easy to **get by** with very little money.

6 After eating out, you should see what the bill **comes to** and then everybody should **chip in** to pay it.

7 It's important to **shop around** and compare prices before you buy something.

8 You should always snap up bargains quickly before they **sell out**.

9 When you **run out of** money, you should immediately ask your parents for more.

10 Some shops try to **rip** teenagers **off** by charging high prices for badly-made clothes.

2 Rewrite each sentence using one of the phrasal verbs above.

1 My brother hasn't got much money but he's surviving.

2 I'm saving some of my allowance for the holidays.

3 That video game is disappearing from the shops really fast.

4 I'll give you back the money you lent me as soon as I can.

5 £30 for that! They charged you far too much!

6 I can't go out because all my money has gone.

7 She needs to spend less on clothes.

3 Complete the questions with one word.

1 Do you set any money .... each week or month? What for?

2 Does anybody need to pay you .... at the moment because you lent them money?

3 Have you ever gone to buy something and couldn't because they'd already sold ....? What was it?

4 Do you think a shop or restaurant has ever ripped you or your family ....? How?

5 When's the last time you chipped .... to buy something with your friends?

Use it ... don't lose it!

4 SPEAKING 👥 **Ask and answer the questions in 3.**

Reach higher ▷ page 138

GREAT LEARNERS
GREAT THINKERS

CASH AND DEBT

Lesson Aim: To think about how to spend money sensibly and avoid debt

Video: Keeping it local

SEL Social and Emotional Learning: Self-management

1 [SPEAKING] How many different currencies from around the world can you name? Which country or countries is each currency used in?

GREAT THINKERS

See-Think-Wonder

2a Look at the image at the top of page 63 and answer the questions.

1 What do you **see**? Describe the things in the image.

2 What do you **think** the things are? Why, how, and where do you think you can use them?

3 What evidence can you give to justify your answers in 2?

4 What do you **wonder** about when you look at the image? What more would you like to know?

5 Now share your thoughts with other students.

2b [VIDEO] Watch a video which explains the image. Were your ideas correct? Does it tell you the things you wanted to know? If not, how could you find out more?

3a [SPEAKING] Are the sentences True (T) or False (F)?

1	Berkshire is a relatively busy, industrialised area of the US.	T / F
2	It's quite common for areas like Berkshire to have their own currency.	T / F
3	Both sides of the BerkShare notes illustrate people connected with the area.	T / F
4	One great thing about the BerkShare scheme is that it encourages shop owners to keep spending the money locally.	T / F
5	When you buy things in a chain store, most of your money goes to another part of the country.	T / F
6	A local currency creates a better bond between shop owners and their customers.	T / F
7	Thanks to technology, almost thirty countries are going to follow in Berkshire's footsteps.	T / F
8	There are more jobs for the inhabitants of Berkshire thanks to this local currency.	T / F

3b [VIDEO] Watch the video again. Check and complete your answers in 3a.

4a [SPEAKING] Using cash instead of a card or electronic payment is often considered to be a good way to spend less. Make a list of other ways to spend less and avoid getting into debt.

4b Read this text. Do any of the ideas in the text also appear in your list in 4a?

How students can avoid debt

$ Plan a budget. Write down your monthly income and expenses to see how much you can spend. Always spend less than you earn!

$ Decide on a certain amount of cash to spend each week in local shops or on the high street. Learn to live within your limits.

$ Avoid external pressure (peer pressure, advertising …) to spend money unnecessarily.

$ There are different organisations that offer help and advice about debt and managing money. Don't be afraid to consult them.

$ Discuss money with your friends. Together, look out for free or cheap things to do and search around for good deals.

5   **SPEAKING**  Discuss these questions.

1   Which do you think is the best piece of advice in the text?

2   What other ideas did you think of that are useful?

3   When you are responsible for controlling your own financial situation, how well do you think you will manage? Why?

GREAT LEARNERS   SEL

Great learners take responsibility for their own actions.

In theory, it is compulsory for UK secondary schools to teach students about personal finance. What do you think about this?

Learner profile >   page 142

Listening

1 **SPEAKING** 👥 Look at the photos and describe what you can see.

2 🔊 **25** Listen to four news stories. For each story (1–4), decide (a) *who* made the discovery, (b) *where* they made it, and (c) *what* it was.

> ☑ **Exam tip**
>
> Look at the next task. Before you listen, it's a good idea to read the statements carefully and underline any important information. When you listen, remember that different speakers may use words that come in other sentences but you are listening for the ideas, not just the words that express them.

3 🔊 **25** Listen again. Which of the four stories and main characters does each statement refer to?

A The financial value of their discovery is still not very clear. 1/2/3/4

B They still need to wait half a year before they can receive their prize. 1/2/3/4

C They had immediate access to the financial value of what they found. 1/2/3/4

D The discovery happened during their holidays. 1/2/3/4

E They are very interested in discovering where the financial prize they received came from. 1/2/3/4

F Their discovery was lucky but not <u>only</u> a question of luck. 1/2/3/4

G There is no real theory now why the prize was where it was found. 1/2/3/4

H They are going to do something to show appreciation for their good luck. 1/2/3/4

4 ⚙ **Critical thinkers**

> In your opinion, should people who find treasure be able to keep it?
>
> What makes you say that?

Grammar in context 2

> **Flipped classroom video** ↻
> Watch the Grammar Presentation video

Modal verbs of speculation and deduction – present and future

1 Look at these sentences and complete rules a–d with the verbs in bold.

1 The cleaner **might** become very rich.

2 This person **must** have a big heart to give away money like that.

3 The story **may** or **may not** end well for him.

4 She **might not** discover the person's identity.

5 It **can't** be easy for him to relax.

6 The treasure **could** be worth £5 million.

a We use ...., ..., and .... when there is a 50% possibility that something is or will be true. The negative forms are .... and .... We cannot use the negative form of ....when there is a 50% possibility that something isn't true.

b We use .... when we are 90% certain that something is true.

c We use .... when we are 90% certain that something isn't true.

d When we are speculating and making deductions, the opposite of *must* is ....

> ☑ **Check it page 68**

2 Choose the best alternative.

1 His parents *might/must* have a lot of money because they have three cars.

2 She *can't/must* sing very well because nobody wants to listen to her.

3 It *may/must* be hard to write a bestseller because not many people manage it.

4 That *can't/mightn't* be Joe's jacket because his is blue and this one's grey.

5 She's seen that band five times. She *can't/must* really like them.

6 It's unusual that the teacher hasn't arrived yet. She *can't/may not* be well, or perhaps she had a problem on the way here.

7 My parents *might/must* let me stay out on Saturday night or they *can't/may not*. I don't really know because I've never asked them before.

3a Look at these objects from the bag of a girl called Sarah. What can you guess about Sarah? Use *must*, *can't* or *may/might*.

3b Complete the sentences with *must*, *can't* or *may/might*.

1 Sarah .... be learning Spanish because she's got a Spanish text book.

2 She .... be Spanish because she's only learning the language now.

3 She .... be very good at Spanish yet because her book is for beginners.

4 She .... like the number 10 or it .... be the number they gave her in a team.

5 She .... be quite well-off because her wallet is very full and she's got a gold credit card.

6 She .... have a full-time job because she's still a student.

7 She .... love cats. Who knows, she .... have a pet cat at home.

Modal verbs of speculation and deduction – past

4 Look at these sentences and complete rules a–c with the verbs in bold.

1 The owner of the coins **must have been** very rich.

2 The gold **can't have had** any connection with the war because it was produced much later.

3 He **may/might/could have forgotten** where it was buried.

4 She **mightn't/may not have seen** the gold if the water in the lake hadn't been so clear.

a We use ...., ..., and .... when there is a 50% possibility that something was true but we cannot use .... in the negative form with this meaning.

b We use .... when we are 90% certain that something was true.

c We use .... when we are 90% certain that something wasn't true.

☑ Check it **page 68**

5 Find and correct the mistakes in these sentences.

1 You must have saw Liam. He was here just a second ago.

2 Let's not buy her that book. I'm not sure but I think she might read it already.

3 You can't finish watching that film already. It lasts two hours and you only started half an hour ago!

4 You look full of energy. You must have a good rest last night.

5 Somebody's taken my physics text book. It must have been Kim because she doesn't study science.

6 I think Joel might seen that film last week.

7 Sam hasn't replied to my message. She mightn't had received it.

8 The exam mustn't have been very hard because everybody got ten out of ten.

6 Complete the text with past modal verbs of speculation and the verbs given.

News   **Technology**   Entertainment   Sport

The mysterious creator of bitcoins

Bitcoins are a well-known cryptocurrency (a digital or virtual currency) but nobody knows who exactly created them. The person used the name Satoshi Nakamoto, so it sounds like he (a) .... (be) Japanese. However, other people are not so sure. They think that the person (b) .... (use) a Japanese pseudonym to confuse people. Journalists found a man called Satoshi Nakamoto in California. At first they weren't sure but they thought he (c) .... (invent) bitcoins because he knew about computer programming. But the man denied it. The 64-year-old Satoshi claimed he (d) .... (do) it because he had been suffering from an illness and didn't even know what bitcoins were until his son told him! What is clear is that, right from the beginning, the mysterious creator of bitcoins (e) .... (want) to remain anonymous because he was careful never to give away any information about his identity. His? Who knows? It (f) .... (be) a woman, not a man. Or some people are sure that a team of people (g) .... (create) bitcoins because the code was too complicated for just one person. One other theory is that perhaps the person or people (h) .... (be) working for a government. One thing seems sure. They (i) .... (make) a lot of money from bitcoins. Some people calculate that they have bitcoins worth billions of dollars!

7 🗣 **SPEAKING** 👥 Look at these situations and write at least two sentences with *must have*, *might have*, and *can't have* to explain or comment on them.

1 Sandra always rides her bike very carefully but yesterday she had an accident.

2 Joe is usually very easy-going but yesterday he was furious.

3 My uncle didn't use to be rich but now he's got a really expensive sports car.

4 My sister is not usually very good at maths but she got full marks in her last exam.

5 Paula used to love chocolate but now she never eats it.

6 The last time I saw my cousin she couldn't speak a word of English but now she's really fluent.

Use it … don't lose it!

8 🗣 **SPEAKING** 👥 Compare your ideas in 7 with the rest of the class and choose the best sentence for each situation.

Reach higher 〉 **page 138**

Developing speaking

Talking about photos 2

1 What words and expressions can we use to talk about similarities and differences between photos? Make a list.

Both photos show ...,

In this photo there is ..., whereas in the other photo there is ...

2 **SPEAKING** 🗢 Use the words and expressions from your list in 1 to talk about the two photos.

3 🔊 **26** Listen to a student talking about the photos and answer the questions.

  1 Which of the things that you mentioned in 2 does the student talk about?

  2 Does the student talk about each photo in detail?

  3 Apart from comparing and contrasting the photos, what question do you think the examiner asked the student?

4 **SPEAKING** 🗢 Discuss which of the two places you would prefer to shop in and why.

✓ Exam tip

When you have to talk about two photos, you shouldn't describe each photo in great detail. Compare and contrast the two photos. Listen very carefully to the examiner's instructions because you may have to answer one or more questions related to the photos. Your marks will depend on completing the whole task, so if you only complete the first part (in this case, comparing the photos), you will lose marks.

5 Look at the lists of words and expressions in the Speaking bank and answer the questions.

  1 What title could you give to each list?

  2 What expressions can you add to each list?

Speaking bank
Useful language to talk about photos

1 ....: In the background, At the top, In the middle

2 ....: Both photos show ..., One similarity between the photos is ...

3 ....: In this photo there is X whereas in the other photo there is Y, Another difference between the photos is ..., This photo is more ... than

4 ....: must (have), may (have), might (have), could (have), can't (have), I'm not sure but ..., I imagine ..., It looks/seems like/as if ...

5 ....: Let me think ..., I mean ..., Well, ...

6 ....: Personally, In my opinion, I think ...

6 **SPEAKING** 🗢 Use expressions from each list in 5 to talk about the photos in 2.

Practice makes perfect

7a **SPEAKING** 🗢 Student A, do the task below using the photos on page 150. Student B, listen to your partner.

> Compare the photographs. Then say why you think people are giving money in these different situations.

7b **SPEAKING** 🗢 Now change roles. Student B, your task is on page 150.

Developing writing

An informal email / A story 2

1 **SPEAKING** 👥 Look at these two writing tasks. Imagine they are options in a writing exam. Which would you choose to answer and why?

> ### Task 1
>
>
>
> You have just received this email from your English friend, Ella.
>
>
> Hi!
>
> My school needs to raise money to be able to start up some new clubs and societies next year. Have you got any ideas about different ways we could raise the money? Please write back and give me any advice you can.
>
> Many thanks!
>
> Ella
>
> Write your reply.

> ### Task 2
>
>
>
> You have seen this announcement.
>
> **Stories wanted**
>
> We would like some stories for our new international magazine for teenagers. Your story must begin with this sentence:
>
> *It was 9 o'clock on Saturday morning and Jo was taking her dog for a walk as she always did at the weekend.*
>
> Your story must include:
> * a surprise
> * a reward
> Write your story.

2a **SPEAKING** 👥 With your partner, brainstorm …

1 useful expressions to use in an informal email.
2 useful language and linkers when writing a story.

2b Check your ideas in the Writing banks on pages 15 and 27.

3 Read the start of two students' answers to tasks 1 and 2. What do you think of the answers and why?

Task 1

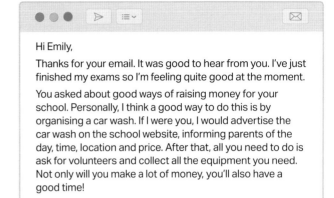

Hi Emily,

Thanks for your email. It was good to hear from you. I've just finished my exams so I'm feeling quite good at the moment.

You asked about good ways of raising money for your school. Personally, I think a good way to do this is by organising a car wash. If I were you, I would advertise the car wash on the school website, informing parents of the day, time, location and price. After that, all you need to do is ask for volunteers and collect all the equipment you need. Not only will you make a lot of money, you'll also have a good time!

Task 2

It was 9 o'clock on Saturday morning and Jo was taking her dog for a walk as she always did at the weekend. It was a beautiful morning and Jo was feeling full of energy as she looked out at the sparkling sea. But just at that moment she heard somebody calling for help. At first, she thought she must have made a mistake because she couldn't see anybody, but then she looked out to sea again more carefully and could just make out somebody struggling in the ocean.

4 Look at the advice in the Writing bank. Do the writers in 3 follow any of it? Give examples.

> ## Writing bank
> ### Useful advice to make texts more interesting
>
> * Use a wide range of vocabulary to avoid repetition, e.g. use *impressive, fantastic, spectacular* instead of *good*.
> * Use adjectives and adverbs to give colour to your descriptions, e.g. *The elderly man walked slowly down the dark, wet road.*
> * Use linkers to make your ideas and arguments clear, e.g. *However, Nevertheless, What's more …*
> * Use words and expressions of time and sequence to make the order of events or arguments clear, e.g. *Firstly, At that moment, Later …*
> * Use comment adverbs and adverbials to express attitudes or opinions, e.g. *Personally, Frankly, To be honest, Interestingly, Fortunately …*
> * Use more varied and complex grammar, e.g. past modal verbs of speculation, a wide variety of past tenses, *not only … but also …*

> **Practice makes perfect**
>
> **5a** Choose your favourite option in 1 and write your email or story. Use the advice in the Writing bank to help you make your writing more interesting.
>
> **5b** When you finish the task, use the Writing checklist on page 141 to check it.

Grammar reference

Modal verbs of obligation, prohibition and advice – present

- We use *have to* to talk about things which are obligatory or necessary. It often describes obligations imposed on us by other people and authorities.
  You have to pay before leaving the shop.

- We use *don't have to* to talk about things which are not obligatory or necessary.
  You don't have to be 18 to open an account.

- We use *must* to talk about rules, regulations and obligations. It often describes obligations that come internally, from ourselves.
  I must remember to buy a present for my friend.

- We use *mustn't* to talk about prohibitions.

- We use *need to* to talk about things which are obligatory or necessary.
  We need to hand in our homework on Wednesday.

- We use *don't need to* or *needn't* to talk about things which are not obligatory or necessary. With *needn't*, we do not use *to* before the infinitive.
  We don't need to go to class at the weekend.
  We needn't go to class at the weekend.

- We use *can't* to refuse permission.

- We use *should, shouldn't, ought to, had ('d) better* to give and ask for advice and recommendations. *Had better* is especially for when we think we should do something because it's a good idea. *Ought to* and *had ('d) better* are slightly less common in negative and question forms.
  You should/ought to/had better save up if you want to buy a new phone.

Modal verbs of obligation, prohibition and advice – past

- We use *had to* to talk about things which were obligatory or necessary.

- We use *didn't have to* to talk about things which were not obligatory or necessary.
  I didn't have to go to school last Friday.

- We use *needed to* to talk about things which were obligatory or necessary.
  I stopped because I needed to rest.

- We use *didn't need to* to talk about things which were not obligatory or necessary. Maybe we did them or maybe we didn't.
  We didn't need to give the waiter a tip (but we did anyway/so we didn't).

- We use *needn't have* + past participle to talk about things that were not obligatory or necessary but we did them.
  You needn't have bought me a present. But thank you!

- We use *wasn't/weren't allowed to* to talk about past prohibitions.
  I wasn't allowed to go to school alone when I was small.

- We use *couldn't* to talk about things that were prohibited or not possible.
  I couldn't go out alone when I was younger.

- We use *should/ought to have* + past participle or *shouldn't have* + past participle to criticise past actions or to say that they were a mistake.
  I should/ought to have been more careful with my money but I spent it all.

Modal verbs of speculation and deduction – present and future

- We use *must* + infinitive without *to* when we are 90% certain that something is true.
  She lives in an enormous house. She must be rich.

- We use *may, might, could, may not, mightn't* + infinitive without *to* when there is a 50% possibility that something is true (or not).

- We use *can't* + infinitive without *to* when we are 90% certain that something is not true.
  She's only fourteen. She can't have a driving licence.

Modal verbs of speculation and deduction – past

- We use *must have* + past participle when we are 90% certain that something was true.
  He hasn't got any money left. He must have spent it all.

- We use *may (not) have, might (not) have, could have* + past participle when there is a 50% possibility that something was true (or not).

- We use *can't have* + past participle when we are 90% certain that something was not true.
  He didn't do very well in the test. He can't have studied much.

Vocabulary

1 Spending and saving money

account (n) · afford (v) · allowance (n) · ATM/cashpoint (n) · bank charge/fee (n) · bargain (n) · budget (n) · cash (n) · coin (n) · change (n) · credit/debit card (n) · discount (n) · get into debt (v) · (bank)note (n) · payment (n) · purchase (n, v) · receipt (n) · refund (n) · sale (n) · save (v) · spend on (v) · spending habits (n) · swipe (v) · take out (money) (phrasal verb) · tax (n) · value/value for money (adj) · waste (money) (v)

2 Idioms connected with money

cost an arm and a leg · snap up a bargain · spend a fortune (on) · throw money down the drain · tighten your belt

3 Phrasal verbs connected with money and shopping

come to · chip in · cut down (on) · get by · pay back · rip off · run out (of) · sell out · set aside · shop around · splash out

On-the-Go Practice

Grammar test

Modal verbs of obligation, prohibition and advice – present

1 **Choose the correct alternative. In two sentences, both alternatives are correct.**

1 You *needn't/don't need* come to class today.

2 You *mustn't/aren't allowed to* take your own food into a restaurant.

3 Usually at university you *mustn't/don't have to* go to classes all day.

4 You *'d better not/shouldn't* hand in your work late.

5 *Should/Ought* we leave at six o'clock?

6 You *don't have to/mustn't* leave your bags unattended at an airport.

/ 6 points

Modal verbs of obligation, prohibition and advice – past and present

2 **Write sentences with the correct form of the words given.**

1 Yesterday I .... (talk) to the bank manager. (have to)

2 I spent all night worrying about the exam, but I .... (worry) because it was easy. (need)

3 Usually students .... (write) their exam answers in red – they should only use black. (must)

4 I .... (read) the instructions but I didn't and I got the whole exercise wrong. (ought to)

5 I'm sorry. I .... (lie) to you. It was wrong. (should)

6 She .... (get) up early this morning so she stayed in bed. (need)

7 We .... (write) the essay this week, we can do it next week if we want. (have to)

/ 7 points

Modal verbs of speculation and deduction

3 **Complete the sentences using the correct form of the verbs given and present or past modal verbs of speculation and deduction.**

1 He won the race. He .... (run) fast!

2 Somebody is knocking at the door. It .... (be) the postman because he's already been.

3 His lips are blue and he's shivering. He .... (be) really cold.

4 Somebody's taken my red pen. Jack .... (do) it because I saw him using one earlier.

5 My friend climbed a mountain that's 5,000 metres high. That .... (be) easy!

6 I don't know when our next match is. We .... (have) one next week but I'm not sure.

7 Mike hasn't replied to my email. He .... (not receive) it.

/ 7 points

Vocabulary test

Spending and saving money

1 **Write simple definitions for these words and expressions.**

1 refund 3 change 5 sale 7 afford

2 receipt 4 bargain 6 value for money 8 get into debt

/ 8 points

Idioms connected with money

2 **Complete the sentences with idioms.**

1 It cost us an .... and a ....

2 That game is half price. I'm going to .... it up.

3 You've already got three. If you buy another, you're throwing money .... the ....

4 Ben lost his job so he'll have to tighten his .... and spend less.

5 His pets live in complete luxury. He spends a .... on them.

/ 5 points

Phrasal verbs connected with money and shopping

3 **Rewrite these sentences without the phrasal verbs in bold. Express the same meaning with different words.**

1 Last week I **splashed out** on a new bag.

2 They **get by** on £500 a month.

3 People are **cutting back** on holidays now.

4 The bill **comes to** £24.

5 There weren't any hats left. They'd **sold out**.

6 Let's all **chip in** and buy a present.

7 They **rip** tourists **off** in that shop.

/ 7 points

Total: / 40 points

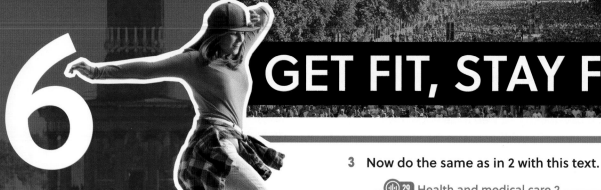

Vocabulary in context

Parts of the body
Health and medical care

1 **SPEAKING** 👥 Draw one of the words in the box for the rest of the class. Can they identify the part of the body?

> 🔊 **27** Parts of the body
>
> ankle • chest • eyebrow • eyelash • eyelid • forehead • heel • hip • kidney • liver • lungs • muscle • nail • ribs • thigh • waist

2 Complete the text with the correct form of the words in the box. Check that you also understand the words in bold. Use a dictionary if necessary.

> 🔊 **28** Health and medical care 1
>
> A and E (accident and emergency) • broken • fracture • injury • operation • painful • painkiller • physiotherapy • X-ray

DOCTOR WEB

| Health news | Doctors near you | A–Z health | 🔍 |

A dislocated shoulder

How does a **dislocated** shoulder happen? It's possible to dislocate your shoulder while playing a contact sport, such as rugby or judo, or in some other (a) .... connected with sport or exercise.

How do I know if I have dislocated my shoulder? It is quite easy to identify a dislocated shoulder because your shoulder will be very (b) .... and it will be difficult to move your arm.

What should you do if you have a dislocated shoulder? The best thing is to go to the (c) .... department immediately. While you are waiting for a doctor to examine you, try not to move your upper arm.

How do you treat a dislocated shoulder? Usually they'll give you an (d) .... to see if you have any (e) .... bones, or have a (f) .... If you do, an (g) .... might be necessary. They will give you (h) .... and perhaps some other medicine to help you relax.

How do you recover from a dislocated shoulder? Once your shoulder is back in place, normally you are able to go home. However, it is often necessary to keep your arm in a **sling** for the next couple of days at least. You might also need (i) .... to rehabilitate the shoulder.

3 Now do the same as in 2 with this text.

> 🔊 **29** Health and medical care 2
>
> ache • exhaustion • fever • get better • infectious • injection • lower • prescription • sick • sneeze • sore • symptom • treat

Flu

Have I got the **flu**? The (a) .... of flu can appear very suddenly. They often include a (b) .... (a **temperature** of 38ºC or above), (c) .... and pains, feelings of **dizziness**, **tiredness** or (d) .... a dry **cough**, a (e) .... throat and a **headache**. You might also feel and be (f) ....

How can you treat flu yourself? You can often (g) .... without seeing a General Practitioner, or **GP**, and should begin to feel better in about a week. If you don't, you should see your doctor. It is a good idea to see a **chemist** as they can advise you how to (h) .... flu and suggest flu remedies, without a doctor's (i) .... To help you recover quickly, try to rest and get as much sleep as possible, keep yourself warm, take paracetamol or ibuprofen to (j) .... your temperature and treat aches and pains. Don't forget to drink plenty of water.

How can you avoid spreading the flu? Flu is highly (k) .... – it's easy to **pass it on** to other people, particularly in the first week. You can pass flu on by **germs** when you cough or (l) .... Use warm water and soap to keep your hands clean since germs can live on hands and surfaces for 24 hours.

How can you prevent flu? It can be a good idea to have a flu **vaccine**. You should get an (m) .... before the start of the flu season.

> **Use it ... don't lose it!**
>
> 4 **SPEAKING** 👥 Ask and answer the questions. Give details.
>
> 1 Have you ever injured yourself playing sport?
> 2 Have you ever been to an A and E department?
> 3 When was the last time you had a fever?
> 4 Are you afraid of injections?
> 5 Have you ever had physiotherapy?

Reach higher ⟩ page 138

Reading

1 **SPEAKING** 👥 How and where would you get clean water and basic medicine in a dystopian future?

2 Read the text and check your predictions in 1.

HEALTH AND MEDICINE IN A DYSTOPIAN FUTURE

It could come from a nuclear war, a meteor or any of the hundreds of disasters that appear in all the dystopian TV series, films and novels that we are obsessed with nowadays. But somehow in those stories, even in the worst-case situations, life seems to
5 go on relatively unchanged. But let's imagine this world for a second. For a few weeks or months maybe, the things we're used to may still be around – bottled water, canned food, medicine, some basic technology. But then? How would we cope if we had to start civilisation again from scratch? If we think about some of
10 the fundamental knowledge needed, it will help our chances of survival.

Health and medicine would be one of our most important challenges as every injury could be fatal. An open fracture of the leg would be lethal unless you received medical treatment since
15 even a small cut could lead to an infection and blood-poisoning. In this imaginary future, infectious diseases would be the biggest problem. Understanding basic sanitation and hygiene could save your life. We all know now that if you wash your hands regularly, you protect yourself from potentially life-threatening diseases
20 and parasites. The other key strategy would be making sure your drinking water wasn't contaminated. It was only as recently as the 1850s that experts realised the importance of these two basic health measures.

It's worth pointing out that if you do pick up some type of food
25 poisoning, you shouldn't need any complex medication to survive. Since the 1970s, the widely adopted treatment is to drink a litre of clean water with a tablespoon of salt and three tablespoons of sugar. As long as you had clean water, you'd generally be OK. But since there would be no water coming from taps, you would have
30 to prepare the water yourself. If you boil water, you make it safe to drink. But you need fuel for that. The simplest method for water

disinfection is a technique being taught around the developing world by the World Health Organisation. Simply fill a plastic bottle with suspect water and leave it in bright sunshine for a day or two.
35 The ultraviolet rays from the Sun pass right through the bottle and kill anything harmful in the water.

Now we have water, but what medicines would be available? Many modern drugs and treatments come from plants, and herbal medicine is as old as civilisation itself. Almost 2,500 years ago,
40 Hippocrates recommended biting the bark of the willow tree to relieve pain and control fever, as they did in Ancient China, too. The essential oil extracted from lavender has antiseptic and anti-inflammatory qualities when used as an external cream, and menthol (from mint plants) can have a cooling effect on the
45 skin to relieve pain. Provided that you had some of these natural resources nearby, you'd have the beginning of a medicine cabinet. But you would need to be careful in case you took too much of any active ingredients.

However, for most serious diseases simple herbal remedies are
50 not effective. Today's medicines are highly complex. When they do contain natural plant extracts, these have been modified to strengthen their effect and/or reduce side effects. This is how willow bark has been transformed into the most widely used drug in history – aspirin – keeping its painkilling properties but
55 reducing the side effect of stomach pains.

In short, if we survived something like a nuclear war, we would need to rediscover all this knowledge and recreate all this technical expertise. So maybe the key lesson is to realise how sophisticated society is today and how many amazing advances
60 have been made over time to improve the quality of our lives. If we look after the incredible world we have today, we won't need to waste time starting again from zero.

3 🔊30 Read the text again. According to the text, are the statements True (T) or False (F)? Write the line(s) where you found the information.

1 In this imaginary future world, even trivial incidents could mean a death sentence. T / F Line: ....

2 There is a simple and ancient way to treat food poisoning. T / F Line: ....

3 An effective low-tech way of disinfecting water has already been developed. T / F Line: ....

4 People have used plants to treat illnesses for thousands of years. T / F Line: ....

5 Patients should apply willow bark, lavender oil and menthol in the same way. T / F Line: ....

6 Today, pharmaceutical companies are not interested in plants or herbs to make their medicines. T / F Line: ....

4 What do the underlined words in the text mean? Guess and then check in your dictionary.

5 🧠 **Critical thinkers**

In your opinion, how important or useful is the information in this text (a) today (b) in a possible dystopian future situation?

What makes you say that?

Reach higher > page 138

Zero, first and second conditionals

1a **Look at the sentences. Which type of conditional is each one?**

1 **If** you **boil** water, you **make** it safe to drink.

2 **If** we **survived** an apocalypse, we **would need** to rediscover all this knowledge.

3 **If** we **look** after this incredible world, we **won't need** to rebuild it from zero.

1b **Read the rules. Which type of conditional does each rule apply to?**

a It describes an improbable or imaginary situation in the present or future, and its consequence.

b It describes a possible situation in the present or future and its consequence.

c It describes something that is generally true.

1c **Explain how we make the zero, first and second conditional.**

☑ Check it **page 80**

2 **Complete each sentence with the zero, first or second conditional and your own idea.**

1 If you never do any exercise, ...

2 If I ate a lot of junk food, ...

3 I won't be very happy if ....

4 You feel tired if ....

5 If I lived in the US, ...

6 I'd be really angry if ....

7 If you mix red and white, ...

8 If I get a ten in my next English exam, ...

3 **Decide if the sentences are correct. Rewrite the incorrect sentences.**

1 What would you do if you injure your knee?

2 If I had a million pounds, I'd buy my teacher a present.

3 If you heat water to 100°C, it would boil.

4 If I am you, I would stay in bed today.

5 She'll buy the coat if it was a bit cheaper.

6 I won't move my arm if I was you.

7 If you don't water flowers, they die.

8 What video game will you buy if you had enough money?

4 **Complete the questions with the correct form of the verbs given.**

1 Which country .... you .... (live) in if you .... (be) free to choose anywhere in the world?

2 If you .... (have) time tonight, which series or film .... you .... (watch)?

3 If you .... (have) the powers of a superhero, what powers .... you .... (like) to have?

4 If you .... (go) out this weekend, where .... you .... (go)?

5 If you .... (be) a journalist and .... (have) the chance to meet any famous person for an interview, who .... you .... (meet) and why?

6 If you .... (be) able to choose a special meal to celebrate an important occasion, what .... you .... (choose)?

7 If you .... (have) homework this weekend, when .... you .... (do) it?

5 **SPEAKING** 👥 **Ask and answer the questions. Then tell the class something interesting you discovered about your partner.**

unless, as long as, provided/ providing (that), in case

6 **Look at the sentences and match the words in bold to the words and expressions in a–c.**

1 A fracture of the leg would be lethal **unless** you received adequate medical treatment.

2 You would need to be careful **in case** you took too much medicine.

3 **Provided/Providing (that)** you had these natural resources, you'd have the beginning of a medicine cabinet.

4 **As long as** you had clean water, you'd be okay.

a *if ... not, except if:* ....

b *if, only if:* ...., ...

c *because maybe:* ....

☑ Check it **page 80**

7 **Choose the correct alternative.**

1 We'll have a picnic *as long as/unless* it's sunny.

2 I wouldn't go to her party *provided that/unless* she invited me.

3 My mum will work overtime *as long as/unless* they pay her.

4 You can't come in *as long as/unless* you have an invitation.

5 Take some sweets *in case/providing that* you start coughing.

6 You can go out with your friends *in case/providing* you come back before 11 pm.

7 I'll make you a sandwich now *as long as/in case* you feel hungry later.

8 I don't care about money *as long as/unless* I'm fit and healthy.

8 Complete the second sentence so that it has a similar meaning to the first sentence, using the word given. Do not change the word given. You must use between two and five words, including the word given.

1 It's obvious that you won't get better unless you take your medicine. (if)

It's obvious that .... your medicine, you won't get better.

2 I'll help you, but only if you listen carefully to me. (long)

I'll help you .... carefully to me.

3 If you don't enjoy hospital dramas, don't watch it. (unless)

Don't watch it .... hospital dramas.

4 Don't speak in a loud voice and you can stay with the patient. (provided)

You can stay with the patient .... quietly.

5 I want to become a doctor but my marks aren't good enough. (if)

I'd become a doctor .... enough.

6 I'll take an extra pen because this one might run out. (case)

I'll take an extra pen .... out.

7 I won't miss class providing I feel better tomorrow. (as)

I'll come .... I feel better tomorrow.

8 Personally, I think you should complain. (would)

I .... you.

9 Complete these sentences with your ideas and information.

1 I'll start saving money in case ...

2 I'll finish my next assignment on time unless ...

3 I'll go out with my friends soon providing ...

4 I'll do sport and/or play video games this weekend as long as ...

5 I enjoy watching series provided that ...

6 I think/don't think I'll go to university when I leave school unless ...

Use it ... don't lose it!

10 SPEAKING 👥 Compare your sentences in 9. Are any the same?

Reach higher ▷ page 138

Developing vocabulary

Idioms connected with health and illness

1 Complete the idioms in bold in the text with the words in the box. Check that you understand the meaning of each expression. Use a dictionary if necessary.

> about · back · out · picture · pull · shape · world

Accidents will happen ... when you drive fast

Matthew Anderson is a popular Australian television presenter and racing car driver. Right now, he's the **(a)** .... **of health**. But in 2019 he suffered a dramatic accident when his car went spinning 200 metres at top speed down a hill. Luckily, he only fractured his knee and was soon **up and (b)** .... It wasn't his first serious accident though. He was lucky to **(c)** .... **through** after the one he had in 2013. As his car went out of control at over 380 kph, he **blacked (d)** .... Even now he doesn't remember exactly what happened to him. It took him about a year to get **(e)** .... **on his feet** after that accident, and he prefers never to talk about it. He used to go running to **keep in (f)** .... , but unfortunately after his latest accident he's had to give up. Apart from that, he's feeling **on top of the (g)** ....!

2 SPEAKING 👥 Look at these idiomatic expressions. Do you think each one is used to describe good or bad health? Use a dictionary if necessary.

> come down with · full of beans · on your last legs · out of shape · under the weather ·

3 Find and correct the mistakes in these questions.

1 What do you do to keep on shape?

2 Have you ever blacked down?

3 What do you do when you start coming up with a cold?

4 Are you feeling full with beans today?

5 Do you know anybody who's feeling out of the weather at the moment?

Use it ... don't lose it!

4 SPEAKING 👥 Ask and answer the questions in 3.

Reach higher ▷ page 138

GREAT LEARNERS
GREAT THINKERS

HEALTHY EATING

Lesson Aim: To think about nutrition and healthy diets
Video: Is a detox diet actually good for you?
SEL **Social and Emotional Learning:** Managing emotional eating

1 **SPEAKING** Read this definition of a detox diet. What do you think of it? Would you consider following a diet like this? Why/Why not?

> Some people believe we need to help our bodies to manage all of the toxins that are all around us in our daily lives – toxins such as junk food, sugar, caffeine and even pollution in the air. They suggest following a detox diet by cutting down on foods that contain toxins and also by consuming other food and drinks which they say help to cleanse any toxins from our bodies.

2a **SPEAKING** You are going to watch a video about six students following two different diets, one a traditional balanced diet and the other a detox diet. Before you watch, discuss which diet you think will be the healthiest and why.

2b **VIDEO** Watch the video. Were your ideas in 2a right?

3 **VIDEO** Watch the video again and answer the questions with B (balanced diet) or D (detox diet).

Which diet ...
1 included wholemeal bread? ....
2 included raw and steamed vegetables and fish? ....
3 involved drinking coconut water? ....
4 negatively affected one student's emotions? ....
5 was easier for the students to follow? ....
6 improved the way one student felt in the mornings? ....
7 had a more positive effect on the liver and heart? ....
8 was better for the students' skin? ....

GREAT THINKERS

The 4 Cs: Connections, Challenges, Concepts, Changes

4 Follow the instructions.
1 Make **connections** between what you learned in the video and your life and/or the life of people you know.
2 Think about ideas or opinions that you want to **challenge** or argue with in the video.
3 Decide which key **concepts** or ideas you think are important and useful to remember.
4 Consider what **changes** you and/or others could make based on what you learned in the video.
5 Now share your ideas in small groups.

5 **SPEAKING** 👥 Read this text about healthy eating. What do you think of the advice?

TOP EATING TIPS
—— FOR TEENS!

Don't skip breakfast. A healthy breakfast gives you some of the important vitamins and minerals you need to start the day with energy.

Eat five a day. Try to eat five portions of fruit and veg each day as they're rich in healthy vitamins and minerals.

Eat healthy snacks. You don't have to give up fizzy drinks, crisps and chocolate completely, but remember that unhealthy snacks can easily lead to consuming too many calories.

Be aware of emotional eating. Sometimes we eat just because of our emotions, not because we're hungry. Be aware that this can sometimes make us eat too many unhealthy snacks.

Beware of new 'wonder' diets. Trendy new diets can be very unhealthy and usually only lead to short-term weight loss anyway. The best diet is a natural, healthy, balanced diet.

Get enough calcium and vitamin D. These both help make sure your teeth and bones are healthy.

6 **SPEAKING** 👥 Think about what you've eaten in the last 24 hours. Using the information in the video and text, evaluate how healthy you think your diet was. What simple changes could you make to improve your diet if necessary?

GREAT LEARNERS **SEL**

Great learners look after their physical health.

How important do you think your physical health is in order to study effectively? Why?

Learner profile ⟩ page 143

Listening

1 Read the text. Can you identify the missing word? It is the man's surname and the name of the sport he invented. Have you ever tried this sport? Would you like to? Why/Why not?

Culture exchange

Sport in the US 1

Joseph .... was born in Germany but lived for over forty years in the US. He founded a studio in New York where he taught people the sport he had created. The main aim of .... is to use the mind to control your muscles, focusing particularly on the muscles that keep the body balanced. Your breathing is really important, too, and you learn to always keep your back in the right position. It has similarities with yoga but the emphasis in .... is on strength more than flexibility. Over nine million people practise .... in the US!

2 🔊31 **You will hear five different people talking about a sport they practise. Which sport does each person do? The first speaker does the sport in 1. Did you guess the sport correctly?**

Speaker	Sport	Statement (A–F)
1		
2		
3		
4		
5		

3 🔊31 **Listen again. Choose from the list what each speaker says and complete the table in 2. Use the letters only once. There is one extra letter which you do not need to use.**

A You have to learn theory and practice before you can do this sport.

B I want to get better at my favourite sport so that I can win matches.

C I couldn't start my favourite sport when I was younger.

D To do my favourite sport well I should have started earlier.

E My favourite sport is more tiring than it looks.

F In the past I took my favourite sport too seriously.

4 🧠 **Critical thinkers**

> In your opinion, which of the five sports is the healthiest and most appropriate for a student to practise?
>
> What makes you say that?

Grammar in context 2

Flipped classroom video
Watch the Grammar Presentation video

Third conditional

1 Look at these sentences and answer the questions.

  1 If I'**d lived** closer to the sea, I **would have begun** surfing much earlier.

  2 If I **hadn't passed** my exams, they **wouldn't have let** me do the course.

  a In third conditional sentences, what tense is the verb in the half of the sentence containing *if*?

  b What verb form do we use in the other half of the sentence?

  c Do we use the third conditional for imaginary situations in the present or the past?

  ☑ **Check it page 80**

2 Write sentences about these past situations using the third conditional.

  1 The team / reach the final / if / they / win last week.
    The team ....

  2 She / go for a run yesterday / if / she / not injure her knee.
    If ....

  3 If / we / eat less last night / we / not feel so full.
    If ....

  4 I / not catch a cold / if / I / wear warmer clothes last night.
    I ....

  5 If / he / drive more slowly / he / not have that accident in 2017.
    If ....

  6 If / she / not come down with the flu on Monday / she / come to school.
    If ....

  7 If / I / need painkillers yesterday / I / take them.
    If ....

3 Look at the situations and write third conditional sentences.

  1 I didn't go for a walk because it was windy.
    If it hadn't been windy, I would have gone for a walk.

  2 We didn't watch the match because we didn't have time.

  3 I didn't go to the hospital because I felt better.

  4 She was on her last legs because she hadn't trained hard for the race.

  5 He didn't go surfing because the waves weren't big enough.

  6 She missed the exam because she felt under the weather.

  7 He didn't go up the tower because he was afraid of heights.

4 Complete the text by putting the verbs in the correct form of the zero, first, second or third conditional.

Culture exchange

Sport in the US 2

The world would be a sadder place for many people if basketball **(a)** .... (not exist). If you do some research into the origins of the sport, you **(b)** .... (see) that it was the invention of one man. That's right. If it **(c)** .... (not be) for James Naismith (1861–1939), basketball would never have existed. Naismith was a Canadian PE teacher who worked in the US. If Naismith **(d)** .... (have) a different profession, I imagine he wouldn't have thought up this new sport. His director gave him 14 days to create a new indoor sport. It had to be indoors because the weather was bad in the winter where they lived. Of course, if you play indoors, you **(e)** .... (not get) cold or wet. The director also wanted the sport to be non-aggressive. If he hadn't told Naismith this, perhaps Naismith **(f)** .... (not make) basketball a non-contact sport. Naismith's original baskets were wooden fruit baskets which didn't have a hole. If we **(g)** .... (have) the same baskets today, we would need a ladder to get the ball back every time a player scored! If basketball hadn't become so popular, maybe people **(h)** .... (forget) about James Naismith a long time ago. But it's thanks to him that one of the world's most popular sports exists.

Collaborative project 3 **page 83**

I wish/If only

5 Look at these sentences and answer the questions.

a **I wish/If only I'd learnt** to swim properly when I was a kid.

b **I wish/If only** I **was/were** taller.

c **I wish/If only** people **wouldn't** make fun of my favourite sport.

1 What tense appears after *I wish/If only* in sentence a?

2 Does this sentence talk about a present or past situation that we would like to be different?

3 What tense appears after *I wish/If only* in sentence b?

4 Does this sentence talk about an imaginary wish for a present or past situation?

5 What verb form appears after *I wish/If only* in sentence c?

6 Do we use sentence c to talk about habitual behaviour that we like or we want to criticise and change?

☑ **Check it** **page 80**

6 Complete the sentences with the correct form of the verb given.

1 If only I .... (have) a motorbike! I'd ride it every day.

2 If only he .... (not shout). I can't concentrate with the noise he makes.

3 I wish we .... (not buy) tickets for the concert. I've just found out we've got an exam the morning after!

4 I wish I .... (go) skiing yesterday. They say the conditions were perfect.

5 If only I .... (be) 18 already. I'd be able to vote.

6 I wish you .... (clean) the kitchen after using it.

7 Complete the text with one word in each gap.

My BLOG

New posts

Study versus Sport   *22nd August*

If **(a)** .... I had more time to do sport this year. I'm in my last year of school and I have lots of exams and assignments. I **(b)** .... I didn't have so many! I used to be in the school basketball team but I stopped. I wish I **(c)** .... given it up. But if I **(d)** .... continued playing, I **(e)** .... have spent far too much time on matches and training, although I still go running and swimming occasionally. I think that as **(f)** .... as you get some exercise from time to time, you can stay more or less fit. I always do sport at least once at the weekend **(g)** .... it's absolutely impossible because of homework and revision. I'm always careful with what I eat, too, and I try to avoid eating too much junk food **(h)** .... case I put on a lot of weight. Provided **(i)** .... you have a balanced diet, you should be able to keep **(j)** .... shape quite easily. The problem is that my mum is always buying me my favourite cakes. I wish she **(k)** .... do that because I find it difficult to resist them! Anyway, providing I take **(l)** .... sport again next year, I'm sure I **(m)** .... be as fit **(n)** .... I was before.

8 Write three true sentences with *I wish*. Write one about a present situation that you would like to be different, one about a past situation, and one about somebody who does something that you would like to change.

Use it ... don't lose it!

9 SPEAKING 👥 Compare your sentences in small groups. Ask follow-up questions to find out more information.

Reach higher **page 138**

Developing speaking

Negotiating and collaborating 2

'I'd like you to imagine that your school wants to encourage students to live healthier lives. Here are some ideas that they are thinking about and a question for you to discuss. Talk to each other about how these ideas could encourage students to live healthier lives.'

Cookery classes at school

A school sports day

A talk by a doctor

A weekend in the country

fitness club
A week's free membership of a gym or sports club

'Now you have a minute to decide which two ideas you think are the best.'

1 SPEAKING 👥 Look at both parts of the task. Make a list of advice on how to do this type of task. Look at the Exam tip on page 26 if necessary.

2 SPEAKING 👥 Now do both parts of the task with your partner.

3 ⏺ 32 Listen to two people doing the task. Do you think they do the task well? Why/Why not? How do you think you did in comparison?

4a Complete the expressions in section 4 of the Speaking bank with these words.

better • best • choice • choose • going • let's • shall

4b SPEAKING 👥 Make a list of expressions for sections 1–3 of the Speaking bank. Then compare your answers with the Speaking bank on page 26.

Speaking bank
Useful expressions for negotiating and collaborating 2

1 Asking your partner's opinion
2 Agreeing
3 Disagreeing
4 Making choices
   a My .... would be (X).
   b I think we should .... (X).
   c I think the .... option is ...
   d In my opinion, (X) is a .... option than (Y).
   e .... choose (X).
   f .... we choose (X)?
   g I'd suggest .... for this/that one.

Practice makes perfect

5 SPEAKING 👥 Do this task with a partner. Remember to use expressions from the Speaking bank.

'I'd like you to imagine that a teacher is planning a class discussion about important everyday activities. Now, talk to each other about why these activities are important.'

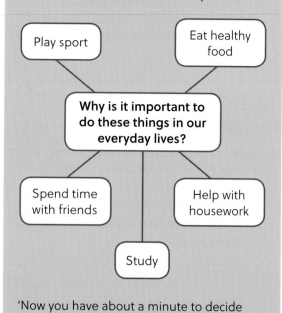

Play sport

Eat healthy food

Why is it important to do these things in our everyday lives?

Spend time with friends

Help with housework

Study

'Now you have about a minute to decide which of these things you think it is most important to do.'

Developing writing

A for-and-against essay

1 Look at the people in the photos above. Do you know who they are? Do you think they deserve to earn a lot of money? Why/Why not?

2 **SPEAKING** Look at this essay title and make notes with arguments for and against the statement.

> 'Doctors should be paid more than top sports stars.'

3 Read this essay. Tick any of the ideas you wrote down that appear in the essay. Do you agree with the writer and their conclusion? Why/Why not?

We all love the excitement of watching our favourite sports stars in action. <u>Therefore</u>, <u>to my mind</u>, it seems fair that they earn a lot of money. <u>However</u>, the problem comes when we think about how much a doctor earns in comparison with our favourite football players or Formula 1 drivers. Is it right that somebody can make more by scoring goals or winning races than by saving lives?

<u>Firstly</u>, it is important to remember that top sports stars are precisely that, at the top of their profession. Not all athletes earn millions a year, only the very best. <u>What is more</u>, to get to the top, all of these sports men and women have made lots of sacrifices and trained to the maximum to be the very best they can, just like doctors. <u>Lastly</u>, because they train hard and look after their health, we could say that they help society by acting as inspirational role models.

<u>On the other hand</u>, what job could be more important than a doctor's, saving lives every day? In order to become a doctor, people have to dedicate years to learning the skills and knowledge they need to help patients. <u>Furthermore</u>, their training never stops. <u>In addition</u>, doctors often have to work overtime, at any time of the day, and in very stressful conditions.

<u>All in all</u>, <u>I believe</u> that top sports stars deserve to earn a lot of money. <u>Nevertheless</u>, society needs to recognise the essential work that doctors do and make sure they are paid at least as well as people like popular sports stars, actors or singers. <u>After all</u>, a world with few doctors but hundreds of sports stars would definitely not be a good place to live.

4 Look again at the essay and answer the questions.
1 What is the purpose of each paragraph?
2 How are for-and-against essays different from opinion essays?

5a Put the <u>underlined</u> words in the essay in the correct section in the Writing bank.

5b Can you add any other linkers or expressions to the different sections?

Writing bank
Useful linkers and expressions in for-and-against essays

1 Introducing and sequencing arguments	4 Expressing consequences
....	....
	and so
Secondly,	as a result
2 Adding arguments	**5 Expressing opinions**
....	....
not only ... but also	In my opinion,
3 Making contrasts	Personally,
....	As far as I'm concerned
On the one hand,	**6 Concluding**
In contrast,	....
Despite/In spite of (+ noun/gerund/ the fact that ...)	In conclusion, To sum up,

6 **SPEAKING** Read the essay task. Make a paragraph plan and write down notes with ideas for each paragraph.

> 'We should always try to avoid any type of stress in our lives.'

☑ Exam tip

Remember that in for-and-against essays, you must think of points for both sides of the argument. You can express your own view in the conclusion.

Practice makes perfect

7a Write your essay individually. Use your notes and the expressions in the Writing bank.

7b When you finish your essay, use the Writing checklist on page 141 to check it.

Grammar reference

Zero, first, second and third conditionals

We use the zero conditional to talk about situations that are generally or always true.

If + present simple, ... present simple
If you don't water plants, they die.

We use the first conditional to talk about possible and probable situations in the future, and their consequences.

If + present simple, ... will + infinitive
If you eat junk food, you will put on weight.

We use the second conditional to talk about imaginary or improbable situations and their consequences. The imaginary or improbable sentences are in the present or future, not in the past.

If + past simple, ... would/wouldn't + infinitive
If I had a beard, I'd look older.

We use the third conditional to talk about imaginary or impossible situations in the past and their consequences. The situations are impossible because we cannot change them now that they have happened.

If + past perfect, ... would/wouldn't have + past participle
If I had studied, I would have passed the exam.

unless, as long as, provided/providing (that), in case

unless = if ... not, except if
We won't be able to swim unless the swimming pool is open.

as long as, provided/providing (that) = if, only if
We'll be able to swim as long as/provided the swimming pool is open.

in case = because maybe
We'll take our swimming costumes in case the swimming pool is open.

I wish/If only

We use *I wish/If only* + the past simple to talk about imaginary situations in the present. It expresses wishes for things to be different in the present.
I wish I was/were on the beach right now.

We use *I wish/If only* + the past perfect to talk about past situations that we would have liked to be different. It expresses regrets.
If only I hadn't spent all my money last weekend.

We use *I wish/If only* with *would/wouldn't* + infinitive to talk about somebody's habitual behaviour that we want to criticise and change.
My dad smokes. I wish he wouldn't do it.

Vocabulary

1 Parts of the body

ankle • chest • eyebrow • eyelash • eyelid • forehead • heel • hip • kidney • liver • lungs • muscle • nail • ribs • thigh • waist

2 Health and medical care

A and E (accident and emergency) (n) • ache (v, n) • broken (adj) • chemist (n) • cough (n, v) • dislocate (v) • dizziness (n) • dizzy (adj) • exhaustion (n) • fever (n) • flu (n) • fracture (n, v) • GP (n) • germ (n) • get better (v) • headache (n) • heal (v) • infection (n) • infectious (adj) • injection (n) • injure (v) • injury (n) • lower (v) • operation (n) • painful (adj) • painkiller (n) • pass on (phrasal verb) • physiotherapy (n) • prescription (n) • relief (n) • remedy (n) • sick (adj) • sneeze (v, n) • sore (adj) • stiff (adj) • stiffness (n) • symptom (n) • temperature (n) • tiredness (n) • treat (v) • treatment (n) • vaccine (n) • X-ray (n)

3 Idioms connected with health and illness

back on your feet (adj) • black out (phrasal verb) • come down with (phrasal verb) • full of beans (adj) • keep in shape (v) • on top of the world (adj) • on your last legs (adj) • out of shape (adj) • pull through (phrasal verb) • the picture of health (adj) • under the weather (adj)

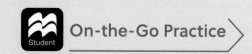
On-the-Go Practice

Grammar test

Conditionals

1 Put the verbs in the correct form. Which type of conditional is each sentence?

1 If I was you, I .... (not eat) that!

2 I would've prepared something special for dinner, if I .... (know) you were coming.

3 If she had told me your number, I .... (call) you last night.

4 If you multiply two by five, the answer .... (be) ten.

5 .... you .... (give) Mark this message if you see him tomorrow?

6 I would have had a good time if I .... (go) out last night.

7 If you find my keys, ... you .... (tell) me?

8 I .... (get) something to eat if I had any money.

/ 8 points

unless, as long as, provided/providing (that), in case

2 Rewrite the sentences using the words given.

1 You won't finish in time if you don't hurry. (unless)

You ....

2 Take your mobile phone because you may need to call me. (in case)

Take ....

3 They will win the match, but only if they do their best. (provided)

They ....

4 We wouldn't need Danny in the team except if someone was ill. (unless)

We ....

5 We'll be able to make sandwiches if Kate remembers to bring the bread. (as long as)

We ....

6 They'll let you in, but only if you have your ID card. (providing that)

They ....

/ 6 points

I wish/If only

3 Write sentences with *I wish* or *If only* for these situations.

1 You aren't fit but you would like to be.

I wish ....

2 He always takes a long time in the bathroom.

I wish he ....

3 You didn't buy tickets for a concert yesterday and now they're all sold out.

If only ....

4 Your parents don't let you have parties at home and you're not happy about it.

If only my parents ....

5 You ate a big lunch and now you regret it.

I wish ....

6 You're allergic to cats but you really like them.

I wish ....

/ 6 points

Vocabulary test

Parts of the body

1 Reorder the letters to make parts of the body.

1	phi	4	nidkye	7	alin
2	gnusl	5	tiswa	8	lemsuc
3	ghiht	6	reedhofa		

/ 4 points

Health and medical care

2 Write one simple sentence to define each word or phrase.

1	stiffness	4	chemist	7	fever
2	A and E	5	prescription	8	ache
3	GP	6	operation	9	pain relief

/ 9 points

Idioms connected with health and illness

3 Rewrite the sentences using an idiom connected with health and illness. Use the word given.

1 Sam is feeling great. (top)

2 Joe has caught the flu. (down)

3 Ella was totally exhausted at the end of the race. (last)

4 I go swimming to keep fit. (shape)

5 I lost consciousness for a second. (out)

6 It looks like he'll be okay after the accident. (pull)

7 You look really well! (picture)

/ 7 points

Total: / 40 points

Reading

In multiple choice reading activities for a long text, remember ...
Read the whole text first to understand the topic and general meaning. Then identify which section(s) of the text relate to each question.

1 SPEAKING 👥 **What are the different ways you think people might escape from a flood?**

2 **Read the text. Then read the questions and choose the best answer.**

Ashura looked with horror out of the small window as the river rose higher and higher. The rains had been going on for days and seemed even worse today. Everyone was asleep but he shouted for them to get up. His mum rushed out of the bedroom and shouted at his sisters. His dad
5 ran out of the hut and down the path to the river. Ashura chased after him.
'It's going so fast – look, it's rushing over the banks,' his dad said, pointing to the other side where they could see neighbours waving. They ran back to the house and started to pack some small bags with their most important possessions.
10 'Quick, quick!' his dad shouted at them all. 'If we leave now we can walk down to the bridge and get to the town. We'll be safe there. Our house is too low. If the water comes over this side, the house will be taken away by the flood. Quickly!'
They all packed their bags but there was a bang and the door fell
15 in, followed by a gush of water. His sisters screamed but he took their hands and pulled them up the tiny stairs. 'Quick,' he said, 'Onto the roof.' He helped his mum and they all went through a small hatch and climbed onto the roof with their belongings.
They could now see the flood waters running beneath the hut as the
20 river had completely come over the banks. Some of their neighbours shouted to them as they went by in boats but nobody had any room to take them.
'Don't worry,' they shouted. 'We'll tell the emergency services you're here. They'll come and get you!'
25 Ashura and his family waited on the roof but they started to get cold and hungry. His sisters were crying and his mum had gone very quiet. Ashura looked around the swilling waters and saw that all sorts of debris was floating past – people's abandoned possessions and parts of the huts they lived in. Suddenly he jumped up.
30 'Be careful,' his dad shouted. 'You'll fall.'
'I've had an idea,' Ashura called as he climbed back into the top room of the hut. When he came back he had a length of old rope with him.
'What are you doing?' his mum asked. 'We need to wait for someone to get us.'
35 Ashura looked around at the waters again and saw his chance. 'Hold me,' he said and he leaned out off the roof and grabbed a wooden door as it went past. His dad helped him drag the door near to the walls and tie it to the hut. Then Ashura grabbed another one. They pulled both the doors up and slowly Ashura started tying the doors together with the rope to make
40 a raft. Then he went down into the house and found a long wooden stick he could use as an oar to guide the raft.
As he climbed back out on the roof, he was worried the raft might not be strong enough for all of them. He didn't tell his dad what he was thinking though. He climbed back on the roof where the family were
45 sitting shivering. He and his dad pushed the raft into the water, holding it with a rope.
'Come on,' he said. 'The waters are rising – we must leave!'

1 Why did Ashura wake his family?
  A He wanted them to see the floods.
  B He knew they needed to escape.
  C He was scared and wanted to be with them.
  D He wanted them to get help.

2 Why do the family pack small bags?
  A because their dad wants them to carry very little
  B because they only have time to take a few things
  C because they think they might be leaving their home forever
  D because their important things take very little space

3 Why didn't the family get on the rescue boats?
  A Because they were full.
  B Because they didn't go to the bridge.
  C Because their friends were angry at them.
  D Because the water was running too fast.

4 What gives Ashura an idea in lines 27–29?
  A the fact he nearly falls off the roof
  B the different objects floating in the water
  C going back into their house
  D seeing how fast the water was running

5 What does 'saw his chance' mean in line 35?
  A He realised he had little time.
  B He found a place to jump.
  C He recognised someone in the water.
  D He noticed the floating door.

6 What do we learn about Ashura in the final paragraph?
  A He is willing to take risks.
  B He feels confident about his design.
  C He is happy that his family trusts him.
  D He values his relationship with his dad.

Sports in your country

 SPEAKING **Starting point**

What facts do you remember about the origins of Pilates and basketball? Try to remember at least two facts about each sport and then check your ideas by looking back at the texts on pages 76 and 77.

 SPEAKING **Project task**

Students at an American school want to know about sports in your country. Which sports are particularly popular? Did any sports have their origins in your country? Use your own knowledge and experience to tell them all about it. Use the Internet to look for any extra information. Prepare one of these:

A poster   **C** video message

B presentation   **D** information leaflet

Research areas

- sports that began in your country – who invented them, when, how, why
- sports that are unique to your country – the rules, the equipment, etc.
- international sports that are popular in your country – when people started playing them, when and why they became popular
- famous teams and players from your country and things that they have won
- typical summer and winter sports in your country

③ Think about …

Virtual Classroom Exchange

Digital skills

Don't only research information online. Look also for useful images or graphics that you can use to clarify or illustrate the information in your project. For example, an image of a sport unique to your country would help to make the sport clear to somebody from another country.

Academic skills

When you search the web for information, it's important to look critically at the information you find. Look at who wrote the information. What makes them 'experts' in the topic?

Collaboration

When you work in a team, it's essential to listen to everyone and let everybody contribute. Sometimes one or two people can dominate in a group, but the best teams have a balance between everybody, even including the quieter members of the team.

Useful language

That's a good idea. But what do you think, (Sara)?, Let's listen to (Oscar), Who hasn't spoken?, It's (Olga's) turn to speak.

Intercultural awareness

Do you think the sports that are popular in your country are as popular in the UK or US, for example? What could explain the similarities or differences? What do you think makes some sports more popular in different countries?

④ **SPEAKING** **Project time**

Do the project. Then present it to the class.

⑤ **Evaluation**

Give each project a mark from 1 to 5 (5 = very good) for these categories.

Content   ☐   Design   ☐

Presentation ☐   Language ☐

7

RAVE REVIEWS

Vocabulary in context
Words connected with film, fiction and music
Adjectives to use in reviews

1 **SPEAKING** Put the words in the columns. Some can go in more than one column.

(( )) 33 Film, fiction and music genres

action • animation • crime • dance • electronic • folk • historical • horror • indie • metal • punk • R&B • rap • rom-com • sci-fi • soul • thriller

Film	Fiction	Music

2 Complete the text with the correct form of the words in the box. Check that you also understand the words in bold. Use a dictionary if necessary.

(( )) 34 Words connected with music

album • chart • download • live • lyrics • make it • performance • record • songwriter • stage • tour • track

Culture exchange

THE ARTS IN IRELAND TODAY 1

Ireland has always been world-famous for its music. The latest Irish band to **(a)** .... is the punk band Fontaines D.C. Grian Chatten is the singer and one of the **(b)** .... in the band. They're all very influenced by poetry, and you can tell that when you listen to the **(c)** .... of their songs. So far, they've **(d)** .... and **released** just one **(e)** ...., called 'Dogrel', available on CD, limited edition yellow **vinyl** or digital **(f)** .... All of the eleven **(g)** .... on it are amazing. It's no surprise that it immediately went into the Top Five of our **(h)** .... The group have just been on **(i)** .... in the UK and the US. Their **gigs** are famous because of the energy put into their **(j)** .... when they get on **(k)** .... You've just got to see them **(l)** ....

3 Now do the same with this text.

(( )) 35 Words connected with film

audience • box office • ending • main • plot • screenplay • sequel • soundtrack • star (v) • villain

Culture exchange

THE ARTS IN IRELAND TODAY 2

Irish actor Cillian Murphy is famous for **(a)** .... in the TV series *Peaky Blinders* as the leader of a group of gangsters. He's also about to be one of the **(b)** .... **characters** in the **(c)** .... to the dystopian future horror movie, *A Quiet Place*. The original film was a surprise **hit** both with **critics** and at the **(d)** ...., earning $340 million! **(e)** .... were silent while watching *A Quiet Place* because it was all about carnivorous aliens hunting humans by sound, which also explains why there was only one song in the film's **(f)** .... Cillian is keeping silent about the **(g)** .... of *A Quiet Place 2*, so we don't know if there'll be a happy **(h)** .... or not. In fact, we don't even know if Cillian will be a hero or a **(i)** .... in the film. The screenplay is **(j)** ...., but we are sure that the actors won't be shouting!

Collaborative project 4 page 109

4 **SPEAKING** Look at the adjectives in the box. Which are positive and which are negative?

(( )) 36 Adjectives to use in reviews

amusing • clichéd • convincing • fast-moving • gripping • hilarious • inspiring • intriguing • moving • predictable • realistic • stunning • well-produced

Use it ... don't lose it!

5 **SPEAKING** Ask and answer the questions.

1 Do you ever buy CDs or vinyl, or do you just download individual tracks or albums?

2 Which adjectives in 4 could you use to describe the latest film you've seen?

Reach higher page 139

Reading

1 **SPEAKING** 👥 Look at the photos and the title of the newspaper article on this page. Who do you think would use a machine like this? Why might it be popular?

2 Read the article and check your answers in 1.

3 🔊 37 Read the article again and answer the questions in your own words.

1 What options does the Short Story Dispenser give you?

2 What made the Canary Wharf Group decide to install these machines?

3 What are the reading habits of Paresh Raichura? Explain them.

4 What are the attitudes of Babita Bismal and Sam Rankin to smartphones?

5 Why did Anthony Horowitz decide to write a mystery story for the vending machine?

6 Why was the idea of writing a story for this machine so attractive to Horowitz?

7 In the last paragraph, what does the writer say about fiction in general?

8 What advantage does the writer think short fiction has over longer fiction?

4 What do the <u>underlined</u> words in the text mean? Guess and then check in your dictionary.

5 🧠 **Critical thinkers**

> In your opinion, should we read more and use our smartphones less?
>
> What makes you say that?

| Home | About | News | The Arts: Trending in fiction | More ▾ | 🔍 |

Free short story vending machines receive rave reviews

1 Vending machines which serve cold drinks and snacks are nothing new. But at Canary Wharf in London there are three brand-new vending machines which offer you free short stories at the press of a button. You choose the length of the story you want to read – one, three or five minutes. Then select a story from genres such as crime, science fiction or romance. Finally, the machine prints out your story on eco-friendly paper and you're <u>all set</u> to read your new story. The Canary Wharf Group said they had decided to install the machines after new research involving 2,000 UK adults found that 36% had <u>given up on</u> at least one book in the last year due to lack of time, and 30% had not finished a book in over six months. However, an incredible 70% said they'd prefer to get lost in a good book than waste time on social media.

2 The reaction to the vending machines has been incredibly positive. Although the fact that the stories are free and print off in a few seconds undoubtedly helps, that's not the only reason. 'Every single day,' says Paresh Raichura, 'I'm <u>on the lookout for</u> something new to read.' On his hour-long commute to Canary Wharf, he picks up a magazine or newspaper, but says: 'I've stopped reading all the long novels I used to read.' Why? 'Too long. Lack of time. Once you start, you can't stop.' Give us something that we can read in the time it takes to listen to a pop song and we might actually make it to the end.

3 'I think it's cool – just to get people reading,' says Babita Bismal, who commutes from north London. 'I have children, and I can see them getting addicted to their phones. I'm almost encouraging them to watch TV instead.' She has printed off a five-minute story – *A Light in the Storm* by Thierry Covolo – and will try it on her 12- and 17-year-olds later. Other commuters feel the same way and are grateful for anything that can pull them away from their smartphones. 'I love reading,' says Sam Rankin, a receptionist and trainee barber, 'but it's so nice to have something on a piece of paper, something <u>tangible</u>. These days everything is on a phone.' She has printed off a one-minute story called *The Death of Mr Robinson* that has been specially written for the project by best-selling novelist Anthony Horowitz.

4 So what's it like for an author to write one of these stories that last just one minute? Horowitz decided to write a crime story for the machine, and admitted it had been a challenge to condense the genre into such a short form. 'It was the challenge of writing a story that could be read between two stations – not just a short story but a very short story,' he said. 'Because I love mystery and <u>whodunnits</u>, the question of if it would be possible to write a proper whodunnit with a solution which made you smile in such a short amount of space was irresistible. The whole <u>notion</u> amused me.' He said it had taken three or four days to write his story. 'The idea of using that little <u>chunk</u> of your day for something that entertains you, something which is, with a very small 'l', literature, is appealing.'

5 Generally speaking, novels have become shorter than, say, a hundred years ago, when there were fewer leisure activities on offer. In this age of browsing and messaging, fiction, whether short or long, can help us relax from the stress and chaos of life. Machines like those at Canary Wharf are clearly a great idea if they inspire and encourage us to read some fiction … even for just 60 seconds a day.

Reach higher ⟩ page 139

Grammar in context 1

Reported speech – statements

1 Look at the sentences and answer the questions below.

1a She said: 'I'm on the lookout for something to read.'

1b She said that she was on the lookout for something to read.

2a He told the journalist: 'It was the challenge of writing a story that could be read between two stations.'

2b He told the journalist that it had been the challenge of writing a story that could be read between two stations.

3a She said: 'I'll try this story on my teenage kids.'

3b She said she would try that story on her teenage kids.

a How do tenses usually change when we go from direct to reported speech?

b What do you think *could*, *would*, *should*, *might*, the past perfect, infinitives and gerunds all have in common when they go from direct to reported speech?

c Do you think tenses change when the reporting verb is in the present or present perfect (e.g. *He says, He has said*)?

d Apart from the tense, what words change when we put sentence 3a into reported speech?

e What is the difference between *say* and *tell*?

f Do we always need to use *that* after *say* or *tell*?

☑ Check it **page 94**

2 How do the words in the box change when they go from direct to reported speech?

> a (week/month/year) ago • here •
> last (week/month/year) • next (week/month/year) •
> now • these • this • today • tomorrow •
> tonight • yesterday

3 Complete the sentences with *said* or *told*.

1 She .... me she might buy tickets for the gig that weekend.

2 They .... they'd been waiting there for ages.

3 She .... she hadn't seen the film the day before.

4 They .... the lyrics of their songs weren't very important.

5 We .... Amy that we'd go to the concert with her that night.

6 He .... her the music festival was the following month.

4 Write the sentences in 3 in direct speech.

Flipped classroom video
Watch the Grammar Presentation video

5 Put the sentences in direct speech into reported speech.

1 'These papers are yours, Oliver.'
Angela told ....

2 'I'm going to start writing a short story next week.'
Simon said ....

3 'The crowd went mad when I played this song last night.'
Mikey said ....

4 'I might see you tomorrow but I'll tell you tonight, Ella.'
Dan told ....

5 'I love listening to hip-hop records.'
James says ....

6 'We must finish this before we can leave, Luke.'
Jenny told ....

6a Using reported speech, write down five things that famous people have said recently. They can be actors, singers, sports stars, etc.

6b SPEAKING 👥 Report back to the class and tell them two interesting things you wrote down.

Reported speech – questions

7 Look at the sentences and answer the questions below.

1a 'Why have you stopped reading novels?'

1b The journalist asked Paresh why he had stopped reading novels.

2a 'Have you read any novels this year?'

2b They asked people if they had read any novels that year.

3a 'Will you read the short story you've just printed out?'

3b He wondered whether I would read the short story I had just printed out.

4a 'Do you prefer reading or playing online games?'

4b They wanted to know whether we preferred reading or playing online games.

a Do tenses and pronouns change in reported questions in the same way as in reported statements?

b Do we use the auxiliary verb *do* in reported questions?

c Do we put the subject before the verb in reported questions?

d Do we use question marks in reported questions?

e What words do we use when with questions that do not begin with a question word?

☑ Check it **page 94**

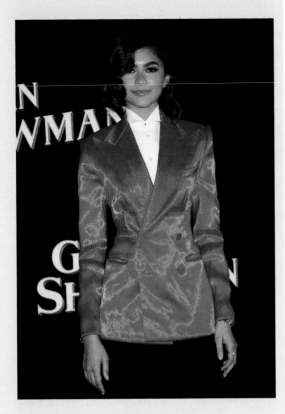

8 Report the conversation using *said*, *told*, *asked* and *wanted to know*.

Olivia: Have you ever seen a famous actor in person?

Tom: Yes, I have. I saw Zendaya last year.

Olivia: Where did you see her?

Tom: I was in France. There was a film festival near where we were staying.

Olivia: Do you always go to France in the summer?

Tom: Yes, we usually go because my grandparents are French.

Olivia: We're probably going to Hollywood next summer. My dad's got a friend who lives in California.

Tom: You're so lucky! I'd love to visit the Walk of Fame one day. Can I come with you?!

Olivia: I'll ask my dad if it's OK!

Use it ... don't lose it!

9 **SPEAKING** 👥 Write five questions about films or series. Then ask your questions to as many people in your class as possible and make a note of their answers. When you finish, write a report about some of the questions you asked and the answers they gave you.

I asked people whether they preferred watching films or series. Three people told me they preferred films but the rest said they liked series more.

Reach higher ▷ page 139

Developing vocabulary

Compound nouns

1 Look at these compounds from pages 84 and 85. Which are compound nouns and which are compound adjectives?

> best-selling • download • eco-friendly • screenplay

2 🔊 38 Listen to the words and mark the stress. Where is the stress in the compound nouns – on the first word, the last word, or both? And in the compound adjectives?

3 Complete the text with the compound nouns in the box.

> blockbuster • box office • breakthrough • cliffhanger • drawback •
> feedback • masterpiece • outcome • sell-out • soundtrack • turnout

INSIDE THE *film industry*

Most film companies aim to produce (a) ...., films that are a big hit with the public at the (b) .... To do that, they often test films in a few cinemas before their official release. At the end of the film, the audience have to give their (c) .... on the film, and their comments can sometimes change a film quite dramatically. The length or title may change, or maybe the music from the (d) .... needs improvements. Often a director needs to introduce a (e) ...., a moment that leaves the audience in complete suspense. However, one possible (f) .... of test screening is that all films become quite similar. Some directors feel that their wonderful film, their (g) ...., can be ruined by paying too much attention to the public's comments. In contrast, others are quite happy with the (h) .... of the process and feel that it can improve the film.

One thing that film directors never really like is having their film chosen for the 'dump months'. These are the months when the (i) .... at cinemas is low. For example, in January and February, relatively few people in the US go to the cinema. In December, on the other hand, it can be difficult to get tickets and there are (j) .... in many cinemas. As a result, companies release their worst films then, the ones that did badly in their test screening. Sometimes there are surprise (k) .... though, when a January film goes on to become a big hit. *The Silence of the Lambs* came out in January and then won the Academy Award for Best Movie!

Use it ... don't lose it!

4 **SPEAKING** 👥 Complete the compound nouns in bold in the questions and use the questions to interview your partner.

1 What is the latest .... **buster** in cinemas at the moment? Have you seen it yet?

2 What do you think are the .... **backs** of watching films at home, rather than in the cinema?

3 What was the .... **out** like in the cinema the last time you went to see a film?

4 What film would you personally say is a **master** ....?

5 What film(s) can you remember where the **sound** .... was especially good?

Reach higher ▷ page 139

GREAT LEARNERS
GREAT THINKERS

HUMAN CREATIVITY

Lesson aim: To think about the importance of creative thinking

Video: A musical with a difference (AKA Can a computer write a musical?)

SEL **Social and emotional learning:** Being curious and creative

1 **SPEAKING** 🧑‍🤝‍🧑 **Ask and answer these questions.**

1   Have you ever seen a musical, either in the cinema or a theatre? What did you think of it?

2   What do you think the elements of a great musical are?

GREAT THINKERS

Think-Question-Explore

2 **SPEAKING** 🧑‍🤝‍🧑 **You are going to watch a video about a musical that was written by a computer. Before you watch, work with a partner and follow these instructions.**

1   What do you **think** you are going to learn about musicals or computers in this video? Make a list with ideas.

2   What **questions** do you have about the topic of the video? Write them down.

3   **VIDEO** ▷ Now watch and **explore** the video and see if it answers any of your questions. If not, which other sources of information could you use to explore the topic?

3a How much information do you remember from the video? Finish these sentences with information about the musical.

1   London's West End is the place where …

2   Benjamin, Nathan, Neil and Luke are four people who …

3   Challenges, some love, and a happy ending are all things which …

4   Greenham is the place where …

5   'Searching the forest of blood' are words that Benjamin …

6   Nick is a person who …

7   The opening night of the musical is a moment which …

8   A little imagination and a lot of hard work are elements which …

3b **VIDEO** ▷ **Watch the video again. When it finishes, check and complete your answers in 3a.**

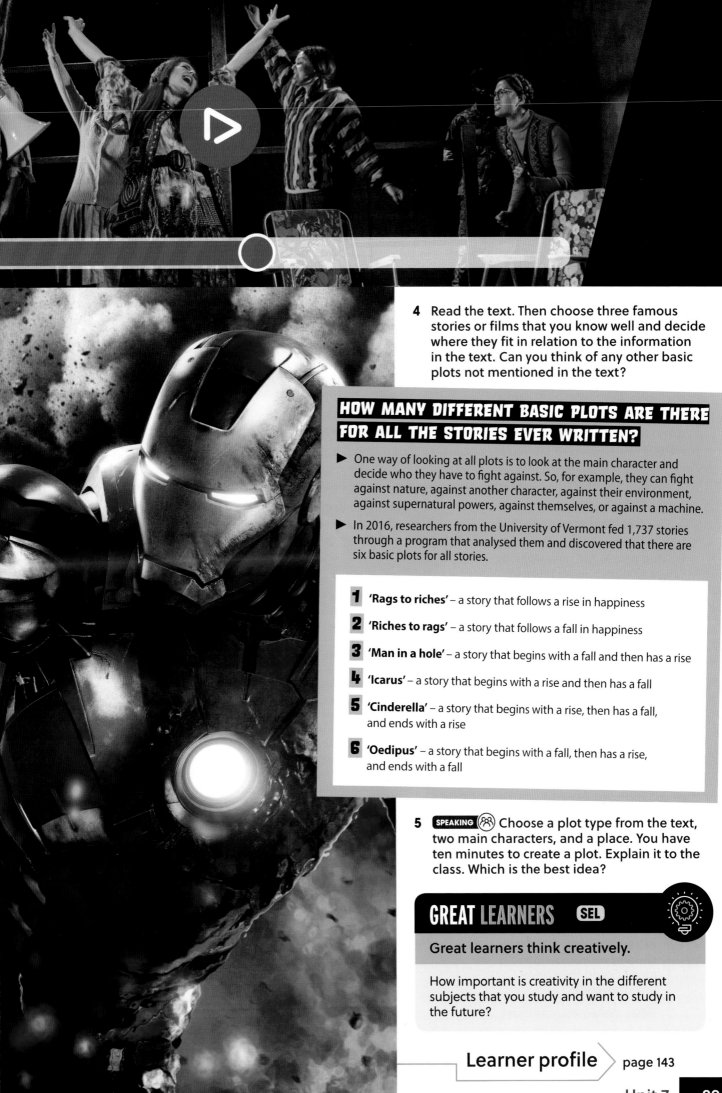

4 Read the text. Then choose three famous stories or films that you know well and decide where they fit in relation to the information in the text. Can you think of any other basic plots not mentioned in the text?

HOW MANY DIFFERENT BASIC PLOTS ARE THERE FOR ALL THE STORIES EVER WRITTEN?

▶ One way of looking at all plots is to look at the main character and decide who they have to fight against. So, for example, they can fight against nature, against another character, against their environment, against supernatural powers, against themselves, or against a machine.

▶ In 2016, researchers from the University of Vermont fed 1,737 stories through a program that analysed them and discovered that there are six basic plots for all stories.

1 **'Rags to riches'** – a story that follows a rise in happiness

2 **'Riches to rags'** – a story that follows a fall in happiness

3 **'Man in a hole'** – a story that begins with a fall and then has a rise

4 **'Icarus'** – a story that begins with a rise and then has a fall

5 **'Cinderella'** – a story that begins with a rise, then has a fall, and ends with a rise

6 **'Oedipus'** – a story that begins with a fall, then has a rise, and ends with a fall

5 **SPEAKING** 🗣️ Choose a plot type from the text, two main characters, and a place. You have ten minutes to create a plot. Explain it to the class. Which is the best idea?

GREAT LEARNERS   SEL

Great learners think creatively.

How important is creativity in the different subjects that you study and want to study in the future?

Learner profile ▷ page 143

Listening

1 SPEAKING 👥 **Ask and answer these questions.**

1 How often do you read fiction? Which genres do you prefer?

2 Do you prefer to read (a) traditional, physical books (b) electronic books, or (c) reading apps on a mobile device (smartphone, tablet ...)? Why?

2a 🔊**39** **Listen to a podcast about story-sharing websites. Are the statements True (T) or False (F)?**

1 They say that fan fiction is the most popular genre on story-sharing websites.   T / F

2 These websites are exclusively for new authors.   T / F

3 Most people, but not everybody, use a smartphone or tablet to read the stories on these websites.   T / F

4 The app 'Tap' gives you access to fictional text messages.   T / F

5 Wattpad encourages detailed feedback from its readers.   T / F

6 The difference in quality between one story and another is a major problem with story-sharing websites.   T / F

7 Beth Reekles' story went straight from a story-sharing website to TV.   T / F

8 Nowadays, TV and film companies often do market research using story-sharing websites.   T / F

2b 🔊**39** **Explain why the false sentences are false. Listen again if necessary.**

3 ⚙️ **Critical thinkers**

In your opinion, are story-sharing websites a good idea? Could they have any drawbacks?

What makes you say that?

Grammar in context 2

Other reporting verbs

1a Look at the sentences. Which of the reporting verbs in bold need an object pronoun (like *told*) and which don't (like *said*)?

1a 'There are thousands of books written by teenagers. And some of them are using smartphones to write their stories.'

1b She **explained** that there were thousands of books written by teenagers. She **added** that some of them were using smartphones to write their stories.

2a 'Not all of the stories are well-written.'

2b She **warned** him that not all of the stories were well-written.

3a 'Don't forget, there's something for everyone.'

3b He **reminded** them that there was something for everyone.

4a 'We have 70 million users.'

4b They **claimed** that they had 70 million users.

1b What about these verbs? One verb can go with or without an object pronoun. Which one?

admit • agree • announce • complain • promise

1c What is the meaning of the reporting verbs in 1b?

☑ Check it **page 94**

2a Choose the best alternative.

SUPERNATURAL SUCCESS STORY

Teenage author Lee Kim (a) *added/announced* at a press conference that there was going to be a TV adaptation of her latest supernatural thriller, *An X-ray of Memories*. She (b) *claimed/warned* that she was surprised but delighted by the news. Lee Kim (c) *agreed/complained* that her story would make a great TV series. She (d) *admitted/promised* that the director had asked her to make some changes to the plot and (e) *added/announced* that she had no problem with that. But, joking with the press, she explained (f) *them/–* that she wanted to act in the series, too, and (g) *agreed/ complained* that she couldn't appear in the series as her favourite character, Tracey. On a more serious note, she (h) *added/warned* her fans that the series wouldn't be exactly the same as the novel. But she (i) *complained/ promised* them it would be just as good.

2b Rewrite the sentences in 2a in direct speech.

(a) *'There's going to be a TV adaptation of my latest supernatural thriller.'*

3 Rewrite the sentences in reported speech using each verb once. Sometimes more than one answer is possible.

admit • announce • claim • complain • promise • remind • warn

1 **Jenny:** 'I'll remember to finish the book today.'

2 **The Prime Minister:** 'We are going to put wi-fi in every school.'

3 **Ben:** 'I didn't know it was illegal to download these songs.'

4 **Tom:** 'The special effects in the film were terrible.'

5 **Ella:** 'I should read more often.'

6 **Mike:** 'Joe, it isn't very good for your eyes to read in the dark.'

7 **Becky:** 'Dad, don't forget. My train arrives at 3 pm.'

Other reporting structures

4a Check that you understand the meaning of the reporting verbs in bold and write each one in the correct list below.

1 He **suggested** taking a look at those websites.

2 He **apologised** for not having more time.

3 He **asked** her to explain story-sharing websites.

4 They **claimed** to have 70 million users.

5 They **criticised** some authors for making mistakes with spelling and grammar.

a verb + infinitive: ...., *agree, offer, promise, refuse*

b verb + object + infinitive: ...., *advise, instruct, tell, order, invite, persuade, remind, warn*

c verb + gerund: ...., *admit, advise, deny, recommend, regret*

d verb + preposition + gerund: ...., *insist on, object to, confess to*

e verb + object + preposition + gerund: ...., *congratulate somebody on, accuse somebody of, warn somebody against*

4b Check that you understand the meaning of the other reporting verbs in lists a–e above.

☑ Check it **page 94**

5 Rewrite the sentences.

1 'Oliver has hidden all my text books.'
   May accused ....

2 'I'll tell you the truth, Dad.'
   Sandra promised ....

3 'I didn't eat all the popcorn.'
   Dylan denied ....

4 'Don't write your essay in pencil, Will.'
   The teacher told ....

5 'I'm sorry I took your laptop without asking, Liam.'
   James apologised ....

6 'Don't go near the edge, Ned, because you could fall.'
   Ned's mum warned ....

7 'Okay, we'll talk about the assignment after school.'
   Cathy and Lucas agreed ....

8 'No, I won't appear in a selfie with all of you.'
   The singer refused ....

6 Choose the correct alternative.

Publishers have to take difficult decisions sometimes. They can't print every novel that comes their way. But there are some occasions where publishers get it very wrong!

● Many publishers said no to the novel *Moby Dick* by Herman Melville. One of them (a) *criticised/explained* that they thought it was a bad idea to write a story about a whale.

● A publisher refused (b) *to publish/publishing* one of Ernest Hemingway's most famous novels, *The Sun Also Rises*. They criticised Hemingway (c) *for/of* writing a book that was both 'tedious and offensive'.

● Poet T. S. Eliot rejected *Animal Farm* by George Orwell. He warned Orwell (d) *against/for* criticising the current political situation in a book about a farm. He (e) *added/warned* that he thought the pigs in the book were too intelligent.

● One publisher (f) *advised/claimed* that John Le Carré and his book had no future. The book, *The Spy Who Came in from the Cold*, became one of the most famous spy novels of all time and an international bestseller.

● Another publisher admitted (g) *to like/liking* F. Scott Fitzgerald's novel, *The Great Gatsby*. But then they suggested (h) *to get/getting* rid of Gatsby, the main character.

● Nearly every big publisher in the UK said no to Harry Potter. One advised the author (i) *not to write/not writing* about a school like Hogwarts. Another recommended (j) *to make/making* the book shorter. Bloomsbury Publishing eventually (k) *announced/offered* that they wanted to publish the book. That's because the boss of the company had given the first chapter to his eight-year-old daughter, Alice. She insisted (l) *in/on* reading the next chapter and then persuaded her father (m) *to print/printing* the book. But even then, J.K. Rowling's editor (n) *suggested/warned* her that it was a bad idea to write full-time. He (o) *explained/reminded* her that authors of children's books didn't usually earn much money. When Harry Potter became such a phenomenal success, many publishers congratulated J.K. Rowling (p) *of/on* writing such a great book and apologised (q) *by/for* turning her down.

7 Complete the sentences with information about yourself. You must use a verb.

1 Teachers usually warn us ....

2 My parents don't usually insist on ....

3 If you want to read a good story, I suggest
   ....

4 The other day somebody persuaded me to
   ....

5 I once congratulated a friend on ....

6 Nobody has ever accused me of ....

7 My parents once refused ....

8 At our school, they always tell you ....

┌─────────────────────────────────┐
│ **Use it … don't lose it!**

8 **SPEAKING** 👥 **Compare your sentences in 7. Choose the most interesting to share with the class.**
└─────────────────────────────────┘

Reach higher ▷ **page 139**

Developing speaking

Discussions 1

1 SPEAKING 👥 Describe the photo in the magazine article. What does it show? Look at the title of the article. What do you think the article is going to say?

2 Read the article. Does the information surprise you? Why/ Why not?

ARE FILM AWARDS FAIR?

N owadays there are more and more complaints that film awards are not very fair. There always seem to be fewer minority actors nominated for the top prizes. And few women win the top filmmaker prize, or any non-acting award. But it seems obvious that films and stories, from fantasy to historical fiction, should represent the world around us in all its diversity. Critics say that the problem with film awards could be that the judges and voters who choose the winners are very often old, white and male. That means they are not representative of film audiences as a whole.

3 🔊40 Listen to a boy and a girl discussing the magazine article and answer the questions.

1 Do the boy and girl generally have similar opinions?
2 What examples do they give to support their arguments?

4 🔊40 Listen to the discussion again. Which expressions in the Speaking bank do you hear?

Speaking bank
Presenting a solid argument

Adding emphasis
- You have to remember that …
- Don't forget that …
- There's no doubt in my mind that …
- I really do think that …
- I'm totally convinced that …
- You can't deny that …
- It's time that (subject + past tense)

Giving examples
- For instance,
- Take …, for example.
- What about the case of …?
- Look at …
- You only have to think of …
- … such as …
- A good example of that is …
- Just to give you an idea …

5 SPEAKING 👥 Work in threes. Discuss your own opinions about the article in 2. Give examples.

✓ Exam tip

Remember that in discussions, you must listen carefully to what your partner or partners say and react to it. Your mark will depend in part on how well you interact with others.

6 Look at these discussion topics. Decide what your opinion is for each one and make a note of your arguments and examples.

1 Superhero films are ruining the cinema because they all tend to be childish and silly.
2 To really enjoy a film, you have to watch it in the cinema, not on a smartphone or tablet.
3 Film adaptations are never as good as the original book.

Practice makes perfect

7a SPEAKING 👥 Work in threes. Discuss the different topics. Remember to use expressions from the Speaking bank.

7b SPEAKING 👥 When you finish, share your ideas with the whole class. Do you have similar opinions or not? Can you change anybody's mind with your arguments and examples?

Developing writing

A review

1 SPEAKING 👥 Look at this notice from an international website for teenagers. Which book would you recommend and why?

REVIEWS WANTED

A book that ALL teenagers should read!

Which book do you think is essential reading for all readers of your age? Write a review telling us about the story and main characters and explain why you think it's such a great book for teenagers.

2 SPEAKING 👥 Read this review of a book for teenagers. Would you want to read this book after reading the review? Why/Why not?

| Latest posts | **Reviews** | About | 🔍 |

1 *The Outsiders* is a brilliant book which S. E. Hinton wrote over 50 years ago, when she was still only 17 years old. Not only is it a fast-moving novel full of action, but it's also a deep and moving story about family, friendship and what it's like, even today, to be a teenager.

2 The narrator of the story is a 14-year-old boy called Ponyboy. Both of his parents died in a car crash and now his older brother, Darry, looks after him. Although Ponyboy doesn't get on very well with Darry, he does have a great relationship with his other brother, Sodapop.

3 Ponyboy, Sodapop and all their friends are 'greasers', teenagers who have long hair and not much money. Their rivals are the 'socs', rich kids who they often fight against. One night, Ponyboy is with a friend when some 'socs' attack them and they fight back in self-defence. From that moment on, Ponyboy's life changes dramatically. Despite the tragic events that take place, there's a happy ending.

4 I really love this book because of Ponyboy, who is both clever and sensitive. In my opinion, he is not only a very likeable character, but he's also a convincing narrator. Neither the 'greasers' nor the 'socs' really hate each other. They all just feel they need to fit in and be part of a group, but they also want to be individuals and find their place in the world.

5 All things considered, I really do believe that this is a brilliant story for teenagers. Seeing this violent world of teenage rebels through Ponyboy's sensitive and perceptive eyes is an unforgettable experience. If you haven't read this story yet, it's time you did!

3 Read the review again and decide what the purpose of each paragraph is.

Paragraph 1: ....

Paragraph 2: ....

Paragraph 3: ....

Paragraph 4: ....

Paragraph 5: ....

4 SPEAKING 👥 Look at the expressions in the Writing bank and answer the questions.

1 Why are the auxiliary verbs *do/did/does* used in the first examples in the Writing bank?

2 When *not only* comes at the beginning of the sentence, do we use the affirmative or interrogative from of the verb after it?

Writing bank
Ways of adding emphasis

- I really **do** think that ..., He **did** have a hard life, The book **does** describe this problem well.
- **Not only** is it fast-moving, **but** it's **also** deep, He is **not only** a complex character, but he's also a great narrator.
- He's **both** clever **and** sensitive, He is **neither** violent **nor** stupid.
- She was **still** only 17 years old, It's **still** thought-provoking today.
- **It's time** you **picked** up this novel, **It's time** we **thought** about questions like this.
- See other expressions in the Speaking bank on page 92.

5 Rewrite each pair of sentences as one sentence, beginning with the expression 'Not only ...' .

1 The book was successful in the US. It was translated into many other languages.

2 Ponyboy gets good marks at school. He writes really well.

3 I've read the book. I've seen the film.

4 I'd recommend this novel. I'd recommend all her other novels.

5 You can understand how he feels. You can understand his actions.

6 Make notes about one of the books you thought about in 1. Organise your notes into paragraphs. Follow the paragraph plan in 3.

☑ **Exam tip**

To make reviews interesting for the reader, use a variety of adjectives and adverbs. Also, don't forget the advice about making your writing more interesting (Unit 5), involving the reader (Unit 4) and using expressions of opinion (Unit 3).

Practice makes perfect

7a Write your review. Use your notes in 6, the expressions in the Writing bank, and the advice in the Exam tip box.

7b When you finish your review, use the Writing checklist on page 141 to check it.

7c Exchange reviews with other students. Which of the books do you want to read?

Grammar reference

Reported speech – statements

When the reporting verb (e.g. *say, tell*) is in the past, the tense of the verb in reported speech usually changes, going one tense 'back'. Some tenses cannot go any further back and so stay the same.

Could, would, should, might, the past perfect and infinitives and gerunds do not change from direct to reported speech.

When the reporting verb is in the present simple or present perfect, the tense of the verb in reported speech usually stays the same.

'I enjoy watching films.' → *He says he enjoys watching films.*

When the reporting verb is in the past but the statement is something which is still true, or is and will always be true, the tense of the verb in reported speech can stay the same.

'I'm American.' → *Hayden said he's American.*

'They make lots of films in India.' → *The guide told us that they make lots of films in India.*

In reported speech, pronouns and possessive adjectives also change.

'I love your smile.' → *Brad said he loved her smile.*

With **say** you do not need to use a personal object to say who the subject is talking to.

He said it was going to be a great film.

NOT He said me it was going to be a great film.

With **tell** you must use a personal object to say who the subject is talking to.

He told me it was going to be a great film.

NOT He told that it was going to be a great film.

Reported speech – questions

The same changes occur with tenses, pronouns and other words as with reported statements.

We do not use the auxiliary verb *do* in reported questions.

'Do you like rap music?' → *She asked me if I liked rap music.*

There is no inversion of subject and verb in reported questions.

'Where are you?' → *He asked me where I was.*

Reported questions are not real questions so they do not need question marks.

NOT She asked me what I needed?

When there is no question word (*who, what, how, why,* etc.), we use *if* or *whether*.

'Can you do it?' → *They asked me if I could do it.*

Reported speech – other reporting verbs

*   add, admit, agree, announce, claim, complain, explain, promise

These work like *say* – you do not need to use a personal object with them. In the case of *promise* you can use a personal object if you want.

*   remind, warn

These work like *tell* – you need to use a personal object with them.

Reported speech – other reporting structures

*   verb + infinitive: *agree, claim, offer, promise, refuse*
    He agreed to go with them.
*   verb + object + infinitive: *advise, ask, instruct, tell, order, invite, persuade, remind, warn*
    She advised him to buy tickets in advance.
*   verb + gerund: *admit, advise, deny, recommend, regret, suggest*
    They admitted stealing the watch.
*   verb + preposition + gerund: *apologise for, insist on, object to, confess to*
    We apologised for arriving late.
*   verb + object + preposition + gerund: *accuse somebody of, congratulate somebody on, criticise somebody for, warn somebody against*
    They accused him of cheating in the exam.

Vocabulary

1 Film, fiction and music genres

action • animation • crime • dance • electronic • folk • historical • horror • indie • metal • punk • R&B • rap • rom-com • sci-fi • soul • thriller

2 Words connected with music and film

album (n) • audience (n) • box office (n) • (main) character (n) • chart (n) • critic (n) • download (n, v) • (happy) ending (n) • gig (n) • hit (n) • live (adv) • lyrics (n) • make it (v) • performance (n) • plot (n) • record (v) • release (v, n) • screenplay (n) • sequel (n) • songwriter (n) • soundtrack (n) • stage (n) • star (v) • tour (n, v) • track (n) • villain (n) • vinyl (n)

3 Adjectives to use in reviews

amusing • clichéd • convincing • fast-moving • gripping • inspiring • intriguing • hilarious • moving • predictable • realistic • stunning • well-produced

4 Compound nouns

blockbuster • box office • breakthrough • cliffhanger • drawback • feedback • masterpiece • outcome • sell-out • soundtrack • turnout

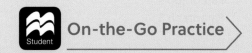

On-the-Go Practice

Grammar test

Reported speech – statements

1 Complete the second sentence so that it has a similar meaning to the first sentence. Use between two and five words, including the word given.

1 'I can't do this exercise,' Ethan said. (able)

Ethan said .... do the exercise.

2 'You must bring your passports,' the teacher said to them. (to)

The teacher told .... bring their passports.

3 'It's on television tonight on Channel 4,' said Ava. (that)

Ava explained it .... on Channel 4.

4 'I failed the exam,' said Daniel. (passed)

Daniel admitted .... the exam.

5 'I'm sure these are our seats,' said Chloe. (was)

Chloe claimed she .... seats.

6 'We might have made a mistake,' Ben said to them. (maybe)

Ben warned them that .... a mistake.

/ 6 points

Reported speech – questions

2 Complete the sentences using reported speech.

1 'Where have you just been?' Charlie asked Holly.

Charlie asked ....

2 'Do you want to go to the cinema tonight?' Harry asked her.

Harry asked ....

3 'Can you speak English?' Lucy asked the boy.

Lucy asked ....

4 'Will it rain next week when we're on holiday?' wondered Dave.

Dave wondered ....

5 'How did the magician do that trick?' Sophie wanted to know.

Sophie wanted to know ....

6 'Are you going to go out this weekend?' Grace asked Jack.

Grace asked ....

7 'What have you been doing all this morning?' Mum asked us.

Mum asked ....

/ 7 points

Reported speech – other reporting structures

3 Complete the text with the correct form of the verbs given. Add prepositions if necessary.

Last year the police (a) .... (promise/do) something about people downloading films illegally. They (b) .... (accuse/one man/make) hundreds of illegal copies of a recent Hollywood blockbuster. They arrested him but he (c) .... (refuse/answer) any of their questions. In the end, he (d) .... (admit/do) it. He (e) .... (confess/copy) nearly one thousand films. He (f) .... (apologise/cause) any problems. The police (g) .... (tell/him/not do) it again.

/ 7 points

Vocabulary test

Words connected with music and film

1 Write simple definitions for these words.

1 audience   **4** box office   **6** critic

2 gig   **5** screenplay   **7** soundtrack

3 lyrics

/ 7 points

Adjectives to use in reviews

2 Put the letters in order to make adjectives. Is each one positive (+) or negative (−)?

1 alihiuosr ....   **4** gunninst ....

2 fanviostmg ....   **5** riabeldecpt ....

3 acisitler ....   **6** hdlicéc ....

/ 6 points

Compound nouns

3 Match the words in the two columns. Which word is not a noun?

1	block	**a**	piece
2	box	**b**	selling
3	master	**c**	buster
4	draw	**d**	come
5	best	**e**	out
6	turn	**f**	office
7	out	**g**	back

/ 7 points

Total: / 40 points

8 TO THE RESCUE!

Vocabulary in context
Natural disasters and extreme weather
Words connected with natural disasters

1 **SPEAKING** Look at the words in the box. Which can you use to describe the photos in 2 and 3? Check that you understand all the words. Use a dictionary if necessary.

41 Natural disasters and extreme weather
avalanche • blizzard/snowstorm • downpour • drought • dust storm • earthquake • epidemic • flood/flash flood • forest fire/wildfire • gale • gust (of wind) • hail • heatwave • hurricane • landslide • thunderstorm • tornado • torrential rain • tsunami • volcanic eruption

2 **Complete the text with the correct form of the words in the box.**

42 Words connected with natural disasters 1
aftershock • casualty • collapse • debris • devastating • put out • survivor • tremor • victim

---

NEWS   VIDEO   SEVERE WEATHER   MORE ▾   🔍

There have been at least eleven deaths and hundreds of (a) .... after last night's (b) .... earthquake, which registered a (c) .... of 7.1 on the Richter Scale. Sadly, the number of (d) .... is still increasing. Meanwhile, the (e) .... of the earthquake are camping out in the street because it is safer than being indoors. The scenes in the street are dramatic, with many cars destroyed by fallen (f) .... from buildings that have (g) .... Firefighters have been working hard to (h) .... fires across the city. The authorities are warning the public that there could be (i) .... in the next few days.

3 **Now do the same with this text.**

43 Words connected with natural disasters 2
aid • ash • destruction • evacuate • evacuee • molten lava • relief worker • spread • supply • sweep down

News   Video   Severe Weather   More ▾   🔍   ✕

One of the country's biggest volcanoes has just erupted. The authorities have warned people to (a) .... the area. At 12:44 pm the volcano threw up a massive cloud of (b) .... Later, a stream of (c) .... started to come down the side of the mountain. Right now, this stream is heading towards the most populated village near to the volcano. Panic had already been (d) .... through the village over the past few weeks. The (e) .... caused by flying rocks and landslides (f) .... the mountain could be terrible. The authorities are busy setting up camps for the hundreds of (g) .... who are expected to arrive in the coming days. However, there are concerns that these camps will not have enough (h) .... of food, water and essential medical (i) .... for so many people arriving. Thousands of (j) .... are travelling to the area to help.

4 **SPEAKING** Ask and answer the questions.

1 Are any types of extreme weather common in the region or country where you live? Give details.

2 Have people ever needed to evacuate the area where you live, or any part of your country? Why?

3 Would you ever consider volunteering to help as a relief worker in an emergency? Why/Why not?

Use it ... don't lose it!

5 **SPEAKING** Talk about a famous natural disaster that was, or is, in the news. Use words from 1, 2 and 3 to help you.

Reach higher ➤ page 139

Reading

1 SPEAKING 👥 Look at the photos on this page. What do you think these things are and how could they help in a natural disaster?

2 Read this article and check your predictions in 1.

3 🔊44 Read the text again and choose the best answer.

1 The first paragraph states that we know for a fact …
   a the reason(s) why there has been an increase in the number of natural disasters in recent years.
   b that natural disasters in the future will become more and more intense.
   c that we will rely more on new technology before, during and after natural disasters.

2 The drone created at the University of Texas is so important because …
   a it helps rescue workers to communicate with each other when satellites stop working well.
   b it helps normal people to continue using their smartphones in disaster zones.
   c it helps to do both a and b.

3 From the text we know that rescue robots …
   a are already being used to find victims in disaster areas.
   b will need to be able to work more independently than they do at the moment.
   c are already 100% prepared to use a wide variety of sensors in real disasters.

4 Anna and Andrea …
   a saw first-hand that there was a need for their invention.
   b went to investigate a disaster area in order to create their invention.
   c made the LuminAID light specifically for disaster zones affected by water.

☑ **Exam tip**

The correct option will probably express the information in the text using different words.

4 What do the underlined words in the text mean? Guess and then check in your dictionary.

5 ⚙ **Critical thinkers**

In your opinion, should big tech companies be spending more money on new technology for disaster relief?

What makes you say that?

Reach higher ⟩ page 139

TECHNOLOGY
— TO THE RESCUE! —

EM-DAT, the International Disaster Database, indicates that the number of disasters has quadrupled since 1970. In 2018 alone, there were over 3,100 floods, storms and other extreme events, according to the World Disasters Report. While experts continue to debate not only the causes for these natural disasters, but whether they are in fact going to become more common and destructive, the one certainty is that the need for technologies to provide prediction, safety, and relief in these disasters will only increase. Here are just some of the latest developments.

▶ DRONES AND WI-FI

For several years now, drones have been used more and more to help with disaster relief, putting humans less at risk. They can be used to assess damaged areas, assist with restoring power, and for search and rescue efforts. And now the University of Texas at Arlington has developed a drone that is able to increase a wi-fi signal up to fifty times its normal reach. This can be vital in an area affected by a natural disaster, because it is such a fast and reliable way to restore communications. It also means that the first relief workers who arrive at the scene of a natural disaster can coordinate easily, making their work much more effective. Meanwhile, strong wi-fi signals will also allow a large communication network amongst the people caught in the disaster area and between them and the outside world, simply by using their smartphones.

▶ RESCUE ROBOTS

Apart from drones, robots are also being developed to help with disaster relief. Between 2012 and 2015, the US Defense Advanced Research Projects Agency (DARPA) held an annual competition aimed at creating humanoid robots capable of performing disaster relief and rescue tasks. The DARPA Robotics Challenge featured robots created by teams from all over the world competing in a series of tasks such as avoiding obstacles, climbing stairs and even driving a vehicle. In Germany there is currently a Rescue Robot League where robots from international teams operate in a simulated disaster area. The robots have to find the simulated victims hidden there using different sensors like video-, infrared-, or 3D-cameras, laser scanners and ultrasound. The ultimate aim is to do so with a higher degree of autonomy and less remote-control than at present.

▶ EMERGENCY LIGHTING

At Columbia University an original way to illuminate a disaster zone has been created by architecture students Anna Stork and Andrea Sreshta. They were inspired to create the LuminAID when they heard about the 2010 earthquake in Haiti. Food and other supplies were being given out to the victims, but nothing was being done to help with the lack of light, a typical problem in disaster zones. Anna and Andrea created a solar-powered inflatable LED that's waterproof and floats. This makes it ideal for floods and storms and makes it easy to be distributed, particularly by air. It is only the size of a wallet when folded. The lights have been distributed in 10 countries so far and the company has also begun a 'Give light, get light' programme which means when you buy a package (priced between $18.95 to $26.95), somebody who needs light is given another package free.

The passive

1a Look at the sentences and answer the questions below.

1 Supplies **were being given** out to the victims.

2 The drone **can be used** by relief workers to restore communication.

3 One day, perhaps victims **will be saved** by humanoid robots.

4 The light **has been created** by two architecture students.

5 They **were inspired** to create their invention in Haiti.

a Are all the sentences in the passive?

b What tense is each sentence?

c How do we form the passive?

d What does *by* introduce?

1b Are these statements True (T) or False (F)?

1 We use the passive when we are interested mainly in an action, not the person who does the action. T / F

2 We use the passive when we don't know the person who does the action. T / F

3 We use the passive when it is obvious who does the action. T / F

☑ Check it **page 106**

2 Complete the sentences by putting the verbs in the correct form of the passive.

1 Some matches in the Rugby World Cup® in Japan 2019 .... (cancel) because of a typhoon.

2 The strength of hurricane winds .... (measure) using the Saffir-Simpson Scale.

3 Houses and flats should .... (build) to resist typical weather in that area.

4 Alaska in the US .... (hit) by a .8 earthquake in 2020.

5 Some experts think the weather .... (control) by humans one day.

6 In 2019, some forest fires could .... (see) from space.

7 In the history of mankind, a number of cities .... (destroy) by volcanoes.

3 Read the text. Find and correct ten mistakes with active/passive verb forms.

Culture exchange

Natural disasters in California

The US state of California has its fair share of natural disasters. 2019 was a particularly tough year. Terrible wildfires were hit large parts of the state. The fires were making worse by strong winds. Many people, including celebrities such as basketball player LeBron James, were evacuated from their homes. Experts believe that more fires are been caused in California by the weather getting hotter and drier each year. Since the 1970s, the average temperatures in spring and summer have gone up by 1°C and the average wildfire season lasts two and a half months longer than it did in the early 1970s. Today twelve times as much is spending by the US Forest Service to stop wildfires as in 1985.

Apart from wildfires, landslides have sometimes being caused in California by flash flooding. And, of course, California has often hit by earthquakes due to its position on the San Andreas Fault. There were two big earthquakes in July 2019. The second one near Ridgecrest lasted twelve seconds and were felt by 30 million people. Luckily, nobody was died. This is partly thanks to the fact that the buildings are usually construct to resist tremors. Unfortunately, even that might not be much use when 'the big one' comes. Experts know that an earthquake eleven times stronger than Ridgecrest will be happened one day, probably in the next seventy years or so. The consequences may be catastrophic but, no, it won't be like in the films, with tsunamis and Los Angeles collapsing into the sea.

The passive – verbs with two objects

4a Look at the sentences. Then read the explanation and answer the question below.

1 They give a free light to those people.

2a A free light **is given** to those people.

2b Those people **are given** a free light.

Some verbs are followed by two objects: one usually a thing and the other a person. When this happens, we can make two different passive sentences (2a and 2b). Which do you think is more common – to use the thing (2a) or the person (2b) as the subject?

4b These verbs can all be followed by two objects. Check their meanings in a dictionary if necessary.

bring • buy • lend • offer • owe • pay • promise • refuse • send • show • teach • tell

☑ Check it **page 106**

5 Rewrite the sentences using the passive. Use the person or people as the subject and use 'by' only when it introduces useful information.

Some of the services of a Non-Governmental Organisation (NGO)

1 Many NGOs give immediate support to first responders.

2 They have taught millions of people lifesaving skills.

3 NGOs have often offered shelter to disaster victims.

4 They will bring food to survivors.

5 They tell young people general safety information.

6 They never refuse medical help to people in need.

7 NGOs promise evacuees as much help as possible.

8 They're always giving training to volunteers.

Use it ... don't lose it!

6 SPEAKING Ask the questions. When the answer is 'yes', find out more details.
Then tell the class one interesting thing you found out about your partner.

Have you ever been ...
1 given a prize?
2 bought a special gift?
3 taught a special skill by somebody in your family?
4 offered a job or special responsibility?
5 sent an interesting or surprise package?
6 told an important secret?
7 paid for doing something?
8 owed money or a favour?

Reach higher ⟩ page 139

Developing vocabulary

Prepositional verbs

1 Complete the text with prepositions.
The preposition depends on the verb in bold which comes before it.

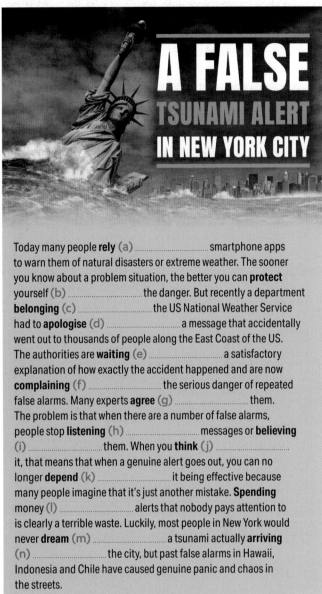

A FALSE TSUNAMI ALERT IN NEW YORK CITY

Today many people **rely** (a) .... smartphone apps to warn them of natural disasters or extreme weather. The sooner you know about a problem situation, the better you can **protect** yourself (b) .... the danger. But recently a department **belonging** (c) .... the US National Weather Service had to **apologise** (d) .... a message that accidentally went out to thousands of people along the East Coast of the US. The authorities are **waiting** (e) .... a satisfactory explanation of how exactly the accident happened and are now **complaining** (f) .... the serious danger of repeated false alarms. Many experts **agree** (g) .... them. The problem is that when there are a number of false alarms, people stop **listening** (h) .... messages or **believing** (i) .... them. When you **think** (j) .... it, that means that when a genuine alert goes out, you can no longer **depend** (k) .... it being effective because many people imagine that it's just another mistake. **Spending** money (l) .... alerts that nobody pays attention to is clearly a terrible waste. Luckily, most people in New York would never **dream** (m) .... a tsunami actually **arriving** (n) .... the city, but past false alarms in Hawaii, Indonesia and Chile have caused genuine panic and chaos in the streets.

2 Complete the sentences so they are true for you. Use a preposition.

1 I occasionally spend money ....
2 I hate waiting ....
3 One day I dream ....
4 I know I can rely ....
5 I never listen ....
6 Once I had to apologise ....
7 I nearly always agree ....
8 I don't usually complain ....
9 I believe ....
10 I've often thought ....

Use it ... don't lose it!

3 SPEAKING Compare your sentences in 2. Tell the class any sentences that you have in common.

Reach higher ⟩ page 139

GREAT LEARNERS
GREAT THINKERS

WEATHER CONTROL

Lesson aim: To think about our relationship with the weather

Video: From supercell storm to tornado

SEL Social and emotional learning: Empathising

1a **SPEAKING** What type of weather conditions do you associate with tornadoes? Make a list.

1b **VIDEO** Watch the video with the sound off. What different weather conditions do you see? Tick the things from your list from 1a and add any others.

2 **VIDEO** Watch the video again. Complete the sentences with between one and three words and/or numbers in each gap.

1 Supercell storms are storms that are produced when warm, ... air is trapped under cold, ... air.

2 Updrafts are produced when air is pulled .... through the storm.

3 In supercell storms, hailstones eventually fall when they become very ....

4 The hailstones can be the same size as ....

5 The maximum length of time that a normal storm lasts is usually ....

6 Supercell storms last longer than normal storms because .... goes up and around the storm.

7 The .... of the winds can be the deciding factor whether a supercell storm becomes a tornado or not.

8 .... % of supercell storms become tornadoes.

3 Read this text. What two examples of controlling the weather does it mention and what were the results?

CONTROLLING *THE WEATHER*

Natural disasters and extreme weather are affecting more and more people. Obviously, a lot of money is spent on rescue and repair after a natural disaster. But what if that money was spent on controlling and preventing extreme weather?

Trying to control the weather is nothing new. On the night before the start of the 2008 Olympic Games®, 1,100 rockets were fired into the sky to make sure no rain fell on the opening ceremony the next day. It worked and the ceremony was a great success.

But what is great weather for some can be disastrous for others. In 2018, in Puebla, Mexico, a giant car factory used sonic cannons to stop hail from falling and damaging newly built cars parked just outside the factory. Months later, farmers in the area protested since the cannons had worked so well that they caused a complete drought in the region surrounding the factory, vastly reducing their crops.

So perhaps the question is not 'Can we change the weather, extreme or otherwise?' but '*Should we?*' Is it ever justifiable to affect the Earth's weather cycles?

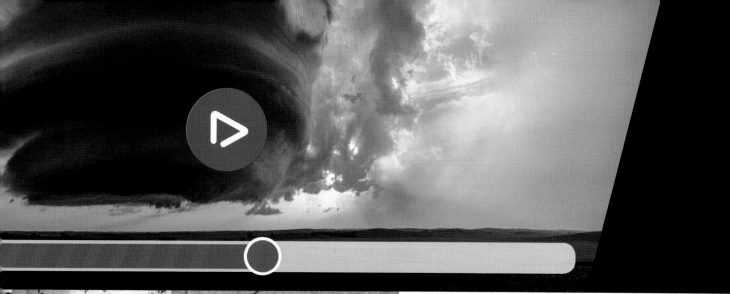

GREAT THINKERS

Sentence-Phrase-Word

4 **SPEAKING** Follow the instructions.

1 Find **one sentence** in the text that you think talks about a key concept.

2 Choose **one phrase** in the text that moved you, interested you, or provoked you.

3 Choose **one word** in the text that you think was central to the idea(s) in the text.

4 Share your sentence, phrase and word with other students. Are they similar or different? What important ideas or themes come out of your discussion?

5a Think of arguments both for and against manipulating the weather. Try to see the question from different points of view (e.g. farmers vs. factory owners).

5b **SPEAKING** Share your ideas. Listen carefully to other people's ideas, but if you don't agree, can you find arguments to persuade them to change their mind?

GREAT LEARNERS   **SEL**

Great learners justify their opinions.

In the final activity, did you give reasons for your opinions? Why is it important to do this?

Learner profile > page 143

Listening

1 SPEAKING 👥 **Look at the photo and answer the questions.**

1 Where and when do you think this photo was taken?

2 The photo shows an important moment in history. What do you think happened and why do you think it was so important?

2 🔊45 **Listen to a programme about the event in the photo and check your predictions in 1.**

> ☑ **Exam tip**
>
> In 'complete the sentence' activities, you can usually write just one word or a short phrase in the sentences, but nothing longer. Perhaps you won't hear the same words that appear in the sentences but you do have to write in the space the exact word or phrase that you hear. Remember that correct spelling is important, too.

3 🔊45 **Listen again and complete the sentences with a word or short phrase.**

The speakers talk about a tragedy that people called the (a) .... of 1900.

The organisation that currently monitors the weather in the US is called the National Weather (b) ....

Isaac Cline influenced the events in Galveston by his written comments in the year (c) ....

Many people who lived in Galveston had wanted to construct a (d) ....

There was a first warning made to Galveston about the storm on (e) ....

The maximum wind speed was (f) .... kilometres per hour.

The main lesson learnt from the tragedy was the need to forget (g) .... when forecasting natural disasters.

Once you know about a future natural disaster, it's essential to prepare for (h) ....

Hurricane Katrina caused destruction in New Orleans in the year (i) ....

4 ⚙️ **Critical thinkers**

> **In your opinion, how much importance should we give to natural disasters that happen a long way from our own home?**
>
> **What makes you say that?**

Grammar in context 2

The passive with *say*, *know*, *believe*, etc. 1

1 **Look at the sentences and answer the questions below.**

1 It **was reported that** the hurricane was heading towards New England.

2 It **is thought that** the winds reached hundreds of kilometres per hour.

3 It **has been claimed that** 6,000 people died.

4 It**'s believed that** this is still a problem today.

a What is the subject in the first part of these sentences?

b Why do we use the passive in the first part of these sentences?

c Why are different tenses used in the first part of the sentences?

☑ **Check it page 106**

2 **Make complete sentences with the different structures in 1.**

All around the world

1 'People in medieval times used to think the Earth was flat.' – something people say

It is said that people in medieval times used to think the Earth was flat.

2 'It's a myth.' – something people think

3 'The Ancient Greeks already knew the Earth was spherical.' – present knowledge

4 'The world is the same shape as a frisbee.' – something people have claimed

5 'Researchers used a telescope to check the atmosphere on Uranus.' – past report

6 'They'll send up a new rocket one of these days.' – present expectation

7 'There are members of the Flat Earth Society all around the world!' – present claim

The passive with *say*, *know*, *believe*, etc. 2

3 Look at the sentences and decide if the statements below are True (T) or False (F).

1 The disaster **is said** to be the worst in US history.
2 Cline **is known** to have written a newspaper article.
3 A seawall **was not thought** to have been necessary.
4 Emergency plans **are believed** to be just as important.

a In each sentence, the subject of the first part of the sentence is also the subject of the verb(s) in blue.   T / F

b After the verbs *reported, known, believed*, etc., we use *to* + infinitive to talk about things in the present, or things that are always true.   T / F

c After the verbs *reported, known, believed*, etc. we use *to have* + past participle to talk about past events.   T / F

d We use *is/are believed/thought* etc. to talk about present beliefs and thoughts.   T / F

e We use *was/were believed/thought* etc. to talk about past beliefs and thoughts.   T / F

☑ **Check it page 106**

4 Rewrite the sentences.

1 They reported that most people had left the city before the eruption.
Most people ....

2 People believe that Krakatoa was the worst volcanic eruption ever.
Krakatoa ....

3 At first, people didn't know the Earth goes around the Sun.
At first the Earth ....

4 It is said that some tourists enjoy visiting the sites of natural disasters.
Some tourists ....

5 It's believed that natural disasters are becoming more frequent.
Natural disasters ....

6 They know that some animals can hear things humans can't hear.
Some animals ....

7 They believe that flamingos flew away before the tsunami.
Flamingos ....

8 People claim that global warming is responsible for many natural disasters.
Global warming ....

5 Read the text and choose the correct alternative.

The rescue dog who became A NATIONAL HERO

A rescue dog named Frida was reported to (a) *become/have become* a national hero in Mexico following the tragic earthquake of 19th September 2017 in Mexico City. (b) *It is/They are* said that dogs have a sixth sense for finding humans. But (c) *it/Frida* is said to have been better than any other dog that the Mexican Navy ever trained before. (d) *It/She* has been claimed that people would like her face to appear on the 500 peso banknote. It is believed (e) *photos of Frida to have/that photos of Frida have* appeared all over the world. She (f) *is/has* known to have saved the lives of 12 natural disaster victims in Mexico and other countries. Another 53 bodies (g) *reported/are reported* to have been found in the debris by Frida. Thanks to her brave work, she is said to (h) *become/have become* a symbol of national pride and hope. It has been (i) *believed/reported* that one man has even got a tattoo of Frida's face! (j) *It is known/Rescue dogs are known* to put themselves in danger to perform their tasks. So for protection, Frida wears special goggles, a jacket and boots. Reporters (k) *say/are said* that the crowd at a football match in Mexico in 2018 gave Frida a big cheer when she appeared on the pitch wearing her protective gear! In 2019, Frida retired.

6 Complete the sentences in a logical way.

1 People from my country are said …
2 It's well known …
3 In the past, it was believed …
4 Last week in the news it was reported …
5 It's often wrongly claimed …
6 I've never been known …

Use it … don't lose it!

7 SPEAKING 👥 Compare your sentences in 6 with a partner. Do you agree with your partner's sentences?

Reach higher ⟩ page 139

Developing speaking

Talking about statistics

1 Look at the pie chart. It shows how much worldwide economic damage was caused by natural disasters between 1995 and 2016. According to the pie chart, are these statements True (T) or False (F)?

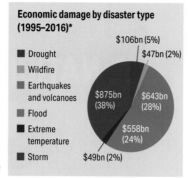

Economic damage by disaster type (1995–2016)*

- Drought
- Wildfire
- Earthquakes and volcanoes
- Flood
- Extreme temperature
- Storm

$106bn (5%)
$47bn (2%)
$875bn (38%)
$643bn (28%)
$558bn (24%)
$49bn (2%)

1 Over one-third of the damage was caused by storms.　　　T / F

2 Just over one-third of the damage was caused by earthquakes and volcanoes.　　　T / F

3 Less damage was caused by earthquakes and volcanoes than by floods.　　　T / F

4 Less than a tenth of the damage was caused by droughts.　　　T / F

5 Just over a quarter of the damage was caused by floods.　　　T / F

6 The majority of the damage was caused by storms and floods.　　　T / F

2a Express the fractions as percentages and vice versa.

1 ¼ = 25%　　　3 10% =　　　5 ½ =

2 20% =　　　4 66.6% =　　　6 80% =

2b 🔊 46 Listen and check. Then practise saying the fractions and percentages.

3 Look at this graph. It shows the number of natural disasters in the US between 1980 and 2016. Read the text below and check that you understand the words in bold.

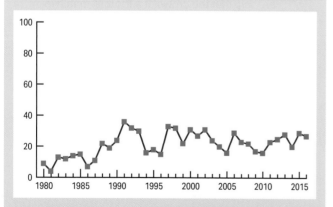

Natural disasters in the US (1980–2016)*

In general, the number of natural disasters **rose significantly** between 1982 and 1985. There was **a significant decrease** in 1986 but **a sharp increase** in the number of disasters from 1988 to 1993. Between 1985 and 1991 the number more than **tripled**. The number of disasters **fell sharply** for three years after 1993. After that there was **a dramatic rise** again. The number of disasters **fluctuated a lot** between 1997 and 2015. It rarely **stayed the same** during that period.

4 Find a word or words in the Speaking bank which mean:

1 go up

2 go from 20,000 to 40,000, for example

3 go from 40,000 to 30,000, for example

4 one in three

5 slowly and in small amounts

6 important

7 in a sudden and surprising way

8 most of the people or things in a group

9 50%

10 three times more

Speaking bank
Words and expressions to talk about statistics

Numbers and proportions
- a half/third/quarter/fifth/sixth etc.
- one in two/three/five/ten etc.
- the majority

Trends
- rise/fall (n/v)
- increase/decrease (n/v)
- stay the same/change little (adj/adv)
- slow(ly)/gradual(ly)/slight(ly) (adj/adv)
- steady (adj), steadily (adv)
- significant(ly)/sharp(ly)/dramatic(ally) (adj/adv)
- double/triple (n/v)
- half (n)/halve (v)
- From (year) to (year)

Practice makes perfect

5a 🗣 SPEAKING 👥 Student A: Look at the pie chart below. Student B: Look at the pie chart on page 149. Then take it in turns to describe your charts. Use the percentages, and words and expressions in the Speaking bank.

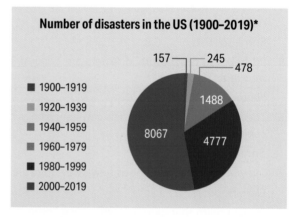

Number of disasters in the US (1900–2019)*

- 1900–1919
- 1920–1939
- 1940–1959
- 1960–1979
- 1980–1999
- 2000–2019

157　　245　　478
1488
8067　　4777

5b 🗣 SPEAKING 👥 Work together. Discuss your opinions of the information contained in the pie charts. What information do you find *surprising, interesting, worrying ...*?

*EM-DAT: The Emergency Events Database – Université catholique de Louvain (UCL) – CRED, D. Guha-Sapir – www.emdat.be, Brussels, Belgium.

Developing writing

An opinion essay 2

1 **SPEAKING** Look at the task. Discuss at least two things that you could write about for each of the points (1–3) in your notes.

> At school you have been talking about climate change and extreme weather. Now your English teacher has asked you to write an essay for homework.
> Write your essay using all the notes and giving reasons for your point of view.
>
> How can we help to save the planet?
>
> Notes
> Write about:
> 1 recycling
> 2 saving energy
> 3 .... (your own idea)

2 **Read this essay. Does the student include any of your ideas in 1? If so, which?**

> Each year the weather is more extreme. _In my opinion_, this is partly because of the effect that humans are having on the planet. _I believe that_ all of us can and should do something about this.
>
> _The first point to make is that_ if we all recycled more, we could make a big impact. By recycling paper, for example, we could protect our forests. _What is more_, if we reused plastic bags and bottles, we could also save precious natural resources. _However_, not everybody does this.
>
> _The next thing to bear in mind is that_ people use energy unnecessarily. For instance, they forget to switch lights off and don't keep doors closed in the winter _even though_ doing these things could help to reduce environmental damage.
>
> _Although_ many students live near school, their parents take them by car each day. If we all walked, cycled or used public transport, we could minimise the pollution caused by exhaust fumes. _Furthermore_, walking or cycling would keep us healthy.
>
> _In conclusion_, some people say that there is nothing that we can do to save the planet. I strongly disagree. If we all take small steps, those millions of small actions can have a major impact on the planet.

3 **Read the essay again. What is the purpose of each paragraph?**

4 **Put the underlined words and expressions in the text in the correct list.**

Expressing opinions: ....
Adding ideas: ....
Putting ideas in order: ....
Contrasting ideas: ....
Concluding: ....

5 **Look at how _although_, _even though_ and _however_ are used in the text and then read the information in the Writing bank.**

Writing bank
Using linkers correctly

- Some linkers **join** two halves of a sentence. They can go at the start or in the middle of the sentence.
  Even though the country is a long way away, we must help it.
  We must help the country _even though_ it is a long way away.

- Other linkers **introduce** a new sentence which refers to the previous sentence. These words are usually followed by commas.
  The country is a long way away. _However_, we must help it.

6 **Look at the linkers in the box and check that you understand their meaning. Then decide if they join two halves of a sentence (J) or introduce a new sentence (I).**

> all things considered · and so · as a result · as far as I'm concerned · consequently · despite (the fact that …) · even though · firstly/secondly/lastly · furthermore · in addition · in conclusion · meanwhile · moreover · nevertheless · on the one/other hand · since · so that · therefore · to sum up · what's more · whereas · while

Practice makes perfect

7a **SPEAKING** Look at the task and think about ideas and information that you could include.

> 'The world is a better place to live in today than it was a hundred years ago.'
> Do you agree?
> Notes
> Write about:
> 1 health
> 2 technology
> 3 .... (your own idea)

7b **Write your essay. Use your notes in 7a, include linkers and use the information in the Writing bank to help you.**

7c **When you finish your essay, use the Writing checklist on page 141 to check it.**

Grammar reference

The passive

subject + *be* + past participle (+ *by* + agent)

Warnings are given. (present simple)

The hospital has been built by the government. (present perfect)

This programme is being watched by millions of people. (present continuous)

Volcanoes weren't understood in the middle ages. (past simple)

New types of energy will be used in the future. (*will*)

We make the passive with the appropriate tense and form of the verb *to be* and the past participle of the verb.

To make questions in the passive, we put the first auxiliary verb before the subject.

Is the news being given on TV?

Has the earthquake been shown on TV?

We use the preposition *by* to introduce the agent, that is, the person or thing which does the action.

We use the passive when:

1 we are more interested in the action than the people who do the action.

   The city was destroyed in 1755.

2 we do not know who exactly does the action.

   Many objects have been stolen.

3 it is obvious or understood who did the action.

   The patient was cured.

The passive – verbs with two objects

Some verbs are followed by two objects, one usually a thing and the other a person.

They told me the truth.

When this happens, we can make two different passive sentences.

I was told the truth.

The truth was told to me.

It is more common to make passive sentences with the person or people as the subject.

Here is a list of common verbs which are followed by two objects:

bring, buy, give, lend, offer, owe, pay, promise, refuse, send, show, tell, teach

The passive with *say, know, believe*, etc.

It + *be* + past participle of *believe, know, think, say, expect, claim, report* + *that*

We use the present of *to be* to talk about present beliefs and thoughts.

It is said that dolphins can communicate.

We use the past of *to be* to talk about past beliefs and thoughts.

It was claimed that the president knew about the situation.

Instead of using the impersonal pronoun *it*, we can use this structure:

subject + *be* + past participle of *believe, know, think, say, expect, claim, report* + *to* + infinitive

With this structure, we use *to* + infinitive to talk about things in the present, or things that are always true.

Dolphins are said to be able to communicate.

We use *to have* + past participle to talk about past events or situations.

The president was claimed to have known about the situation.

We use these structures to talk about what people in general say, think or believe about something.

Vocabulary

1 Natural disasters and extreme weather

avalanche · blizzard/snowstorm · downpour · drought · dust storm · earthquake · epidemic · flood/flash flood · forest fire/wildfire · gale · gust (of wind) · hail · heatwave · hurricane · landslide · thunderstorm · tornado · torrential rain · tsunami · volcanic eruption

2 Words connected with natural disasters

aftershock (n) · aid (n) · ash (n) · casualty (n) · collapse (v) · debris (n) · destruction (n) · devastating (adj) · evacuate (v) · evacuee (n) · molten lava (n) · put out (phrasal verb) · relief worker (n) · spread through/across (phrasal verb) · supply (n, v) · survivor (n) · sweep down (v) · tremor (n) · victim (n)

3 Prepositional verbs

agree with · apologise for (something) · arrive at/in · believe in · belong to · complain about · depend on · dream of · listen to · protect (somebody/something) from (somebody/something) · rely on · spend on · think about/of · wait for

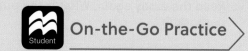

On-the-Go Practice

Grammar test

The passive

1 Rewrite the sentences. Change the form from active to passive or passive to active.

1 A boat rescued the boy and girl.
2 A Japanese company is going to rebuild the damaged towers.
3 The airport had been designed by a famous architect.
4 The waves won't have destroyed the port.
5 A survivor of the tragedy is presenting the awards tonight.
6 They should have written a report about the catastrophe.
7 The school might be opened by a local politician.

/ 7 points

The passive – verbs with two objects

2 Put the words in the correct order. Then make the sentences active.

1 will sent be an email You important
   You will be sent an important email. We will send you an important email.
2 was a birthday camera given for I my
3 disasters They being shown a are about natural film
4 parents stories children Young often are told their by
5 sister lent I by money was some my
6 We taught mathematics a were teacher by new
7 a job He has offered government been the by

/ 7 points

The passive with *say*, *know*, *believe*, etc.

3 Find the mistakes in these sentences and rewrite them correctly. There may be more than one way to do this.

1 It is often claimed Paris to be one of the most beautiful cities in the world.
2 Galileo Galilei is said to invent the telescope.
3 Yesterday a young boy reported to have started the fire.
4 Avalanches are said that they are caused by loud noises.
5 A long time ago the Moon is believed to be made of cheese.
6 The eruption of Krakatoa is thought to turn the skies orange in 1883.

/ 6 points

Vocabulary test

Natural disasters and extreme weather

1 Complete these expressions for natural disasters or extreme weather.

1 flash ....
2 wild ....
3 dust ....
4 land ....
5 torrential ....
6 volcanic ....
7 a gust of ....

/ 7 points

Words connected with natural disasters

2 Match the definitions to words on page 106.

1 someone who is injured in an accident
2 make a fire stop
3 gradually cover or affect a larger area
4 someone who helps after a disaster
5 leave a place because it is dangerous
6 broken pieces that are left when something large has been destroyed

/ 6 points

Prepositional verbs

3 Match the verbs and prepositions.

Verb		Preposition	
1	apologise	a	about
2	belong	b	to
3	rely	c	with
4	complain	d	on
5	dream	e	for
6	agree	f	of
7	spend	g	on

/ 7 points

Total: / 40 points

Test yourself Unit 8

▪ Reading

In activities where you have to write words in gaps, remember ...

Read the text first to understand the context and purpose. Before you complete each gap, make sure you read along the whole sentence to check your answer makes sense.

1 Read the text quickly. Who do you think it is written for? What is the purpose of the text?

2 Complete the text with one word in each gap.

HOME   HOW TO ...   ABOUT   🔍
HOW TO BE A BOOK REVIEWER

Lots of us would like to be able to review books and get paid for it. But it's not always easy to see (a) .... you can start to do this job. The first (b) .... you have to do is, of course, read a lot of books and a great variety of genres. At the same time, read (c) .... people's reviews and make a note of what you like and don't like about these reviews. Then make a start (d) .... submitting some reviews to book retailer websites. Obviously you won't get paid for these, but it's a good way to start because if people like your reviews, then the booksellers will start (e) .... notice you. You could also start a book review blog. It's a good idea to specialise in certain types of books (f) .... then you will become an expert. Publishers read blogs and, if you have enough views, you can ask publishers to send (g) .... books to review. By now, you will (h) .... well established and in a good position to apply to become a professional book reviewer in, for example, magazines or journals.

3 SPEAKING 👥 What kind of books would you like to review? Why?

In activities where you have to complete gaps with sentences, remember ...

Check every sentence in each gap. Don't ignore one because you have already selected it.

4 Read the text quickly. Is the topic focus on (a) how to start your own business, (b) the change in how businesses can be run or (c) what you need to be successful?

5 Six sentences have been removed from the article below. For each question, choose the correct answer A–G. There is one extra sentence which you do not need.

YOUNG BUSINESS OWNER

Maya Penn was a teenager when she set up her own business.

Do you think all companies should give some of their profits to charity organisations? Well, young people are leading the way on this. Take the example of Maya Penn. (1) .... She used to experiment with scraps of fabric she found round the house and started to make headbands from these scraps. She made so many and her friends so admired them that she started to sell these and her fledgling business really took off. (2) ....

But she was also very concerned about the environment, so when she set up her business this was always an important part of her thinking. For example, she discovered that a lot of the fabric dyes were chemical and harmful to the environment so she decided to use only material that had been dyed with eco-friendly colouring. (3) .... What she has demonstrated is a new way of doing business which is that, instead of starting a business that does just one thing, the business can accomplish several things at the same time. That's why her company is called Maya's Ideas. (4) ....

Maya has developed a website for her business, which she coded and designed herself, and this gives her the opportunity to explore multiple ideas, many of which come from the people who engage with her and her current business. She can add products and projects as she develops them and it seems to work that the business is running in multiple different directions. She also has a strong social media presence so that people of her own generation can really connect with her.

Maya's experience has raised an interesting point about how businesses might be conducted in the future. In the past we believed that we had a particular path or skill set and that we had to choose to do one thing, and to become very good at it, and that was our life. (5) .... But Maya has shown how you can take your passion and turn it, not only into a business, but one which helps people. You don't have to choose!

Maya's approach is so valuable that she has now become famous in the business world. (6) .... Her products have expanded so she sells fashion and accessories as well as running the non-profit arm of her business. She was asked what her top tips were for starting a business and she advises keeping a journal where you write down all your ideas, however small. She also warns about using social media and believes that, although it's a huge part of how businesses connect with customers, you should always be careful about what you post as it can strengthen or damage your reputation in the business world.

A She also decided to give a percentage of her profits to organisations that protected the environment.

B Any hobbies we had were very much seen as a free-time activity and not to be taken too seriously.

C It isn't focused on one single product and the concept allows her to add more projects as she develops them.

D She decided to change her business model and how she paid people who work for her.

E Maya has always been interested in art but when she was eight she was also very interested in fashion.

F She's given TED Talks, appeared in financial journals, written books and was interviewed by Oprah Winfrey.

G At 14 she was earning the typical salary of an adult.

The arts in your country

Virtual Classroom Exchange

1 SPEAKING Starting point

What do you remember from the Cultural exchange texts about the arts in Ireland on page 84? What were the names of the Irish group and actor that appeared in the texts?

2 SPEAKING Project task

Use your own knowledge and search the Internet for information about bands, singers, musicians or actors that are popular with teenagers in your country so that you can recommend them to teenagers from other countries. Choose a maximum of four people.

Prepare one of these:

A poster   C video message

B presentation   D information leaflet

Research areas

- basic information and personal details about the person or band
- how they began and how they became popular or famous
- their best and most famous works (albums, series, films, etc.)
- a critical appreciation
- why you think they are popular

3 Think about …

Digital skills

When you find a piece of information that you want to use in your project, search for at least one other source that confirms that information.

Academic skills

When you find and give information, it's important to separate facts from opinions. Facts include objective information such as dates and statistics which we can show to be true. Opinions are subjective beliefs and ideas. In this project, you are asked to write facts in some sections but opinions in others.

Collaboration

When you work in a team, it's OK to disagree with others. But it's always better to be polite and constructive.

Useful language

I see what you mean, but …, I agree up to a point, but …, That's true, but you could also argue that …, Another way of looking at it is …, Yes, but it's also true that …

Intercultural awareness

Look at sources <u>in English</u> to find out if anything has been written about the people you have chosen for your project. If so, what does it say about them? Do you think the facts or opinions are accurate? If not, do you think people from the UK, US or other countries will like the people you have chosen? Why/Why not?

4 SPEAKING Project time

Do the project. Then present it to the class.

5 Evaluation

Give each project a mark from 1 to 5 (5 = very good) for these categories.

Content ☐

Presentation ☐

Design ☐

Language ☐

9 TECH TALK

Vocabulary in context

Technology and IT
Adjectives to describe technology
Words connected with technology

1 **SPEAKING** 👥 Take it in turns to describe one of the things in the box and say what it does. Can your partner identify the word?

🔊47 Technology and IT
desktop • earphones • external hard drive • headphones •
pen-drive • remote control • satnav • smart speaker • webcam •
wireless charger • wireless network

2 **SPEAKING** 👥 Choose a good example of an object for each adjective in the box. Say some of your examples. Can your partner guess the correct adjective?

🔊48 Adjectives to describe technology
bendy/flexible • brittle • chunky • cutting-edge • durable •
eco-friendly • heavy-duty • high-resolution • lightweight •
metallic • rustproof • tough • unbreakable • waterproof

3 Complete the text with the correct form of the words in the box.

🔊49 Words connected with technology
cloud • earbud • firewall • freeze • net • storage • stream •
tweet • virus

4 **SPEAKING** 👥 Match the words in box A to the words in box B to make compound nouns. Use each word only once. Then check you understand them.

A battery • book • click • down/up •
drop-down • land • operating •
touch • up • USB

B bait • charger • date • line • load •
mark • menu • port • screen • system

Use it ... don't lose it!

5 **SPEAKING** 👥 Ask and answer the questions.

1 Do you ever bookmark websites? Which ones?

2 What do you use to listen to music – earbuds, earphones or headphones? Why?

3 How often do you use a landline?

4 How often are you a victim of clickbait? What makes you click on a story?

5 What do you normally download?

Reach higher ⟩ page 140

TechFacts ✕ 🔍

TECHNOLOGY AND NATURE

Many words used for technology originally came from nature. But a 2019 study by researchers at the University of Leeds has found that we now use many of these words much more frequently with their new, technological meaning.

● In the 1990s, a (a) .... was only a small river, but now 64% of the times it is used, it describes how we play online video or audio on our computer so that we can see or hear it continuously.

● In the past, we used (b) .... to describe a thing for catching fish, for example. But now 37% of all uses are to talk about the Internet.

● 23% of all of the uses of (c) .... are to talk about online data (d) ...., keeping data safe outside your own computer. It's no longer just that fluffy white thing in the sky.

● The word for the part of the plant that opens up to form a leaf or flower is part of the word (e) ...., the wireless earphones that have become so popular.

● 99% of the uses of the word (f) .... are to talk about short social media posts, not the sound made by birds.

● If the images on our computer stop moving, we say the computer has (g) ...., as if it had turned to ice.

● Originally a (h) .... was literally something built to stop flames spreading from inside a building, but now we use it for a computer program that stops hackers entering your system. And while we're on that subject, it's interesting that we say a computer has a (i) ...., as if it were a living thing that had become ill.

Reading

1 SPEAKING 👥 Describe the photos on this page and say what you think they show.

2 Read the text and choose the best title. Don't worry about the missing sentences.

1 The discovery of graphene
2 How graphene will shape the future
3 Graphene and other miracle materials

3 🔊50 Read the text again and choose from sentences a–g the one which fits each gap. There is one extra sentence which you do not need to use.

a The problem is that it's brittle.
b They could become part of our clothing, or even of our bodies, so that we can charge our devices wherever we are.
c They did this by playing about with sticky tape, pulling off and separating tiny flakes of graphene that were just one atom thick.
d The problem was working out how to extract it from graphite.
e Scientists are already creating screens that you can fold easily.
f In short, the possibilities are endless.
g And it is no longer the only 2D material in existence:

4 What do the underlined words in the text and 3c mean? Guess and then check in your dictionary.

5 🧠 Critical thinkers

In your opinion, which of the practical applications of graphene mentioned in the text are the most and least useful or interesting?

What makes you say that?

TECH WORLD

Science | Culture | Technology | More ▾

You may already know that pencils are made of graphite. But it might be news to you that with a simple stroke of a pencil you can create a material which scientists and engineers around the world are all suddenly talking about. The material, graphene, was discovered by scientists around 1859. (1) .... Then, in 2004, it was isolated by Professor Andre Geim and Professor Konstantin Novoselov. (2) .... The two scientists, who were researchers at the University of Manchester, won the Nobel Prize in Physics in 2010 for this amazing work, creating the world's first 2D material.

Some people believe that combining all of graphene's amazing properties could change the world as dramatically as the first Industrial Revolution did. A vast number of potential new products, processes and industries all stem from its amazing properties. It is many times stronger than steel (some say 300), yet it is incredibly lightweight and flexible. It is electrically and thermally conductive (meaning that electricity and heat can flow through it easily), but it's also transparent and incredibly thin.

It seems there are literally no limits to graphene's potential applications. You could use it to produce handy devices like tablets or smartphones that you can fold up or bend round your wrist. Today's screens are made with highly conductive material. (3) .... Graphene, meanwhile, could be used to cover screens and make them unbreakable.

Graphene could also be used to create the circuits for our computers and improve their speed since research has shown that graphene chips are much faster than existing ones made from silicon. This has already made it possible for scientists at the University of Manchester to produce a tiny graphene transistor, smaller than any other.

If you want to increase the lifespan of batteries, graphene could be the answer, making it not only faster to charge devices, but also helping devices to conserve energy for greater periods of time. Look no further than Northwestern University in the US where researchers have produced graphene batteries that can go for seven days without recharging. (4) .... Batteries could become flexible and light. Applied to transport, lighter batteries could reduce the weight of cars or planes. Graphene could make the wings of planes much lighter, protect the plane from lightning, and allow the plane to cut down on fuel. In other words, it could help produce the most environmentally friendly and best planes ever in terms of safety, strength and weight.

As we can see, graphene is turning science and technology upside down. (5) .... as Konstantin Novoselov has explained, we used to be limited by the materials which existed in nature, but now, by combining different 2D materials, anybody can produce exactly the type of material which they need. One recent experiment involved feeding graphene to spiders. The result was a web that Spider-Man would be proud of. The silk in the web had three times the strength of natural web silk, making it as strong as steel, and bulletproof, too.

If you're still not convinced, how about using graphene to provide a layer on our skin that mosquitoes are unable to bite through? Contact lenses made from graphene could give you night vision. It could revolutionise sport with stronger, faster and better tennis rackets, skis, bikes or Formula 1 racing cars. (6) .... And it's all thanks to two scientists with some sticky tape and a playful attitude to science.

Reach higher ⟩ page 140

Grammar in context 1

Relative clauses

1 **Look at the sentences and answer the questions below.**

1 We used to be limited by the materials **which** existed in nature.

2 Now anybody can produce exactly the type of material **which** they need.

3 Graphene, **which** is incredibly lightweight, is also transparent.

4 Their experiment, **which** involved sticky tape, led to graphene being isolated.

5 They are the two scientists **who** isolated graphene.

6 These two scientists, **who** were researchers, won the Nobel Prize® in Physics in 2010.

a Which relative clauses are defining, giving us essential information about someone or something? Do they have commas?

b Which relative clauses are non-defining, giving us extra, non-essential information about someone or something? Do they have commas?

c When do we use the relative pronoun *which* and when do we use *who*?

d When do we use *whose, when, where* or *why*?

e Can we replace *which* or *who* with *that* in any of the sentences? If so, which and why? If not, why not?

f Can we omit the relative pronoun in any sentences? If so, which and why? If not, why not?

☑ **Check it page 120**

2 **Decide if the sentences are correct. Rewrite the incorrect sentences.**

1 That's the park where I used to go to.

2 A: Which book did you lose? B: The book, which is about computer science.

3 My new phone, that is really lightweight, is quite durable.

4 There's the IT teacher that I spoke to her yesterday.

5 This is the library that I usually study in.

6 That's the person who I sent the message to.

7 She's the person which computer I borrowed yesterday.

8 I've got a new phone that it takes great pictures.

9 They're the two people who's invention became really popular.

10 I'm going to watch the series that you recommended.

3a **Replace the relative pronoun in bold with *that* where possible in the text.**

WHY STEALING GPS DEVICES IS A BAD IDEA

Two thieves (a) **who** robbed a tech company in California made a big mistake. They stole technology (b) **which** was worth hundreds of pounds. But they didn't realise that the technology (c) **which** they had stolen included GPS tracking devices. These devices, (d) **which** can track the owner's movements, informed the company exactly where the thieves had gone with the stolen property. The company, (e) **whose** name is Roambee, immediately informed the police, (f) **who** went directly to the place (g) **where** the thieves were hiding. The police found other things (h) **which** the robbers had stolen from other businesses. At that time, the tech company, (i) **which** was just beginning, had been thinking of ideas (j) **which** they could use to promote their tracking devices. They had been planning an exhibition (k) **which** would show how effective their tracking devices were. In the end, the theft and recovery of the stolen tracking devices gave them the kind of publicity (l) **which** money just can't buy!

3b **Look at the original text again. Omit the relative pronouns where possible.**

> **Use it … don't lose it!**
>
> **4** **Rewrite the sentences as one sentence using a non-defining relative clause.**
>
> ### Earbuds are for ears, not stomachs!
>
> 1 Ben Hsu swallowed an earbud. He's from Taiwan.
>
> 2 Ben was listening to music one night. His earbuds were white.
>
> 3 Ben fell asleep in his bed. He was resting there.
>
> 4 The earbud still worked in his stomach. It was made by Apple®.
>
> 5 Ben used Apple®'s tracking feature to help him find it. The tracking feature forces the earbud to make a sound.
>
> 6 He heard a noise coming from inside him. The noise was a beeping sound.
>
> 7 Ben is going to be more careful with his earbuds. He was very surprised by the experience.

Reach higher ▷ page 140

5 Choose the best answers (A, B, C or D) to complete the text.

Culture exchange

The screen habits of UK teens

The statistics keep changing, and fast. But the latest information **(1)** .... we have is that British teenagers now spend more than nine hours a day online. In a 2013 survey by Logicalis Group, a number of UK teenagers, **(2)** .... ages were between 13 and 17, answered a series of questions about their screen habits. They **(3)** .... the researchers the amount of time they spent on social media websites. The average answer was one hour and 40 minutes a day, **(4)** .... is approximately the same amount of time that they spend streaming videos and music over the Internet. The 1,000 teens who took part in the survey also admitted **(5)** .... an average of 72 minutes a day playing video games and 55 minutes messaging their friends. One interesting thing we can see about today's teens, **(6)** .... they are online, is that they are very good at multi-tasking. That means that their nine hours of digital engagement takes less than nine hours in real time **(7)** .... they may be texting or playing a computer game while they stream music, for example.

Although parents often worry that teens spend too much time online, there is some research from 2017 from the University of Oxford **(8)** .... suggests that some screen time is beneficial for them. Their well-being increases as their screen time increases. **(9)** ...., this is only up to a certain point and then it becomes bad for you. It depends **(10)** .... how long they spend on the activity. It has been calculated that four hours and 17 minutes is the maximum amount of time that teens should spend on a computer on weekdays.

1	**A** what	**B** –	**C** where	**D** when
2	**A** who	**B** whose	**C** their	**D** when
3	**A** said	**B** explained	**C** answered	**D** told
4	**A** –	**B** that	**C** which	**D** what
5	**A** spending	**B** spend	**C** spent	**D** that
6	**A** than	**B** when	**C** that	**D** which
7	**A** since	**B** meanwhile	**C** furthermore	**D** however
8	**A** that	**B** –	**C** who	**D** it
9	**A** However	**B** Although	**C** Even	**D** Despite
10	**A** in	**B** of	**C** on	**D** for

> ☑ **Exam tip**
>
> If you aren't sure which answer is right, think about why other answers are definitely wrong and eliminate them first.

Reach higher ⟩ **page 140**

Developing vocabulary

Phrasal verbs connected with technology and computers

1 Complete the phrasal verbs in the sentences with the correct form of the verbs in the box. Check that you understand the phrasal verbs.

> back · log · pick · pop · run (x2)

I never knew that!

1 In 2019, there was a smartphone battery that only .... **out of** power after 15 hours. In the future, batteries will last much longer.

2 A typical smartphone can .... **up** a signal from a tower up to 72 kilometres away.

3 Ethan Zuckerman is the person who invented those irritating adverts that suddenly .... **up** online. He has now apologised for inventing them!

4 Novelist Mat Johnson nearly lost a complete novel he had written because he had forgotten to .... **up** his files!

5 The Internet .... **on** electricity. But because electricity is extremely light, all of the electricity needed for the Internet worldwide would only weigh about as much as an apricot.

6 Before the World Wide Web existed, you had to actually .... **on** to different computers to access the information in them.

2 Look at the sentences. Guess the meanings of the phrasal verbs from the context.

1 An alarm **goes off** when you press this button.
2 To buy this app, you have to **set up** an account.
3 The image is really small so you need to **zoom in**.
4 Use the mouse to **scroll up**, **down** or **across**.
5 He quickly **keyed in** all the data.

> **Use it ... don't lose it!**
>
> **3** SPEAKING 👥 Complete the questions and then use them to interview your partner.
>
> 1 How often do you back .... the work you do on a computer?
>
> 2 Has your smartphone battery ever run .... at a critical moment?
>
> 3 Do you get annoyed by adverts popping .... on your computer or laptop? Do you do anything to stop them?
>
> 4 How long does it usually take before your phone runs out .... power?

Reach higher ⟩ **page 140**

 # GREAT LEARNERS GREAT THINKERS

SOCIAL MEDIA

Lesson aim: To reflect on the use of media for study and pleasure

Video: The Social Media Challenge

SEL **Social and emotional learning:** Establishing boundaries and limits

1 **SPEAKING** Ask and answer these questions.

1 How often do you use social media each day?

2 What do you use social media for?

3 Do you generally think using social media is a good or bad thing? Do you think you use it too much?

2 **VIDEO** Watch the video and answer the questions.

1 What is the challenge that Mon has set herself?

2 Why didn't she use the recipe she found on the Internet?

3 Does she manage to overcome the challenge?

4 What is her simple conclusion about social media at the end of the video?

3 **VIDEO** Watch the video again. Why does Mon mention these things, people or places?

1 Portugal

2 Norway

3 the effect that skiing has on her

4 household chores

5 her mother and sister

6 photos of her embroidery

7 the integration of social media into your daily life

GREAT THINKERS

Generate-Sort-Connect-Elaborate

4 **SPEAKING** Follow these instructions.

1 **Generate** ideas about any ways that you can use social media or new technologies for study, at home or in class.

2 **Sort** your ideas in 1 into groups, e.g. ways of communicating with people or ways of accessing information and knowledge. Classify your ideas into the categories in the mind map on page 115.

3 **Connect** any ideas from different categories that you think have a link.

4 **Elaborate** on your ideas by expanding them and taking them in new directions.

SOCIAL MEDIA **AND** TECHNOLOGY

5 SPEAKING 👥 **Look at your diagram and answer these questions.**

1 Which ideas do you already use? How useful and effective do you find each one?

2 Which ideas could you use, but don't yet? Would you ever try them? Why/Why not?

3 Which ideas have you tried but don't regularly use? Why not?

4 Are there any ideas that are impossible for you to try? Why? Do you think they may be possible for you one day?

5 Can you think of any ideas that don't exist yet, but you wish they did? Explain them.

GREAT LEARNERS SEL

Great learners can make reasoned use of new technologies.

Why is it important to think critically about different ways of using technology for study?

Learner profile > page 143

Listening

1 **SPEAKING** 🗣 **Look at the statement and discuss your opinions. Do you agree with the statement? Why/Why not?**

> 'Nowadays we rely too much on technology in our daily lives'.

2 🔊**51** **Listen to a podcast where four people give their opinion about the statement in 1. Does each speaker agree (A) or disagree (D) with it? If they do agree, do they think it's a real problem (P) or not (NP)?**

Speaker 1: _A/D_ _P/NP_
Speaker 2: _A/D_ _P/NP_
Speaker 3: _A/D_ _P/NP_
Speaker 4: _A/D_ _P/NP_

3 🔊**51** **Listen again. Which speaker says these things?**

A	Technology helps us to use our minds in new ways.	1/2/3/4
B	I think it's a good idea to be ready to live without technology in general.	1/2/3/4
C	Technology has changed how, where and when we can learn new things.	1/2/3/4
D	The drawback with technology is that it stops our minds from getting enough exercise.	1/2/3/4
E	Technology means we don't have to store so much data in our memories.	1/2/3/4
F	Technology allows me to put my essential tasks first.	1/2/3/4
G	Technology's biggest strength is now its weakness.	1/2/3/4
H	We have too much confidence in technology giving us the right answer.	1/2/3/4
I	Having access to technology doesn't mean we should forget our own responsibilities.	1/2/3/4
J	I know that my opinion about technology is shared by others.	1/2/3/4

4 🧠 **Critical thinkers**

> In your opinion, which of the arguments that the speakers give are most valid?
>
> What makes you say that?

Grammar in context 2

Flipped classroom video
Watch the Grammar Presentation video

Gerunds and infinitives 2

1a **Read the pairs of sentences. In which pair do the two sentences have the same meaning?**

1a I stopped **to think** about it.
1b I stopped **thinking** about it.
2a We've started **to multitask**.
2b We've started **multitasking**.
3a I remember **to do** all my chores.
3b I remember **doing** all my chores.
4a I won't forget **to read** about the virus.
4b I won't forget **reading** about the virus.
5a I like **to drive** without a satnav.
5b I like **driving** without a satnav.

1b **Match the verbs + gerund/infinitive to the correct meaning.**

1	stop to do	a	you stop one activity because you want or need to do another activity
2	stop doing		
		b	you are doing something and then you stop
3	remember to do	a	you do something and then you remember it later
4	remember doing	b	you remember you need to do something and then you do it
5	forget to do	a	you don't do something that you intended to do
6	forget doing	b	you did something but now you don't remember it
7	like to do	a	you do something because you enjoy doing it
8	like doing	b	you do something because you think it's useful or a good idea

☑ **Check it page 120**

2 **Choose the correct alternative.**

1 I like _to charge/charging_ my phone at night.
2 I stopped _to watch/watching_ the video because I had an exam the next day.
3 Did you forget _to text/texting_ him? Don't worry. I'll send him a message now.
4 I remember _to play/playing_ video games when I was only four.
5 I can't do PE. I forgot _to bring/bringing_ my trainers.
6 Can you remember _to switch/switching_ the computer off when you finish?
7 If your eyes hurt, you should stop _sitting/to sit_ in front of a screen.
8 My dad likes _to read/reading_ sci-fi books. I don't know how he can enjoy them so much.

3 Complete the second sentence so that it has a similar meaning to the first sentence, using the word given. Do not change the word given. Use between two and five words.

1 I think playing e-sports is really good fun.
   (like)
   I .... e-sports.

2 My dad had a break from writing and made the dinner.
   (to)
   My dad stopped .... the dinner.

3 I broke my first tablet. I'll never forget.
   (remember)
   I .... my first tablet.

4 Help me with my homework. Please don't forget!
   (remember)
   Please .... with my homework.

5 I didn't work on my assignment last night because I didn't remember.
   (forgot)
   I .... assignment last night.

6 She thinks it's important to wear smart clothes for work.
   (likes)
   She .... for work.

7 Suddenly it was impossible for us to receive a signal.
   (up)
   Suddenly we stopped ....

8 Don't worry. Yesterday I made a copy of all the data. I didn't forget.
   (up)
   Don't worry. Yesterday I .... all the data.

9 They became silent when their friend started singing.
   (stopped)
   They .... when their friend started singing.

10 I dropped my phone in the water. I'll always remember it.
   (forget)
   I'll .... in the water.

4 Find ten mistakes with gerunds or infinitives in the text. A number of mistakes may depend on the rules that you studied for gerunds and infinitives on page 12.

Latest   **Featured article**   Archive

SMARTPHONES ARE CHANGING THE SHAPE OF OUR HEADS!

Maybe it's time young adults stopped to spend so much time on their phones because it seems to be having an effect on their skulls. We all know that look at a small screen can be bad for your eyes. But did you know when we look at a screen, we put extra pressure on the place where our neck muscles meet our skull? This seems to be responsible for produce a small difference in the shape of the back of our heads. It is becoming more and more normal finding this in people between the ages of 18 and 30. David Shahar, an Australian scientist, has decided investigating this new phenomenon. He's interested in see how big the change could become. He believes that the changes will definitely become bigger and bigger, but says they won't be big enough being dangerous. But, anyway, maybe it's time to think about spend less time on your smartphone. Even if you really like to play games on your phone, remember doing other things too.

5 Write complete sentences about these things.

1 something unusual you remember doing when you were at primary school

2 something that you remembered to do last week

3 something important that you once forgot to do

4 something that you like doing

5 something that you like to do because you think it's a good idea

6 something that you did when you were younger but that you stopped

7 something that you were doing yesterday and then you stopped to do something else

Use it ... don't lose it!

6 **SPEAKING** 👥 Compare your sentences in 5. Ask follow-up questions.

I remember collecting stickers of football players when I was at primary school.

Did you ever finish collecting them all?

Yes, one year. But it took a long time!

Reach higher ＞ page 140

Developing speaking

Discussions 2

1a SPEAKING 👥 Look at the photo of an e-sports tournament. What do you know and what do you think about e-sports?

1b Read this article. Does it tell you anything that you didn't know about e-sports?

| News | Reviews | Articles | More ▾ | | Q |

E-SPORTS IN THE NEWS

What are e-sports? They are video games played competitively at a professional level. Most popular e-sports are team-based games played in leagues or tournaments throughout the year, leading to one final event. The two main types of games are first-person shooters and MOBAs (Multiplayer Online Battle Arena). But there are also sports, fighting and strategy games.

How popular are they? Incredibly popular! Thousands of people (mostly young) go to watch the tournaments live in massive arenas. Many people watch live online, too. The players can earn good salaries, and the winners can win huge prizes.

Why are they in the news right now? Because people are talking about making e-sports a new event in the Olympic Games. Some people are really excited about the possibility. Others are not impressed.

1c SPEAKING 👥 Should e-sports be part of the Olympic Games®? Discuss, giving reasons for your opinions.

2 🔊**52** Listen to two people discussing whether e-sports should become an Olympic event or not. What is each person's opinion? Do they mention any of your ideas in 1c?

3a 🔊**52** Listen again. Which expressions in the Speaking bank do you hear?

Speaking bank
Clarifying and checking understanding

Useful expressions for:

1 ....

- Do you see what I mean?
- Do you get what I'm saying?
- Are you following me?
- Are you with me?
- What I mean/meant is/was …
- Yes, that's exactly what I mean/meant.
- That's not quite what I mean/meant.

Useful expressions for:

2 ....

- Are you saying that …?
- If I understand you correctly, …
- In other words …
- What do you mean when you say …?
- I'm not sure what you mean by …
- Could you go over that again?
- Sorry, I'm not with you.
- I don't understand what you're getting at.

3b Complete the headings in the Speaking bank with a or b below.

a asking someone to clarify something

b checking someone has understood you

4 Look at these questions. Prepare notes with your answers and different arguments to justify your opinions.

1 In general, are video games too violent?

2 Do violent video games produce violent teenagers?

3 Should violent video games be banned?

Practice makes perfect

5 SPEAKING 👥 Take it in turns to discuss the questions. Use your ideas from 4 and the Speaking bank to help you.

Developing writing

A report

1 **SPEAKING** 👥 **What do you think would be the most important and useful things to include on a school website? Discuss the ideas below and add any other ideas you have.**

- a photo gallery
- videos of school events
- a student vlog
- a list of special events at the school
- a history of the school
- school clubs, teams and societies
- lunch menus
- information about the staff

2 **Read this writing task. What style do you think you should use to do this task – formal or informal?**

> Your school has a website, but not many people visit it. The head of your school has asked you to speak to as many students as possible and then write a report saying:
> - why the current website is not very popular
> - how the website could be improved to attract more visitors in the future
>
> Write your **report**.

3 **Read this student's report. What style is it written in? Does the student mention any of the things you talked about in 1?**

Improvements to the school website

Introduction
The aim of this report is to outline our opinion of the current school website and to suggest how it could be improved in order to attract more visitors in the future.

The current website
At the moment, the website is designed in a very old, traditional way which is not sufficiently attractive or dynamic. Furthermore, nearly all the students that we interviewed said that they found it difficult to navigate. Another drawback with the current website is that not all of the information there is up to date, which a large number of people consider to be a major problem.

Suggested improvements
Nearly all the students we spoke to suggested a more dynamic design for the website. It has been mentioned by many students that there should be a section for news about trips, concerts, sports competitions and other events. This section should be updated every week, so that people revisit the website regularly. A few people suggested that the website could also include a vlog prepared by students from different years. This would, without doubt, be appealing to both students and parents.

Conclusion
To sum up, as we have previously mentioned, most of the students we spoke to feel strongly that the website has to be both more attractive and more informative. All things considered, our main recommendation is that the information which is posted there is fresh and frequently updated.

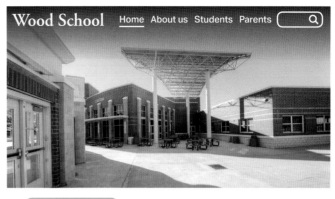

Wood School   Home   About us   Students   Parents   🔍

☑ **Exam tip**

When you write a report, give it a title. Divide the report into paragraphs and give each paragraph a heading.

4 **Read the report again and find examples of the expressions or advice in the Writing bank.**

Writing bank
Using formal language and expressions in reports

- Remember not to use contractions in formal language.
- Use passive and impersonal structures to express a more serious, formal style.
- Use linkers of addition, contrast and consequence to structure your arguments clearly.
- Use determiners and quantifiers (*all*, *each*, *every*, *none*, *a large number of ...*) to say how general your comments are.
- Begin your report with expressions such as: *The aim/ purpose of this report is to outline/describe/present the findings ..., This report is intended to ...*
- End the report with expressions such as: *As I/we have previously mentioned ..., I/we (would) suggest/ recommend ..., My/our main recommendation/ suggestion is ..., All things considered, All in all, ...*

Practice makes perfect

5a **Read the task below and write your report. Use the model to help you and include expressions from the Writing bank.**

> An international company wants to know about the use of new technologies in schools around the world. You have been asked to write a report about:
> - which types of technology you use to study in and outside the classroom and how you use them.
> - what the attitude of students towards the use of technology for studying is, and what the ideal use of technology for studying would be.
>
> Write your **report**.

5b **When you finish your report, use the Writing checklist on page 141 to check it.**

Grammar reference

Defining relative clauses

William Gilbert was the first person who/that investigated electricity scientifically.

We use **who** and **that** for people, **which** and **that** for things, **whose** for possessions, **where** for places, **when** for times, and **why** for reasons.

In defining relative clauses we can omit **who**, **which** or **that** when followed immediately by a noun or pronoun.

That's the device that she invented. = That's the device she invented.

That's the device which I use the most. = That's the device I use the most.

but

That's the device that is popular.
NOT That's the device is popular.

That's the device that helps me the most.
NOT That's the device helps me the most.

Instead of **where** or **when** we can use **which/that ... in**.

That's the year when I was born.

That was the year which I was born in.

That's the city where I was born.

That's the city that I was born in.

We do not use commas in defining relative clauses.
We use defining relative clauses to give essential information about the person, thing, place, time or reason in the other half of the sentence.

Non-defining relative clauses

William Gilbert, who was born in 1544, investigated electricity scientifically.

We use **who** for people, **which** for things, **whose** for possessions, **where** for places, and **when** for times.
We do not use **that** in non-defining relative clauses.

In non-defining relative clauses we cannot omit the relative pronoun.
NOT That device, she invented ten years ago, is really useful.

We always use commas in non-defining relative clauses.

We can use **which** to refer back to the whole of the sentence.

People spend all their money on mobile phones, which I think is ridiculous.

We use non-defining relative clauses to give extra, non-essential information about the person, thing, place or time in the first half of the sentence. The commas work in a similar way to parentheses, showing that the information is not vital to the sentence.

Gerunds and infinitives 2

Some verbs go with the gerund or the infinitive and there is no difference in meaning.

She started to work there in 2014. = She started working there in 2014.

Other verbs: *begin, can't bear, can't stand, continue, hate, love, prefer*

Some verbs go with the gerund or the infinitive but there is an important difference in meaning, e.g.

stop *to do*: you stop one activity because you want or need to do another activity

stop *doing*: you are doing something and then you stop

remember *to do*: you remember you need to do something and then you do it

remember *doing*: you do something and then you remember it later

forget *to do*: you don't do something that you intended to do

forget *doing*: you did something but now you don't remember it

like *to do*: you do something because you think it's a good idea

like *doing*: you do something because you enjoy doing it

Vocabulary

1 Technology and IT

desktop • earphones • external hard drive • headphones • pen-drive • remote control • satnav • smart speaker • webcam • wireless charger • wireless network

2 Adjectives to describe technology

bendy/flexible • brittle • chunky • cutting edge • durable • eco-friendly • heavy-duty • high-resolution • lightweight • metallic • rustproof • tough • unbreakable • waterproof

3 Words connected with technology

battery charger (n) • bookmark (n, v) • clickbait (n) • cloud (n) • download/upload (v) • drop-down menu (n) • earbud (n) • firewall (n) • freeze (v) • landline (n) • net (n) • operating system (n) • storage (n) • stream (v) • touch screen (n) • tweet (v) • update (v) • USB port (n) • virus (n)

4 Phrasal verbs connected with technology and computers

back up • go off • key in • log on • pick up • pop up • run on • run out (of) • scroll up/down/across • set up • zoom in

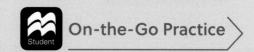
On-the-Go Practice

Grammar test

Relative clauses 1

1 **Choose the correct alternatives. If you think both are possible, choose both.**

1 The man *who/–* came to fix our smart TV knew about laptops, too.

2 The other day, *when/which* I saw you in the shopping centre, I bought a tablet.

3 The classroom *where/which* we leave our bags in is only used by the English department.

4 This unusual invention, *that/which* comes from Japan, could be really popular one day.

5 The blog *that/–* she writes is really interesting.

6 Does anybody know *who's/whose* pen this is?

/ 6 points

Relative clauses 2

2 **Use a defining relative clause to write a sentence about each person, place, time or thing.**

1 Brazil is a country ....

2 2020 was the year ....

3 Chocolate is a type of food
....

4 Judo is a sport ....

5 Cleopatra was a queen ....

6 Milk is a drink ....

7 Plastic is a material ....

/ 7 points

Gerunds and infinitives 2

3 **Put the verbs in the correct form.**

1 Can you remember ....
(switch) off the light when you leave?

2 She really likes .... (paint).
It's her favourite hobby.

3 We stopped .... (write) when the exam finished.

4 Don't forget .... (go) to the meeting tomorrow.

5 I know Harry was at school yesterday because I remember ....
(see) him.

6 I like .... (do) homework on Friday evening so that I'm free at the weekend.

7 The musicians stopped ....
(play) because they'd already been playing for two hours.

/ 7 points

Vocabulary test

Technology and IT

1 **Re-order the halves of the expressions to make six types of everyday technology.**

1 head network   4 desk cam

2 hard phones   5 web speaker

3 wireless drive   6 smart top

/ 6 points

Words connected with technology

2 **Which word from page 120 is being defined?**

1 easy to break – adjective

2 a telephone that is not a mobile phone – noun

3 when the image stops moving on a computer – verb

4 synonym of flexible – adjective

5 mark a page on the Internet so you can easily find it again – verb

6 extremely modern and advanced – adjective

7 make something like a computer program more modern – verb

8 a computer program that stops people entering a computer illegally – noun

/ 8 points

Phrasal verbs connected with technology and computers

3 **Choose the correct alternatives.**

1 He backed *off/up* the files on a flash drive in case he lost them.

2 It's strange that my mobile can't *pick/run* up a signal here because there must be coverage.

3 Can you print *up/out* a copy of those lyrics so I can keep them?

4 An advert suddenly *popped/set* up on the screen.

5 All cars will run *on/up* electricity one day.

6 You need to zoom *up/in* to see the image more clearly.

/ 6 points

Total: / 40 points

NEWS JUST IN!

Vocabulary in context

News sections
Words frequently used in news headlines

1 **SPEAKING** 👥 Look at the different sections that often appear on a news website or in a newspaper. Give examples of what information you can usually find in each section.

> 🔊 **53** News sections
>
> arts • business • columnists • digital archive • editor's blog • entertainment • environmental issues • features • gossip • have your say • health • life and style • money and finance • obituaries • science and tech • showbiz • sport • travel • trending topics • weather forecast • world news

2 **SPEAKING** 👥 Which sections in 1 do you prefer to look at and why?

3 Headlines often use words that are short and dramatic to catch people's attention quickly using little space. Look at these examples.

> 🔊 **54** Words frequently used in news headlines 1
>
> **axe:** cut, reduce • **back:** support •
> **blast:** explosion • **blast:** make strong criticism •
> **clash:** (have a) violent disagreement •
> **hit:** affect badly • **link:** (make a) connection •
> **plea:** (make a) request • **pledge:** make a promise •
> **probe:** (make an) investigation •
> **riddle:** mystery • **spark:** cause

4 Here are some more words frequently used in headlines. Match them to 1–10 below. Use a dictionary if necessary.

> 🔊 **55** Words frequently used in news headlines 2
>
> aid • ban • blaze • boost • boss/head • drama • key • PM • quit • wed

1	tense situation	6	Prime Minister
2	marry	7	prohibit, prohibition
3	manager/director	8	leave, resign
4	help	9	increase, encourage(ment)
5	important, essential	10	fire

5 Newspaper headlines also use grammar in special ways. Look at how they do this.

a Words like articles or auxiliary verbs are omitted.

> **President shot during speech but continues**

b The present simple is used for current or recent events.

> **TORTOISE SMASHES THROUGH BRICK WALL**

c The infinitive is used for future events.

> **HUMANS TO REACH MARS BY 2035**

d The headlines are not usually complete sentences. Nouns are used as adjectives and are often put one after another.

> **WORLD ECONOMY COLLAPSE FEAR**

e Direct speech can be used without inverted commas.

> **It wasn't my fault, says driver**

Use it ... don't lose it!

6a **SPEAKING** 👥 Invent three headlines using the vocabulary in 3 and 4 and the grammar information in 5. Then write a short explanation of your imaginary news.

6b **SPEAKING** 👥 Read your explanations to another pair. Can they guess the headlines?

> *The director of a phone company is going to marry a famous tennis player.*

> *Phone boss to wed tennis star*

Reach higher ⟩ page 140

Reading

1 **SPEAKING** 👥 Look at the photos and headlines on this page. What do you think each news story will be about?

2 Read the news stories. Are they similar to your predictions?

●●● **Latest news** ✕   🔍

UN-NEWS-UAL NEWS FROM THE NATURAL WORLD!

WATER BEARS LAND ON MOON

A spaceship launched from Florida on 22ⁿᵈ February left some of the world's toughest animals on the Moon. It was to land there on 11ᵗʰ April. When it was about to make its final
5 descent, it suffered technical problems and crashed. As part of an ambitious plan to create a 'back-up Earth', the spacecraft was going to land a time capsule with 30 million pages of information about our planet, samples of human DNA, and several thousand tardigrades, also known as water bears.
10 These had been selected for the trip as they are the most indestructible creatures on Earth. Although the spacecraft crashed at high speed, the experts who sent up the creatures believe their cargo may have lived. Tardigrades are able to survive for up to 30 years without food or water and endure
15 extreme conditions like the deep icy waters of Antarctica or the frozen vacuum of space.

The animal's secret lies in its ability to enter a state of suspended animation. They can then reanimate with just a drop of water. They began their mission to the Moon by being
20 dried out and placed in a hard, clear material called resin. If this had broken during the crash, the tardigrades would be on the Moon's surface right now, but not doing much. That's because they would only become active and reproduce if they had three basic things first – food, air, and, above all, water. So if they
25 were found and brought back to Earth, they could come back to life. Experts at Oxford University estimate that they will survive on Earth until the Sun dies, some ten billion years from now. The only threat to their existence would be from an event causing Earth's oceans to boil away, leaving no chance of reanimation.

EXOTIC FRUIT SPARKS UNIVERSITY EVACUATION

30 Australian fire and rescue teams told everyone to leave the University of Canberra's library when someone reported a strong smell of gas. But a short while afterwards, they were all in for a big surprise. The library announced on social media that a durian fruit had caused the
35 drama. This happened on Thursday as classes were ending for the term and students were preparing for an exam period. They were starting their exams the following Monday. The day after the evacuation, the library was back in use, provided the students could face the smell. Some people think durians have a very pleasant smell and taste, but
40 others compare the aroma to 'onion with socks.' If it didn't have such a strong smell, they wouldn't have been banned from some trains in Singapore or from many hotels across Asia.

The library evacuation is not the first time the fruit has caused problems. In November, it caused a delay to an Indonesian flight.
45 Online videos showed travellers and airline staff about to fight because the passengers were unwilling to take off with two tonnes of the fruit in the cargo hold. Some people thought the flight would be their last because of rumours that 2.7 tonnes of durian caused the tragic crash of another plane, something later shown without question to
50 be untrue. Nevertheless, the sacks of fruit were eventually removed from the plane. The durian fruit is regarded by many as the 'king of fruits', particularly, but not only, in Southeast Asia. In 2019 somebody paid a record price of nearly £40,000 for a rare variety at a festival in Rayong, Thailand. And in China a popular fast food chain has added
55 'durian chicken nuggets' to its menu. The nuggets are covered in breadcrumbs on the outside and filled with just a hot, creamy durian paste. Reactions have been mixed, as so often happens with this curious, divisive fruit.

---

3 🔊56 Read the news stories again. Are these statements True (T) or False (F)? Write the number of the line(s) where you found the answer.

1 The introduction of tardigrades onto the Moon was completely accidental.   T / F Line(s): ....

2 Tardigrades can survive without water for much longer than most animals.   T / F Line(s): ....

3 Tardigrades are guaranteed to survive in the future, whatever happens to the Earth.   T / F Line(s): ....

4 On Friday, conditions in the University library were exactly the same as always.   T / F Line(s): ....

5 We know for a fact that durian fruits were not responsible for causing an air tragedy.   T / F Line(s): ....

6 The name of the new durian chicken nuggets is misleading.   T / F Line(s): ....

> ☑ **Exam tip**
>
> In True/False activities, read the text quickly once to get a general idea. Then read the statements. Find the sections of the text where you think the answers come and read these in more detail.

4 **What do the underlined words in the text mean? Guess and then check in your dictionary.**

5 🧠 **Critical thinkers**

> In your opinion, can we learn anything important by reading unusual news stories like these?
>
> What makes you say that?

Future in the past

1 Sometimes when we are talking about the past, we want to talk about something that was in the future at that time, something which had not happened yet (and perhaps never did). Look at the sentences and identify the six structures used to talk about future activities in the past.

1 The spacecraft was going to land a time capsule on the Moon.

2 It was about to make its final descent.

3 It was to land on the Moon on 11th April.

4 Some passengers thought the flight would be their last.

5 They were starting their exams the following Monday.

6 They were all in for a big surprise.

☑ Check it **page 132**

2 Complete the text with these words and expressions.

> about • be • finishing • in for • to • was going •
> were • would (x2)

News   Business   Science   Health   Art   More ▾   Q

Builder finds surprise message

In Germany in 1930, a group of workers were
(a) .... to complete some work that they
were carrying out on the roof of the cathedral in
the town of Goslar. They were (b) ....
the repairs the next day and decided to leave some
kind of souvenir there. So they wrote a message
and put it in a bottle. One of the authors was an
18-year-old man called Willi Brandt. In 2018 some
workers (c) .... to carry out similar repairs
on the same roof. Of course, they had no idea what
(d) .... to happen. During the repairs
they (e) .... not only find the 88-year-old
bottle and message – one of the workers was
(f) .... a bigger surprise. He was Peter
Brandt, Willi's 52-year-old grandson! Peter used to
work with his grandfather, but knew nothing about
the message. In their note, Willi and his colleagues
wrote that they hoped that the future would
(g) .... much brighter for their children and
grandchildren. The local authorities announced that
the message and bottle were (h) .... be
kept in a safe place in the town.
The longest that it has taken a message in a bottle
to be found is 132 years. When some German sailors
threw a message into the sea in 1886, they almost
certainly had no idea that a family in Perth, Australia
(i) .... take so long to find it!

3 Decide if the sentences are correct. Rewrite the incorrect sentences.

1 She had no idea that her next match would be so memorable.

2 They revised a lot because they knew they were for a very tough exam.

3 The weather was bad but it was to become much worse in the next few hours.

4 The young player looked like he was about getting angry.

5 She couldn't do the interview because she was filming an advert the next morning.

6 He felt certain he was winning the award the following year.

4 Use your imagination to complete the sentences.

1 I never thought it would happen, but one day …

2 I was going on holiday the next day, but …

3 I knew it was going to be a great day because …

4 I was going to meet my friends in the park when …

5 I was about to start my homework, but …

6 We knew we were in for trouble because …

7 It was to be a moment they would remember for the rest of their lives because …

┌─ Use it … don't lose it! ─┐

5 SPEAKING 🗣 Compare your sentences. Choose the best sentence for each situation.

Reach higher ⟩ page 140

Mixed conditionals

6 Look at these sentences and answer the questions.

1 If it **didn't have** such a strong smell, they **wouldn't have banned** it from trains and hotels.

2 If the resin **had broken** during the crash, the tardigrades **would be** on the Moon's surface right now.

3 If I **was** a fan of exotic fruit, I **would have tried** durian when I went to Asia last year.

4 If I **had studied** biology last year, I **would know** more about the natural world.

a Are mixed conditionals a mixture of first and second conditionals, or second and third conditionals?

b Which sentences describe an imaginary past situation and its present consequence?

c Which sentences describe an imaginary present situation and its past consequence?

☑ Check it **page 132**

7 Which sentence endings are possible? How is the meaning of each sentence different?

1 If I knew a famous person …
   a I would interview them for the school magazine.
   b I'll interview them for the school magazine.
   c I would have interviewed them for the school magazine.

2 I would have gone to the concert if …
   a I like hip-hop.
   b I liked hip-hop.
   c I had liked hip-hop.

3 Your leg would hurt if …
   a you break it.
   b you broke it.
   c you had broken it.

4 I wouldn't be happy if …
   a I had lost the match.
   b I lost the match.
   c I lose the match.

5 If I'd learned to play the guitar …
   a I'll play at school concerts.
   b I would play at school concerts.
   c I would have played at school concerts.

8 Look at the situations and complete the sentences using mixed conditionals.

1 They don't know where the concert is. That's why they haven't arrived.
   If they knew where the concert was, _____

2 They didn't interview the singer because they can't speak English.
   If they _____

3 I don't have any tea here because I didn't know you liked it.
   If I _____

4 Jim loves playing the guitar so he bought an expensive one.
   If Jim _____

5 Kim spent lots of time studying medicine and now she's a doctor.
   If Kim _____

6 His new book is great because he spent years writing it.
   If he _____

7 Liam has a new tablet because he broke his old one.
   Liam _____

8 I have to revise now because I didn't remember to do it yesterday.
   If I _____

Developing vocabulary

Collocations connected with the news

1 Complete the text with these words. Check that you understand each complete expression in bold. Use a dictionary if necessary.

chief · daily · front · hot · issue · item · make · subscription

News   About   More ▾   🔍

The news in the news 1

Often the (a) _____ -**page news** in most newspapers is sad, scary or upsetting. But not in a newspaper called *The Happy Newspaper*. All the stories that (b) _____ **the headlines** there have to be upbeat and positive. Each (c) _____ **of news** has to prove that there is a lot of good happening in the world, according to (d) _____ **editor** Emily Coxhead. The newspaper isn't a (e) _____ **newspaper**. It's only published every three months. But over 2,000 people have **taken out a** (f) _____ to the paper, receiving a new (g) _____ four times a year, (h) _____ **off the press**.

2 Now do the same with this text.

breaking · broadcast · bulletin · informed · newsflash · newsreader · press conference · sensationalist · turn

News   About   More ▾   🔍

The news in the news 2

Today, with the Internet and special channels that only (a) _____ news, we're used to 24-hour news. But is this a good thing? Yes, the news companies **keep you** (b) _____. But sometimes it seems they're just filling up the time with (c) _____ **stories** created to shock the public and keep them watching. One minute there's a **news** (d) _____ about a famous singer who fell over in a concert. The next minute they interrupt a programme with a (e) _____ about a pair of famous actors **holding a** (f) _____ to announce their separation. Is that really news? In today's world of 24-hour news, can you imagine a day when there is no interesting (g) _____ **of events** anywhere in the world? Just picture 24 hours with no important (h) _____ **news** to announce! Well, on 19ᵗʰ April 1930, that's what happened. The BBC (i) _____ had nothing to say. 'There is no news,' he announced. The rest of the programme was filled with piano music.

3 Complete the questions with an appropriate word from 1 or 2.

1 How do you _____ yourself informed?
2 In your country, what type of news is important enough to get a _____ that interrupts normal programmes?
3 What events became front- _____ news last week?
4 Which famous people are making the _____ at the moment?
5 How do *you* find out about the latest _____ news?

Use it … don't lose it!

4 SPEAKING 👥 Ask and answer the questions in 3.

Reach higher ⟩ page 140

GREAT LEARNERS
GREAT THINKERS

HAPPY AND SAD NEWS

Lesson aim: To consider the importance of (optimistic) journalism
Video: *The Happy Newspaper*

SEL **Social and emotional learning:** Positive thinking

1 **SPEAKING** 👥 Discuss your opinions of *The Happy Newspaper* mentioned in the text on page 125. What type of person do you expect Emily Coxhead, the newspaper's editor, to be?

2 **VIDEO** ▷ Watch the video and answer the questions.

   1 Is Emily the type of person you predicted in 1?

   2 What is Emily's final message about good and bad news at the end of the video?

3 **VIDEO** ▷ Complete each space with one or two words or a number. Watch the video again if necessary.

   1 Emily likes to drink .... and eat ....

   2 Her newspaper has .... pages.

   3 Many people wrongly believe *The Happy Newspaper* is an .... or a ....

   4 Social media and the news were giving her the idea that only .... were happening in the world.

   5 Emily's favourite story came after a problem when an .... affected penguins.

   6 Emily thinks traditional newspapers are often .... and ....

   7 Emily began *The Happy Newspaper* by .... a simple sketch and posting it on her ....

   8 She wasn't going to put out a newspaper because of the .... in Paris but a .... inspired her to carry on.

   9 Emily says she isn't trying to cover over the terrible things with .... and ....

GREAT THINKERS

Think-Question-Explore

4 **SPEAKING** 👥 You are going to read a short text about journalists in prison around the world. Before you read, follow these instructions.

   1 What do you **think** you know about this topic? Make a list with ideas.

   2 What **questions** do you have about the topic? Write them down.

   3 Now read and **explore** the text opposite and see if it answers any of your questions. If not, try to **explore** other sources to find the information.

REPORTING IN SAFETY

In its global annual survey, the Committee to Protect Journalists (CPJ) found 245 imprisoned journalists in 2019, only a little below the 2016 record of 273. The survey indicates a continual increase in the number of journalists accused of reporting news that is 'false' or 'fake'. According to the CPJ, the growing number of jailed journalists reflects crackdowns on people expressing strong disagreement with the authorities in a number of countries. These authorities typically claim that they only imprison journalists who are trying to destabilise their country. The survey did not include journalists who disappeared or were 'arrested' by non-government organisations. According to the 2019 Annual Report by the partner organisations of the Council of Europe's Platform for the Protection of Journalism and Safety of Journalists, reporters are receiving more and more threats of violence as they investigate news for the public good. The Council of Europe says that urgent action is now required to assure that journalists can freely carry out their work safely, in protected environments and without obstruction.

5 Read the text about journalists again. Which do you think are the most important arguments in the text?

6 **SPEAKING** Discuss these questions.

1 How important do you think journalism is as a profession?

2 Would you like to be a journalist? Why/Why not?

GREAT LEARNERS **SEL**

Great learners are informed and knowledgeable.

How important do you think it is to follow the news and know what is happening in different parts of the world? Why?

Learner profile page 143

Listening

1 **SPEAKING** 👥 How do you think you can tell if a photo or news story is real, not fake? Make a list of ideas.

2 🔊57 Listen to a programme about analysing the news. Do they mention any of your ideas in 1?

3 🔊57 Listen again and choose the correct answers.

1 The presenter says they are talking about the news because …
   a there is more news available now than in the past.
   b everybody loves the fact that you don't have to pay to get the latest news.
   c it's a controversial topic at the moment.

2 Jessica says that citizen journalism …
   a is any type of journalism that spreads quickly amongst the public.
   b manages to do one of the things that all news services want to do.
   c means that we will not need professional journalists in the future.

3 Jessica says that ordinary people who write online news stories …
   a don't always get the facts right but they try.
   b don't always worry about getting the facts right.
   c are legally responsible for their own stories.

4 Jessica says that bias is …
   a when people let their own personal preferences or situation influence what they write.
   b when people from different backgrounds and professions write about the same subject.
   c a natural thing that all journalists should accept when they write their articles.

5 Jessica says we …
   a can still rely on images and videos to give us more genuine information than written articles.
   b will no longer be able to trust any image or video that we see in news stories.
   c will need to use special techniques in the future to know if an image or video is genuine or not.

☑ **Exam tip**

Remember to listen for the right person giving the answer. Different options or ideas may appear, but make sure you listen to what the person in the question says.

4 🧠 **Critical thinkers**

In your opinion, is fake news a serious problem today?

What makes you say that?

Grammar in context 2

Flipped classroom video
Watch the Grammar Presentation video

Question tags

1 Look at these sentences and the question tags they contain. Then decide if the statements below are True (T) or False (F).

1 There's a problem with that, **isn't there**?
2 We can't trust them anymore, **can we**?
3 They say a picture speaks louder than words, **don't they**?
4 We won't be able to travel, **will we**?
5 I'm right in saying that, **aren't I**?
6 Anybody can report the news, **can't they**?
7 Nobody is sure about the news now, **are they**?

a We use question tags when we want somebody to confirm what we are saying. T / F
b We use subject pronouns at the end of question tags. T / F
c We use auxiliary or modal verbs in question tags, not main verbs. T / F
d Usually the question tag in an affirmative sentence is negative and the question tag in a negative sentence is affirmative. T / F
e In sentences with *I am* the question tag is *am not I*? T / F
f In sentences with *nobody*, *somebody* or *everybody*, we use the pronoun *they*. T / F

☑ Check it **page 132**

2 Complete the sentences with question tags.

1 You don't believe that things like that could happen,
2 Anybody can do that,
3 We should practise using question tags,
4 I've seen you before,
5 You told me the same story yesterday,
6 Nobody came to school last weekend,
7 We're all going to be famous one day,

3a 🔊58 You will hear this sentence twice. In each case, does the intonation go up or down? When does the speaker seem certain that they know the answer?

Everybody likes chocolate, don't they?

3b 🔊58 Listen again and repeat the sentences.

4a Write three sentences with question tags about things that you know about your partner, and three things that you aren't sure about.

4b **SPEAKING** 👥 Now ask your partner your questions. Remember to use falling intonation when you are quite certain of your partner's answer and rising intonation when you aren't so sure.

You hate watching the news, don't you?

Indirect questions

5a Look at these sentences. They are all indirect questions. Write the direct questions.

1 I'd like to ask you <u>what you think about the news today</u>.

2 I wonder <u>if you could give us any final words of advice</u>.

3 I wonder <u>what the purpose of the article is</u>.

4 Have you got any idea <u>how they create these fake videos</u>?

5 Do you know <u>how they do it</u>?

6 Can I ask <u>if you have any advice for dealing with fake news</u>?

5b Answer the questions.

a In the underlined part of each sentence, does the subject come *before* the verb (like in a statement) or *after* the verb (like in a question)? Why?

b Sentences 1–3 do not have a question mark at the end of the sentence, but sentences 4–6 do. Why?

c Are indirect questions usually more formal and polite than direct questions or less formal and polite?

☑ **Check it page 132**

6a Look at this real news headline and story.

| About | New posts | Archive | 🔍 |

WOMAN SURPRISED BY PET 'DOG'

Two years after
receiving what she thought was a puppy dog, Su Yun realised that her pet was actually a black bear. First, she noticed that the animal had an enormous, insatiable appetite. Later, she became suspicious when she saw her pet walking around the house on two legs. Su Yun decided to contact …

6b Imagine you are going to interview Su Yun. Complete the second sentence so that it has a similar meaning to the first sentence.

1 Where did you get the animal from?
Can you tell me ....

2 Was it a friendly animal?
I'd like to ....

3 How much was it eating a day?
I wonder if you could tell us ....

4 What did you do when you realised it was a bear?
I wonder what ....

5 Is it still living in your house?
Can I ask ....

6 Has this ever happened to anyone else?
Have you got any idea ....

7 What did your friends and family think?
I'd love to know ....

8 How big will it grow?
Do you know ....

7a 🔊 SPEAKING 👥 Look at this headline and photo of a person from a news story. Write six indirect questions to ask him.

'Bananaman' chases and catches shoplifter!

7b SPEAKING 👥 One of you is the reporter and the other is 'Bananaman'. Role-play your conversation and then perform it for the class.

8 Write indirect questions using the words given.

1 Have you ever appeared in the news? **I'd like to ask …**

2 How often do you watch the news on TV? **Can I ask …**

3 Are you interested in going to concerts or plays? **I wonder if you could tell me …**

4 What do you think of celebrity gossip? **Can you tell me …**

5 What series are you going to watch next? **Have you any idea …**

6 How many people in the class pay attention to film reviews? **Do you know …**

7 Have you got a news app on your phone? **I'd like to know …**

Use it … don't lose it!

9 SPEAKING 👥 Take it in turns to ask and answer the indirect questions in 8.

Reach higher ⟩ page 140

Developing speaking

Presentations 2

1 **SPEAKING** 👥 Read the text. Then discuss with your partner what the words and expressions in bold mean. What similarities and differences are there between the British press and the press in your country?

Culture exchange

The British press

British newspapers are often divided into two general categories: quality newspapers and tabloids.

Quality newspapers are newspapers that contain serious and intellectual news and articles. Some of these quality newspapers are called **broadsheets** because they have large pages. However, many quality newspapers now have smaller pages than in the past, in part to make them easier for commuters to read on public transport.

Tabloids are newspapers that have small pages. Originally, the name tabloid referred to the size of the paper, but now we use the expression **tabloid journalism** to talk about a type of journalism that pays special attention to sensationalist stories, crime, showbiz gossip, football and television. This is also called **'the popular press'**. There have been many complaints in the past from famous people (including the royal family) about the invasion of their private lives by this type of press.

Today fewer newspapers are sold in the UK than in the past. One factor explaining this is that many **free newspapers** are given out to commuters in big cities. But the main reason is competition from online news. Nearly all British newspapers have their own websites, some free, some partially free, and some which you have to pay to access.

Collaborative project 5 > page 135

2 **SPEAKING** 👥 Think of arguments for and against the following statement. Generally, do you agree or disagree with it?

'The press should always be free to write what they like.'

3 🔊 **59** Listen to somebody giving a presentation on this topic. Do you agree with what they say? Why/Why not?

4 🔊 **59** Listen again and complete the expressions in the Speaking bank.

Speaking bank
Opposing points of view

Presenting opposing points of view
- It is true that …
- You can't deny that …
- There's no _____ that …
- You can't _____ with the fact that …
- I accept that …

Responding to opposing points of view
- But that doesn't mean that …
- However, …
- Let's not _____ that …
- I would still say that …
- Even so, I still believe that …
- Having _____ that,
- That doesn't alter my opinion that …

5 Look at this statement. Individually, think of arguments for and against it. Then decide what your opinion is.

'Posting your news on social media, and responding to other people's news, is a real waste of time.'

6 Make notes for a presentation. Follow this guide.
1 **Introduction:** State your overall opinion.
2 **Make your main points and justify them:** Do this by presenting one or two opposing points and respond to them.
3 **Conclusion:** Restate your opinion.

7 Think of expressions that are useful at each stage of your presentation and note them down.

Practice makes perfect
8 Give your presentation to the class. Use your ideas from 7 and the expressions from the Speaking bank to help you.

An article 2

1a SPEAKING (8) Brainstorm people or things that are trending at the moment, things that are new and popular in the worlds of entertainment (series, films, music, video games, etc.), fashion or sport.

1b Compare answers with the rest of the class. Have you chosen similar things?

2 Look at this writing task. Underline the key information that you need to include in your article.

> ### Articles wanted
>
> **What's hot right now? And what's not?**
>
> We want to know who or what the latest crazes are. Write an article telling us who or what YOU think is just the best right now and why. Then tell us what you think is yesterday's news – something that's just not as good as it used to be.
>
> Write your article and send it to us today!

3 Read this article. Does it include all the necessary information?

The Name of the Wind

Let me begin by saying that I'm really into fantasy, sci-fi and comics. So, in this article, I'd like to talk about what's hot and what's not in those worlds.

(a) _Despite/Despite the fact that_ I really enjoy fantasy series like _Game of Thrones_, I often find them too dark and depressing. There are so many stories and films based in tragic, sinister, dystopian worlds (b) _and so/whereas_ that's why I'm really excited about the latest trend – 'hopepunk'. The idea of hopepunk is that stories, films and series should have positive, optimistic messages. One of my favourite books is _The Name of the Wind_ and it's soon (c) _being/been_ made into a TV series. It's time we had more stories like this, that show that life isn't just full of violence.

As I said before, I'm a big fan of superhero films. (d) _However/Although_, what is no longer cool is the obsession with having so many remakes of old films. (e) _As far as I'm concerned/Furthermore_, there have been too many films telling the same story again and again with different actors. Just look at Batman and Spider-Man, for instance. We already know those plots (f) _as/so_ why don't they try to create original ones that we've never seen before?

(g) _All in all/Moreover_, I think there are lots of exciting projects for stories, films and series about to appear in the near future. (h) _However/Therefore_, it's important to remember that what we want is for people to keep on coming up with fresh, original and positive ideas, not just remakes.

4 Look again at the article and choose the correct alternatives. Think about the meaning of the words and how they function in a sentence, for example if they are followed by a comma or not.

5 Put these titles in the correct places in the Writing bank.

 a Addition   **e** Reason

 b Consequence   **f** Concluding

 c Opinion   **g** Contrast

 d Sequencing arguments

> ### Writing bank
> **Linkers – a review**
>
> **1** ....
> firstly, secondly, lastly
>
> **2** ....
> however, nevertheless, although, even though, despite, whereas, while, on the one/other hand
>
> **3** ....
> what's more, furthermore, moreover, in addition, not only ... but also
>
> **4** ....
> therefore, and so, as a result, consequently
>
> **5** ....
> because, as, since
>
> **6** ....
> as far as I'm concerned, personally, in my opinion
>
> **7** ....
> all in all, all things considered, to sum up, in conclusion

6 SPEAKING (8) Put these stages of writing a text in order.

 a Organise your notes into logical paragraphs. ☐

 b Make notes. ☐

 c Check your text for mistakes, edit it, and check that you have answered the questions. ☐

 d Write the first version of your text. ☐

 e Brainstorm ideas. [1]

 f Write the final version of your text. ☐

> **Practice makes perfect**
>
> **7a** Follow the instructions for the writing task in 2 and write your article. Use the model to help you and follow the correct procedure in 6. Include expressions from the Writing bank.
>
> **7b** When you finish your article, use the Writing checklist on page 141 to check it.

Grammar reference

Future in the past

I was going to speak to him but he walked away.
My American friend was arriving the next day.
I knew it would be a good day.
I was about to leave the house when my mum called.
The meeting was to take place on Tuesday.
They were in for some bad weather.

- Sometimes when we are talking about the past, we want to talk about something that was in the future at that time, something which had not happened then and perhaps didn't actually happen in the end.
- We use *was/were to* when there was an arrangement for something to happen. It is more formal than the other expressions.
- We use *was/were about to* for things that were going to happen very soon after.
- We use the past continuous for confirmed plans and arrangements in the past.
- We use *was/were in for* to talk about surprising, shocking and often unpleasant events.

Mixed conditionals

If + past simple, ... would/wouldn't have + past participle
If I wanted a coffee I would have asked for one.
If + past perfect, ... would/wouldn't + infinitive
If I had passed my driving test, I'd drive to university.

Mixed conditionals are a mixture of the second and third conditional. They can describe an imaginary present situation and its past consequence.
If I liked that group I would have gone to see them in concert.
Or they can describe an imaginary past situation and its present consequence.
If I had had breakfast, I wouldn't be hungry now.

Indirect questions

I'd like to ask you where you are from.
I wonder if you could tell us what you thought of the show.
I wonder what you prefer.
Do you know whether they won?

In the second part of these sentences we do not put the verb before the subject because they are not direct questions.

We use question marks when the first part of the sentence is a question (e.g. *Do you know ...?, Can you tell me ...?*). Remember that the second part of these sentences are not direct questions.

When there is no question word (*who, what,* etc.), we use *if/whether.*
I'd like to know whether you agree.

We use indirect questions in more formal situations and to be more polite. We can also use indirect questions to ask a big favour from someone we know well.
Dad, I was wondering if I could take the car tonight.

Question tags

I'm late, aren't I?
I'm not late, am I?
You like rock music, don't you?
You don't like classical music, do you?
She could do the exercise, couldn't she?

In question tags we use pronouns, not names or nouns.

We make question tags with auxiliary or modal verbs, not main verbs. If there is no auxiliary or modal verb in the first part of the sentence, we use the appropriate part of the auxiliary *do.*

In affirmative sentences, the question tag is usually negative. In negative sentences, the question tag is usually affirmative.

With *I am,* the question tag is *aren't I?*

With *everybody, nobody* and *somebody,* we use the pronoun *they.*

We reply to question tags using the auxiliary or modal verb, not the main verb.
You don't like classical music, do you? No, I don't./Yes, I do.

We use question tags to change a statement into a question. The question is to confirm what we are saying.

Vocabulary

1 News sections

arts • business • columnists • digital archive • editor's blog • entertainment • environmental issues • features • gossip • have your say • health • life and style • money and finance • obituaries • science and tech • showbiz • sport • travel • trending topics • weather forecast • world news

2 Words frequently used in news headlines

aid (n) • axe (v) • back (v) • ban (n, v) • blast (v) • blaze (n) • boost (n, v) • boss/head (n) • clash (v) • drama (n) • hit (v) • key (adj) • link (n, v) • plea (n, v) • pledge (n, v) • PM (n) • probe (n, v) • quit (v) • riddle (n) • spark (v) • wed (v)

3 Collocations connected with the news

breaking news (n) • broadcast the news (v) • chief editor (n) • daily newspaper (n) • front-page news (n) • hold a press conference (v) • hot off the press (adj) • issue (n, v) • item of news/news item (n) • keep somebody informed (v) • make the headlines (v) • news broadcast (n) • news bulletin (n) • newsflash (n) • newsreader (n) • sensationalist story (n) • take out a subscription (phrasal verb) • turn of events (n)

On-the-Go Practice

Grammar test

Future in the past

1 **The sentences below all talk about future activities in the past. Complete each sentence with one word.**

1 He thought the Sun .... shine the next day, but it was really cloudy.

2 They ran to catch the train because it .... going to leave at that moment.

3 The interview was .... start at 10 am, but she was late.

4 They thought the party .... starting at 9 pm, but they were wrong.

5 He was laughing so hard that he was about .... cry.

/ 5 points

Mixed conditionals

2 **Complete the sentences with the correct form of the verbs given.**

1 I .... (be) tired now if I'd gone to bed late.

2 Dylan would be studying at university if he .... (pass) his entrance exam last June.

3 If I knew your number, I .... (call) you last night.

4 If they .... (win) the lottery last week, they'd all be millionaires.

5 I .... (finish) my assignment last week if I were more organised.

/ 5 points

Indirect questions

3 **Put the words in order to make indirect questions.**

1 you can me tell want what you

2 are I to would know how like you

3 know you what is time it do

4 you idea coffee any whether have he drinks

5 to how know want you I did that

/ 5 points

Question tags

4 **Choose the correct alternative.**

1 Nobody knows how to do it, *does he/do they*?

2 You never arrive on time, *do/don't* you?

3 He's made a lot of mistakes, *hasn't/isn't* he?

4 I'm not ready to do the exam, *am/aren't* I?

5 There's a lot of good news today, isn't *it/there*?

/ 5 points

Vocabulary test

News sections

1 **Which section of a news website would you look at to ...**

1 read about somebody who has just died?

2 read about the private life of a famous actor?

3 find out if it will rain tomorrow?

4 find out about a new TV series?

5 add your own comment about a news story?

6 read a longer article that explores a story in more depth?

/ 6 points

Words frequently used in news headlines

2 **Match words 1–8 to their meanings a–h.**

Headline word		More common equivalent	
1	axe	a	marry
2	plea	b	important, essential
3	wed	c	support
4	back	d	fire
5	key	e	cut, reduce
6	clash	f	request
7	quit	g	leave, resign
8	blaze	h	disagree violently

/ 8 points

Collocations connected with the news

3 **Choose the correct alternative.**

1 Tomorrow they're going to hold a *press conference/ headline* about the increase in organised crime.

2 There has been an interesting turn of *events/ news* in the negotiations.

3 We have an interesting *article/item* of news coming up now.

4 This news is hot off the *press/press conference*.

5 We'll keep you *aware/ informed* of any new developments in the situation.

6 Because of one stupid mistake he has become *front-page/bulletin* news.

/ 6 points

Total: / 40 points

Reading

Reading exam tip

In activities where you have to change a word to fit the text, remember …
Read the text first to understand the context and main point(s). Think about the type of word which is missing.

1 Complete the text with the correct form of the words given.

Virtual travel

People today want to know a lot about the places they are going to visit before they (a) .... (actual) book a trip or holiday. They want to know exactly what their hotel room will look like or what a tour will feel like so that nothing is (b) .... (expect). This means that potential customers are very (c) .... (care) before they commit to a booking and will gather a lot of information from reviews, images, (d) .... (describe) and opinions on social media. Virtual reality allows this investigative process to be (e) (shorten) .... and so the opportunities provided by technology are changing the way the travel industry operates. A key feature is the virtual reality booking process where, as you go through the steps to book your holiday, you can, for example, explore (f) .... (vary) rooms and facilities in a hotel and sample the local (g) .... (attract) as well as getting key information – all in the same place. The question is, if virtual reality can very (h) .... (close) replicate the experience of 'being there', will we still want to go there?

Reading exam tip

In matching activities, remember …
The words in matching texts may not be the same. Look for synonyms in the texts.

2 Match the people A–D with questions 1–10. The people may be chosen more than once.

THE BEST NEWS SITES
Four young people talk about the news sites they recommend.

A Pierre Dupont

I love *BuzzFeed* and I get all my news from it. I don't like the traditional news sites because they're quite boring in the way they present the news. People think *BuzzFeed* is only for unimportant news and making lists of silly things, but they've done some really good journalism and investigative work. I used to follow the news sites of the traditional newspapers but when *BuzzFeed* broke a story about a sports hero of mine I realised how good they were. I also think it's important that it's free – the ads don't bother me at all. I don't think websites like Google News™ are updated quickly enough and I tend to access the site all day in between work or during my lunch break.

B Sarah Holster

I usually read *The Guardian* every day because it's free online and it's updated a few times a day. It does have a lot of ads and I wish they didn't interfere with your reading so much. But generally I like the site – it's very easy to find the news you're interested in. I don't think I'd believe one of the newer online sites because they just want you to click on them to promote their ads, and I don't know where they get their stories from. It's funny because I never used to follow the news at all, but *The Guardian* has really converted me because of the way it looks.

C Maria Figueras

I get all my news from Google News™. I think it's the best way to do it because they gather together all the news from other sites, so what you read on there must be true. If a lot of news sites report something then it's more likely to be accurate I think. I tend to look at it last thing at night so I get my 'news' late but it gives me time to explore all the stories. I think there's much more on the site than you would find on a normal news site. I know some people think it's a very boring layout and presentation – but I don't really care about that as it's the information I want.

D Sanjeev Anand

I get all my news from Twitter®. I realise it's not formal news in the way that you have reports and so on, but it's the most brilliant way to find out what's going on. For a start, it's instant so you see something is happening before more traditional news sites. Then you get a lot of people putting references to articles and comments in so you know you're getting the full picture. Obviously, it depends who you follow but you can get all the major news sites on Twitter®. It's good because I can easily check the news on my phone wherever I am and I like following the links until I find the information I need – it's like detective work.

Which person …

1 likes to read the news constantly? ....
2 prefers reading the news at the end of the day? ....
3 is irritated by the number of adverts? ....
4 appreciates the convenience of the site? ....
5 thinks that news on the site must be true? ....
6 values the immediacy of the news on the site? ....
7 enjoys the less serious aspects of the site? ....
8 likes the layout of the news site? ....
9 changed their mind after reading some news? ....
10 thinks news from many sources is better? ....

Exam success
Listening and Writing ⟩ page 148

The press and news in your country

Virtual Classroom Exchange

1 SPEAKING Starting point

Look back at the text about the British press on page 130. At the moment, do you know enough to write a similar text about the press and news in your country?

2 SPEAKING Project task

A UK school is doing some research. They want to know about the press in your country and how teenagers follow the news. You are going to use your own knowledge and experience to search the Internet for information and answer them. Prepare one of these:

A poster   **C** video message

B presentation   **D** information leaflet

Research areas

- your country or region's main newspapers – physical or online
- the most important news channels, news readers and news programmes on TV
- any other online news sources
- some statistics and information about how and how much people in your class and/or teenagers in general follow the news

3 Think about ...

Digital skills

When you look at a website, it's important to think critically about what you find there. Does the website appear to be reliable? Who is the author of the website? Does the website seem to have any particular bias? Compare any surprising information you find there with other websites or sources.

Academic skills

Think about the best way to present different types of information. For example, it may be clearer to present some information or statistics by using a graph, diagram or illustration. Also, when you give data or statistics, don't forget to mention the source (the place where you found them).

Collaboration

When you work in a team, it can be helpful to take action and make suggestions early instead of waiting until problems develop. If nobody else is volunteering, you can politely offer to take the initiative.

Useful language

I don't mind doing ..., I'm happy to ..., Why don't I ...? If you want, I'll ..., Would you like me to ...?, If you like, I can ...

Intercultural awareness

In 2017, a survey by the European Broadcasting Union found that the British public distrusts its written press more than any other country in Europe. What might explain this distrust? How do you think your country compares and why?

4 SPEAKING Project time

Do the project. Then present it to the class.

5 Evaluation

Give each project a mark from 1 to 5 (5 = very good) for these categories.

Content ☐   Design ☐

Presentation ☐   Language ☐

Reach higher

UNIT 1

Vocabulary in context (page 6)

Write one subject that you can study at school or university for each letter of the alphabet. Leave any difficult letters.

A – architecture, B – business studies, C – chemistry

Reading (page 7)

Write one or two sentences to explain why each of these things, numbers or places is mentioned in the forum on page 7.

1 hockey
2 RoboCup
3 chocolate
4 the UN
5 the Canary Islands
6 £30,000

Grammar in context 1 (page 9)

Write a true sentence about yourself using the word given and the present perfect simple or present perfect continuous.

1 never
2 already
3 since
4 just
5 yet
6 for

Developing vocabulary (page 9)

Write an unusual short story containing as many examples of words or expressions that we use with *do* and *make*. How many can you include?

'Yesterday I did a difficult maths exam. I tried to do my best but …'

Grammar in context 2 (page 12)

Complete this exam advice with the gerund or infinitive form of the verbs given.

1 Make sure you have enough time .... (finish) the exam.
2 .... (start) the exam before you have read all the questions is a bad idea.
3 We suggest .... (take) more than one pen or pencil to the exam.
4 Don't write too fast or carelessly to avoid .... (create) a bad impression.
5 Think about .... (leave) yourself time .... (check) your work before you hand it in.
6 Check you know how many questions you need .... (complete) because sometimes they aren't all obligatory.

UNIT 2

Vocabulary in context (page 18)

Which words from page 18 could you use to talk about these jobs? Write lists.

1 server in a fast food restaurant
2 worker in a car factory
3 company director
4 firefighter

Reading (page 19)

According to the information from the texts on page 19, do these statements talk about Lidia Huayllas (LH), Laila Shabir (LS), both (B) or neither (N)?

1 They are working to inspire more girls or women to follow their example.   LH/LS/B/N
2 They are married.   LH/LS/B/N
3 They always had a clear idea what job they would finally do.   LH/LS/B/N
4 They are thinking of retiring.   LH/LS/B/N
5 We know they had some training specifically for the job they do today.   LH/LS/B/N
6 They always work alone.   LH/LS/B/N

Grammar in context 1 (page 21)

Choose the best alternative. If you think both alternatives are correct, choose both.

1 When I was small, I *used to/would* have a skateboard.
2 My brother *lived/used to live* in France for a month.
3 When I was ten, I *used to/would* play computer games for hours.
4 Once, my friend *met/would meet* a famous actor.
5 At primary school, I *used to/would* go home for lunch.
6 In the past, everything *used to/would* be cheaper.

Developing vocabulary (page 21)

Complete the phrasal verbs with the correct form of the appropriate verb.

1 Don't stop trying! .... at it!
2 I'm ambitious. I want to .... ahead and be the boss one day.
3 Don't forget to .... in this section of the questionnaire with your address.
4 They offered me a promotion but I .... it down.
5 You need a lot of money to .... up a new business.
6 We need to work faster if we want to .... up with our competitors.

Grammar in context 2 (page 24)

Write sentences in the past perfect simple or continuous using the ideas in bold to explain the situations.

1 Why was the little girl upset? **somebody steal sweets**
2 Why were her hands dirty? **work all morning in the garden**
3 Why did she feel really sleepy? **study for hours**
4 Why didn't he want to read the book? **read it twice before**
5 Why were their arms tired? **do exercise all afternoon**

Vocabulary in context (page 32)

Write a definition or an example sentence to show the meaning of these words.

1	crew	3	delay	5	voyage
2	tyre	4	off-peak	6	commute

Vocabulary in context (page 32)

Read the dictionary and answer the questions on page 32.

excursion (n) a short journey that you take for pleasure, or a short visit to an interesting place, for example one arranged by a tourist organisation: *an excursion to Edinburgh Castle*

journey (n) an occasion when you travel from one place to another, especially when there is a long distance between the places: *We had a long journey ahead of us.*

travel (n) the activity of travelling: *Foreign travel never really appealed to him until he retired. Our agency deals mostly with business travel.*

trip (n) an occasion when you go somewhere and come back again: *a fishing/camping/sightseeing trip*

voyage (n) a long journey, especially by boat or into space: *the long voyage home*

Reading (page 33)

Answer the questions for the text on page 33.

1 Why are countries so interested in stopping the sale of petrol or diesel cars?
2 Why won't electric cars solve all the problems of pollution?
3 What type of autonomous cars exist at the moment?
4 What reasons explain why in the future sharing cars might be more popular than buying them?
5 Why does the writer say that maybe in the future there won't be any cars?

Grammar in context 1 (page 34)

Complete the sentences with *will*, *going to*, or the present continuous.

1 I decided years ago that I .... (drive) an electric car when I am older.
2 Scientists believe that cars .... (become) better drivers than people.
3 When you .... (be) old enough, you'll be able to ride a motorbike.
4 It's clear that car computer systems .... (need) good Internet connections.
5 Next year the city .... (open) a new public transport system.

Developing vocabulary (page 35)

Which prefix can we use to add each meaning below to another word? Write at least one example word for each prefix.

1	after	3	incorrect, wrong	5	too much
2	before	4	below	6	again

Grammar in context 2 (page 39)

Write six predictions about life in the year 2099: two with the future continuous, two with the future perfect simple and two with the future perfect continuous.

UNIT 4

Vocabulary in context (page 44)

Write one adjective from page 44 which is either similar to or the opposite of the adjectives (1–6) below and write S (similar) or O (opposite) after your adjective. Then tick the adjectives you could use to describe yourself.

1 humble   S / O   4 introverted S / O
2 broad-minded   S / O   5 diplomatic   S / O
3 untrustworthy S / O   6 relaxed   S / O

Reading (page 45)

Answer the questions for the text on page 45.

1 How does Lucy describe her attitude to parties?
2 How is the difference between shyness and introversion explained?
3 Why do some people believe that society should pay more attention to introverts?
4 What talents does Lucy think quiet people bring to collaborative assignments at school?

Grammar in context 1 (page 47)

Write six sentences comparing two famous people. Three sentences must contain comparative adverbs, one must contain a comparative adjective, one *less* and another *not as*.

Developing vocabulary (page 47)

Make nouns from these words using suffixes. You may need to change the spelling. Sometimes you can make more than one noun from each word.

act • appear • confident • create • different • educate • electric • employ • happy • improve • invent • investigate • mad • music • relevant • science

Grammar in context 2 (page 51)

Write one sentence about yourself ...

1 to talk about a present ability.
2 to talk about a possible future ability.
3 using an infinitive to talk about an ability.
4 to talk about a general ability in the past.
5 to talk about the ability to do something on one specific occasion in the past.

UNIT 5

Vocabulary in context (page 58)

Write a sentence to explain the difference or relationship between these words.

1 receipt/refund
2 discount/sale
3 cash/coin
4 tighten your belt/throw money down the drain
5 follow a budget/get into debt
6 be a bargain/cost an arm and a leg

Reading (page 59)

Write sentences to explain why each number is mentioned in the texts on page 59.

1 1661   3 2012   5 1696
2 80%   4 20%   6 240,000

Grammar in context 1 (page 61)

Write these sentences in the past.

1 She must arrive on time every morning.
2 Do you have to go to the meeting?
3 We mustn't wear jeans and T-shirts.
4 I don't need to get up early (but I do).
5 She doesn't need to wear a uniform (so she doesn't).
6 We ought to work as a team.

Developing vocabulary (page 61)

Look at the definitions. What is the phrasal verb from page 61?

1 give someone the same amount of money they lent you
2 save money from a larger amount to use it later
3 reduce the amount of money you spend
4 buy something expensive
5 have just enough money so that you can do what you need to
6 contribute money to help to pay for something

Grammar in context 2 (page 65)

Invent and write a sentence to say that you …

1 are 90% certain that something is true.
2 are 50% certain that something was true in the past.
3 are 90% certain that something was not true in the past.
4 think there is a 50% possibility that something isn't true.
5 are 90% certain that something was true in the past.
6 think there is a 50% possibility that something was not true in the past.

UNIT 6

Vocabulary in context (page 70)

Write a definition or an example sentence to show the meaning of these words.

1 prescription   4 eyelid
2 fracture   5 infectious
3 ribs   6 GP

Reading (page 71)

Answer the questions for the text on page 71.

1 Why does the writer stress the importance of washing your hands in this dystopian world?
2 Why does the writer mention the 1850s?
3 What is the technique for disinfecting water without using fuel?
4 How does this technique work?
5 What are the problems with simple herbal remedies?
6 What is the writer's main message in the last paragraph?

Grammar in context 1 (page 73)

Complete the sentences in a logical way.

1 If you dislocate your shoulder, …
2 If I catch a cold next week, …
3 If my friend had terrible flu, …
4 Unless you have clean drinking water, …
5 I would be happy on a desert island as long as …
6 On a desert island, I would take a knife in case …

Developing vocabulary (page 73)

Correct these expressions to create six idioms connected with health and illness. Write a short explanation to show the meaning of each idiom.

1 to be full of the world
2 to be back on your health
3 to be on your last beans
4 to be the picture of legs
5 to be under the feet
6 to be on top of the weather

Grammar in context 2 (page 77)

Rewrite the incorrect sentences.

1 I wish I'm on a beach right now.
2 I wish you didn't interrupt me when I'm talking.
3 If only I studied more last night.
4 If only I'd won that competition last week.
5 If only I can pass my exams without studying.
6 I wish you'd tell me the truth yesterday.

UNIT 7

Vocabulary in context (page 84)

Which word does not belong in the group?
Write a sentence explaining why.

1 indie folk rom-com R&B
2 songwriter track audience villain
3 clichéd fast-moving gripping intriguing
4 gig soundtrack screenplay main characters
5 album CD download box office

Reading (page 85)

Imagine that the company that makes the short story vending machines wants to introduce them into your city. Where do you think it would be a good idea to install them? Do you think they would be popular? Would you use them? Write four or five sentences to answer the questions and give reasons.

Grammar in context 1 (page 87)

Report the conversation using *said*, *told*, *asked* and *wanted to know*.

Olivia: (1) Have you ever been to a music festival?

Tom: (2) Yes, I have. (3) I went to one last year.

Olivia: (4) Who was the best band?

Tom: (5) I really enjoyed Billie Eilish. (6) I may see her again if it's not too expensive.

Developing vocabulary (page 87)

Match the words to form compound nouns.
Write a synonym or short explanation for each compound.

1 block   A come
2 draw   B out
3 break   C hanger
4 cliff   D buster
5 turn   E back
6 out   F through

Grammar in context 2 (page 91)

What comes after each of these reporting verbs – (a) an infinitive, (b) a gerund, or (c) a preposition plus a gerund? Write one example sentence for each.

1 confess   3 deny   5 claim
2 offer   4 insist   6 regret

UNIT 8

Vocabulary in context (page 96)

Write a sentence to explain the difference or relationship between these words.

1 tremor/aftershock
2 volcanic eruption/ molten lava
3 evacuate/evacuee
4 blizzard/avalanche
5 flood/flash flood
6 survivor/casualty

Reading (page 97)

Which of the technologies described in the text on page 97 do you think is the most useful and why? Write four or five sentences explaining the characteristics of the technology that you think make it so useful.

Grammar in context 1 (page 99)

Rewrite the sentences using the passive. Use the person or people as the subject.

1 The government has sent food and medicine to the victims.
2 They're offering the survivors financial aid.
3 My teacher has given me information about earthquakes.
4 Perhaps they'll offer the casualties medical help.
5 They told her the news when she arrived.
6 The government have promised the scientists money.

Developing vocabulary (page 99)

Complete the sentences with the correct preposition.

1 Most people **agree** .... my theory.
2 People used to **believe** .... supernatural causes for natural disasters.
3 The strength of a volcano **depends** .... different factors.
4 The experts **apologised** .... not warning people about the tsunami.
5 Nobody **dreamt** .... something so big as a 40-metre wave.
6 Nobody knew who the dog **belonged** ....

Grammar in context 2 (page 103)

Rewrite the sentences.

1 They say that toads sense earthquakes. **Toads** ...
2 They know that bees are very important for the environment. **Bees** ...
3 People believed that the Titanic was unsinkable. **The Titanic** ...
4 They didn't know Everest was the highest mountain until 1852. **It** ...
5 They say that Pompeii is one of the most popular attractions in Italy. **Pompeii** ...
6 It's believed that a meteorite caused the extinction of dinosaurs. **A meteorite** ...

Reach higher

UNIT 9

Vocabulary in context (page 110)

Complete these words connected with technology. Write a short explanation of each word.

1 ....-resolution
2 ....weight
3 ....bait
4 ....screen
5 ....-............ menu
6 .... date

Reading (page 111)

Write one or two sentences to explain why each of these things, numbers, people or places are mentioned in the text on page 111.

1 Konstantin Novoselov
2 300
3 small transistors
4 Northwestern University
5 planes
6 Spider-Man

Grammar in context 1 (page 113)

Rewrite the sentences as one sentence using a non-defining relative clause.

1 The inventor of the remote control didn't like TV. His name was Robert Adler.

2 Remote controls were originally called 'space commands'. They first appeared in 1956.

3 Robert Adler went to university in Vienna. He was born there.

4 Adler was a brilliant physicist. He invented more than 180 different things.

5 In 2007, Robert Adler died. He was ninety-three that year.

6 Adler wasn't very interested in his own invention. It changed the way we live.

Developing vocabulary (page 113)

Write an unusual short story with as many of the phrasal verbs on page 113 as possible.

When my alarm clock went off yesterday morning, I got up, switched on my laptop and logged on to check my emails ...

Grammar in context 2 (page 117)

Decide if the sentences are correct. Rewrite the incorrect sentences.

1 I have to go back home because I forgot switching the lights off.

2 Can you remember bringing me my book tomorrow because I need it?

3 I think it's time to start revising for the exam.

4 Stop to play that song because it's awful.

5 I'll always remember to meet you last summer.

6 I love video games so much that I'll never stop playing them.

UNIT 10

Vocabulary in context (page 122)

Write one sentence explaining what you think these newspaper stories are about.

1 President pledges flood aid
2 New exams plan backed by universities
3 New virus sparks hospital bed fears
4 Investigators probe corruption claims

Reading (page 123)

Answer the questions for the texts on page 123.

1 What were the aims of the spaceship that was launched on 22nd February?

2 Why were tardigrades chosen for this mission?

3 Why did they evacuate the university library?

4 How did the evacuation affect students and how much disruption did it cause?

Grammar in context 1 (page 124)

Complete each expression of the future in the past in the text with just one word.

On Tuesday a baseball team was training. The next day they were (a) .... an important match. But next to the baseball field, a mother was (b) .... to leave her daughter at school. She had no idea what (c) .... happen next. She accidentally knocked her daughter over with her car! The team heard the accident and ran to help. They were (d) .... for a shock. The girl was under a wheel. The players quickly lifted the car. Thanks to them, the girl was (e) .... to survive!

Developing vocabulary (page 125)

Write a definition to explain each collocation connected with the news.

1 hot off the press
2 press conference
3 newsflash
4 newsreader
5 front-page news
6 take out a subscription

Grammar in context 2 (page 129)

Complete the second sentence so that it has a similar meaning to the first sentence, using the word given. Use between two and five words.

1 Was Mike talking to a friend?
   I'd like to .... to a friend. (whether)

2 What do other people think of incidents like this?
   I .... of incidents like this. (wonder)

3 Is it the first time this has happened?
   Do you .... the first time this has happened? (if)

4 Why did you give the picture to an expert?
   Can I ask .... the picture to an expert? (why)

Writing checklist ☑

Great writers check their work carefully to find and correct any mistakes before they complete their final version. Here are the top ten things to check:

1 Content

Check that you have answered the specific question and done everything that appears in the task.
Think about these things:

- Is it easy to understand your ideas and opinions?
- Have you given reasons or examples to illustrate your ideas?
- Have you used the correct number of words?

2 Style

Make sure that you have written in an appropriate style for the task (e.g. formal/informal). Is your writing interesting, informative, descriptive ...?

3 Paragraphs and organisation

Check that you have paragraphs made up of different sentences talking about one main topic or idea. Make sure the paragraphs are in a logical order.

4 Linkers

Check that you have used a variety of linkers (e.g. *firstly*, *furthermore*, *however* ...) to join your ideas clearly and appropriately.

5 Grammar

Check for any mistakes with verb agreement, tenses, prepositions, word order, regular and irregular forms, etc. Be particularly careful with the new grammar you have just learnt in the unit.

6 Vocabulary

Use a wide range of vocabulary and try not to repeat the same words. A dictionary and thesaurus can help. See www.macmillandictionary.com

7 Spelling

If you aren't sure how to spell a word, check in a dictionary. See www.macmillandictionary.com

8 Punctuation

Check your use of commas, full stops, question marks, exclamation marks, etc.

9 Capital letters

Make sure you have used capital letters correctly (e.g. for the first word in the sentence, names, nationalities, days of the week, months, etc.).

10 Presentation

Decide if it is easy to read your handwriting. Are you proud of the presentation?

Model texts

- an informal email
- a story
- an opinion essay 1
- an article 1
- a formal email
- a for-and-against essay
- a review
- an opinion essay 2
- a report
- an article 2

— Workbook

Unit 1

Great learners are good decision-makers.

"It is essential to learn to make good decisions in life, not just at school or in your studies. The decisions you make have all sorts of consequences that can affect your future and your happiness. Consider all the facts, but also your feelings too. And if you make a wrong decision, stay positive and learn from it. It will almost certainly help you make better decisions in the future."

How good are you at making decisions? Grade yourself from 1 to 5.

| 1 | 2 | 3 | 4 | 5 |

Unit 2

Great learners are reflective.

"It is important to be able to give honest consideration to your own strengths and weaknesses. Knowing the things that you are good at can help give you confidence. Being aware of your weaknesses can help you to improve and develop in those areas."

Are you good at being reflective? Grade yourself from 1 to 5.

| 1 | 2 | 3 | 4 | 5 |

Unit 3

Great learners are good at problem-solving.

"In many situations in life, there is not just one easy solution. You have to analyse the situation from different angles and use creativity, common sense and imagination to find intelligent solutions for the problem in question. It's also important to listen to other people and their opinions and ideas."

How good are you at problem-solving? Grade yourself from 1 to 5.

| 1 | 2 | 3 | 4 | 5 |

Unit 4

Great learners are open-minded and positive towards others.

"Stereotypes can sometimes help us to generalise, but they can also simplify our thoughts and reactions in unhelpful and inflexible ways. Great learners remain open-minded towards other individuals because each individual is different. They also remain positive towards other, different individuals and communities."

Are you open-minded and positive towards others? Grade yourself from 1 to 5.

| 1 | 2 | 3 | 4 | 5 |

Unit 5

Great learners take responsibility for their own actions.

"When we are very young, our parents are legally responsible for us, and our family and teachers often help us to do most things. But as we grow up, we have to take on more and more responsibility for our own actions, including our studies, our health and our finances. To make good decisions, we need to talk to others, listen to experts and then make sensible decisions for ourselves, not make excuses or pass on the responsibility for our own actions onto others."

Do you take responsibility for your own actions? Grade yourself from 1 to 5.

| 1 | 2 | 3 | 4 | 5 |

Unit 6

Great learners look after their physical health.

"Healthy eating and physical exercise are not just good for your body but for your mind, too. A balanced diet can actually help your brain to function better, and it can also improve your mood. Physical exercise can improve concentration, too. So, always remember the old expression, 'a healthy mind in a healthy body'."

How good are you at looking after your own health? Grade yourself from 1 to 5.

| 1 | 2 | 3 | 4 | 5 |

Unit 7

Great learners think creatively.

"Creativity is obviously important in the arts, but thinking creatively is incredibly important in all areas of study and life, not just the arts. Coming up with new, original ideas can be just as important as knowledge since thinking creatively can help you to find solutions to all sorts of problems that face us in life."

Are you a creative thinker? Grade yourself from 1 to 5.

| 1 | 2 | 3 | 4 | 5 |

Unit 8

Great learners justify their opinions.

"It's easy to give an opinion or to say you agree or disagree with something. But to show that you have understood a complex question, or to convince somebody that your opinion has a solid and valid foundation, it's important to give logical, objective reasons and arguments to justify your opinion."

Are you good at justifying your opinions? Grade yourself from 1 to 5.

| 1 | 2 | 3 | 4 | 5 |

Unit 9

Great learners can make reasoned use of new technologies.

"New technologies are a powerful tool that can help more effective learning. The important thing is to think critically about which technologies are useful and when. Some technology can speed up your work, and some may be a distraction. Think objectively to weigh up your decisions."

Is your use of new technologies reasonable? Grade yourself from 1 to 5.

| 1 | 2 | 3 | 4 | 5 |

Unit 10

Great learners are informed and knowledgeable.

"Whatever you enjoy studying now, want to study in the future, or would like to do professionally, it is all, to some degree, related to and influenced by current affairs, things happening nationally and internationally. By exploring questions and events happening locally and globally, you will gain knowledge and develop understanding in a wide variety of areas."

Do you keep yourself informed and knowledgeable? Grade yourself from 1 to 5.

| 1 | 2 | 3 | 4 | 5 |

Listening

7 🔊 **For each question, choose the correct answer.**

1 You hear two friends talking about a music concert. How does the boy feel?

   A worried that he won't remember the songs

   B nervous about performing for the first time

   C concerned that too few people will attend

2 You hear part of an interview with a designer. What does he enjoy about his career?

   A He can work on something different every day.

   B The possibility of working by himself rather than with a company.

   C He can make a lot of money quickly.

3 You hear a news report about a travel company. Why is the company changing its location?

   A to reduce costs

   B to increase customers

   C to change the business

4 You hear a student talking about the environment. Why did he take part in a project?

   A It offered an opportunity to work abroad.

   B It allowed him to work in a team.

   C It was a chance to learn new skills.

5 You overhear a dad talking to his son. What is he talking about?

   A his son's poor behaviour

   B his son's progress at school

   C his son's relationship with his friends

6 You hear a girl talking about a summer camp she went to. What did she dislike about it?

   A being with so many other people

   B being forced to do some activities

   C being in the same place for so long

7 You hear part of a programme on the natural world. What is the presenter doing?

   A giving information about an extreme place

   B describing a problem with a natural feature

   C giving reasons for visiting extreme places

8 You hear two students talking about a future career. What do they agree about?

   A positive they'll be accepted on the course

   B relieved that the training is very thorough

   C confident that they have the necessary skills

Writing

8 **Read the task and write your essay. Write your answer in 140–190 words.**

In your English class you have been talking about education. Now your English teacher has asked you to write an essay for homework.

Write your essay using all the notes and giving reasons for your point of view.

> Some people think it's not important for everyone to go to university.
> Do you agree?
>
> Notes
> Write about:
> 1 get a good education
> 2 learn as you work
> 3 .... (your own idea)

9 🗣 SPEAKING 👥 **Exchange essays with a partner. Use the Writing checklist on page 141 to check your partner's essay and give suggestions to help them improve.**

Listening

6 🔊 **ES2** **You will hear a student talking about a man called Phineas Gage whose personality changed. Complete the text with a word or short phrase in each gap.**

Phineas Gage

When he was 25, Gage was very well thought of by his (a) ....

The explosion where he was working meant a large amount of (b) .... flew into the air.

Immediately after the accident, people thought Gage was fine because he was still (c) ....

A sign that Gage was changing was that he told (d) .... that didn't make any sense.

One apparent impact on his thinking ability was noticed because he struggled to calculate (e) ....

Gage became important as it was the first time the link between the brain and (f) .... was established.

People queried the value of the study into Gage because it didn't have good (g) ....

Although the fact Gage changed was accepted, there are doubts about how (h) .... that change was.

The case is important in showing how a myth is created from a small amount of (i) ....

The positive outcome was the insight the case gave scientists in understanding how (j) .... -making happens in the front part of the brain.

7 SPEAKING 👥 **Talk about personality.**

1 How far do you believe your personality can change?
2 What kind of events might make you change your personality?

Writing

8 **Read the task and write your essay. Write your answer in 140–190 words.**

In your English class you have been talking about travel. Now your English teacher has asked you to write an essay for homework.

Write your essay using all the notes and giving reasons for your point of view.

> Some people think that we shouldn't travel by plane anymore.
> Do you agree?
>
> ---
>
> Notes
> Write about:
> **1** the distance of some travel
> **2** the need to protect the environment
> **3** .... (your own idea)

9 SPEAKING 👥 **Exchange essays with a partner. Use the Writing checklist on page 141 to check your partner's essay and give suggestions to help them improve.**

Speaking

3 SPEAKING 🗣 **Read the task below. You are going to talk about this for two minutes.**

Imagine that your school has raised some money through a school fair and now has to decide what to spend the money on. Here are some ideas for spending the money. Talk to each other about the benefits of each idea.

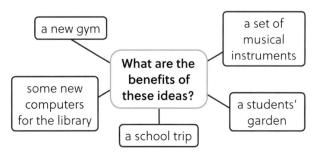

a new gym — **What are the benefits of these ideas?** — a set of musical instruments

some new computers for the library

a students' garden

a school trip

4 SPEAKING 🗣 **Now decide which two ideas would most benefit the students. You have one minute.**

5 SPEAKING 🗣 **Discuss with your partner. Did you each:**

- use correct grammar and vocabulary?
- take turns and listen to your partner?
- ask your partner questions?
- make suggestions?

Listening

6 🔊 ES3 **You will hear five short extracts in which people are talking about sports courses they attended. Choose from the list (A–H) what each speaker says about a course. There are three extra letters in the list that you do not need to use.**

A I was surprised that the course improved my performance.

B I was impressed that I could perform so well on the course.

C The course showed me how much mental activity was involved.

D The course was more complicated than I expected.

E I think the course offered more than I needed.

F I was pleased that the course helped me in a competition.

G The course has renewed my interest in my main sport.

H In the end I was glad I had to start from the beginning again.

Speaker 1 ☐
Speaker 2 ☐
Speaker 3 ☐
Speaker 4 ☐
Speaker 5 ☐

7 SPEAKING 🗣 **If you had the opportunity to do a sports course, which sport would you choose? Why?**

Writing

8 SPEAKING 🗣 **How important is it to take exercise to stay healthy? Give reasons.**

9 **Individually, read the announcement and write an email. Remember to use some of your ideas in 8.**

You have received an email from your English-speaking pen friend.

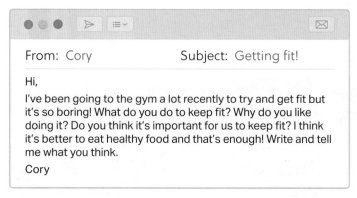

From: Cory   Subject: Getting fit!

Hi,

I've been going to the gym a lot recently to try and get fit but it's so boring! What do you do to keep fit? Why do you like doing it? Do you think it's important for us to keep fit? I think it's better to eat healthy food and that's enough! Write and tell me what you think.

Cory

Write your email in 140–190 words.

10 SPEAKING 🗣 **Exchange emails with a partner. Use the Writing checklist on page 141 to check your partner's email and give suggestions to help them improve.**

Speaking

6 You are going to talk about ways to protect the planet. Look at the questions below and think about what you could say in response to each of them.

- Do you think we should all do something to protect the planet or just governments?
- What do you think is the easiest thing individuals can do to help?
- Why do you think some people don't help with protecting the planet?
- How far do you think natural disasters are caused by climate change?
- Do you think countries should help each other in protecting the planet?
- What is one thing you would like to do to help protect the planet?

7 SPEAKING Discuss the questions in 6.

8 SPEAKING What is important in this part of the exam? How could you improve your answers? Think about:

- the range of grammar and vocabulary you used
- whether you fully answered the question you were asked
- if you made your opinion clear
- if you gave enough reasons or examples.

Writing

9 SPEAKING What do you think makes a good film? Why?

10 Individually, read the advert and write a review. Remember to use some of your ideas in 9 and make a recommendation.

You see this advert on an international film magazine website.

| HOME | FILM REVIEWS | FILM NEWS | ABOUT | Q |

REVIEWS WANTED!

We are looking for reviews of films for teenagers. Your review should include information about the plot, the acting, any special effects and any other important features. Would you recommend this film to other teenagers?

The best reviews will appear on this site next month.

Write your review in 140–190 words.

11 SPEAKING Exchange reviews with a partner. Use the Writing checklist on page 141 to check your partner's review and give suggestions to help them improve.

Listening

Writing

3 SPEAKING How important do you think it is for teenagers to know about world news?

4 ES4 You will hear a student called Harry who's talking about working for a teen news programme. Listen and choose the correct answers.

1 Harry says the focus of the news on the programme is …

A making sure the information is clear for a teenage audience.

B pointing out why the news is important for teenagers.

C ensuring all the facts are covered.

2 Why has the news programme become so popular?

A Each report is quite short.

B Only stories of interest are shown.

C Teenagers talk to each other about the news.

3 Why is having teenage presenters popular?

A They can both write and deliver the reports.

B They are role models for the audience.

C They are the same age as the audience.

4 Harry says teenagers are better presenters because …

A they find talking to the camera easy.

B they are used to working outside.

C they have a lot of followers on social media.

5 Harry says the programme covers a range of topics including …

A local news headlines

B film and theatre reviews

C training courses for teens

6 The news programme won an award for …

A the depth of its news stories.

B the number of public interest programmes.

C the balance of the way it structured its reports.

7 Harry says that sponsorship works well for the programme because …

A the companies have little individual influence.

B the adverts support the range of reporting.

C the programmes refuse to let them push products.

5 SPEAKING What would you like to learn that is new for you? How would you learn this?

6 SPEAKING What do you think can go wrong with technology? What might the effect of that be?

7 Individually, read the advert and write a story. Remember to use the correct sequence of tenses and some of your ideas in 6.

You see this advert in an English language magazine for young people.

Stories wanted!

We are looking for stories for our new English language magazine. Your story must **begin** with this sentence:

Celia switched the computer off and went to the door, but as she was closing it she heard the computer start up again.

Your story must include:

• a prize

• a happy ending

Write your story in 140–190 words.

8 SPEAKING Exchange stories with a partner. Use the Writing checklist on page 141 to check your partner's story and give suggestions to help them improve.

UNIT 3

Developing speaking
Exercise 5c, page 40

Student B:

> Compare the photographs and say what can be difficult about doing these things.

a

b

UNIT 4

Reading
Exercise 1, page 45

PERSONALITY TEST

Answer each question A or B. Then read the key below.

1 At the weekend I would prefer to **(A)** *stay at home watching a series with a friend or two* / **(B)** *go to a party*.

2 I feel **(A)** *very nervous* / **(B)** *quite comfortable* when speaking in public.

3 At school I prefer working **(A)** *individually* / **(B)** *in groups.*

4 I prefer **(A)** *listening to people talking about themselves* / **(B)** *telling people things about myself.*

5 I prefer **(A)** *relaxing weekends with time to think* / **(B)** *weekends with lots of activities in large groups.*

Key Look at your answers. If you answered A more often, you are more likely to be an introvert. If you answered B more often, you may be more of an extrovert.

UNIT 8

Developing speaking
Exercise 5a, page 104

Student B

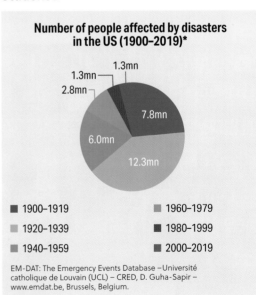

Number of people affected by disasters in the US (1900–2019)*

1.3mn
1.3mn
2.8mn
7.8mn
6.0mn
12.3mn

■ 1900–1919   ■ 1960–1979
■ 1920–1939   ■ 1980–1999
■ 1940–1959   ■ 2000–2019

EM-DAT: The Emergency Events Database −Université catholique de Louvain (UCL) − CRED, D. Guha-Sapir − www.emdat.be, Brussels, Belgium.

Communication activities

Exam success Units 3–4

Speaking
Exercise 4, page 56

Student B:

These are two photos showing different people. Compare the photos and say what you think these people are like.

UNIT 5

Developing speaking
Exercise 7a and 7b, page 66

Student B:

Compare the photographs. Then say how you think the people are feeling and why.

Irregular verbs

Infinitive	Past simple	Past participle
be	was/were	been
beat	beat	beaten
become	became	become
begin	began	begun
break	broke	broken
bring	brought	brought
build	built	built
burn	burnt	burnt
buy	bought	bought
catch	caught	caught
choose	chose	chosen
come	came	come
cost	cost	cost
cut	cut	cut
do	did	done
draw	drew	drawn
drink	drank	drunk
drive	drove	driven
eat	ate	eaten
fall	fell	fallen
feel	felt	felt
find	found	found
fly	flew	flown
forget	forgot	forgotten
forgive	forgave	forgiven
get	got	got
give	gave	given
go	went	gone
grow	grew	grown
hang out	hung out	hung out
have	had	had
hear	heard	heard
hide	hid	hidden
hit	hit	hit
hurt	hurt	hurt
keep	kept	kept
know	knew	known
lay	laid	laid
learn	learned/learnt	learned/learnt
leave	left	left

Infinitive	Past simple	Past participle
let	let	let
lie	lay	lain
lose	lost	lost
make	made	made
mean	meant	meant
meet	met	met
pay	paid	paid
put	put	put
read	read	read
ride	rode	ridden
ring	rang	rung
run	ran	run
say	said	said
see	saw	seen
sell	sold	sold
send	sent	sent
set up	set up	set up
shine	shone	shone
shoot	shot	shot
show	showed	shown
sing	sang	sung
sit	sat	sat
sleep	slept	slept
speak	spoke	spoken
speed	sped	sped
spell	spelt	spelt
spend	spent	spent
split up	split up	split up
stand up	stood up	stood up
steal	stole	stolen
swim	swam	swum
take	took	taken
teach	taught	taught
tell	told	told
think	thought	thought
understand	understood	understood
wake up	woke up	woken up
wear	wore	worn
win	won	won
write	wrote	written

Macmillan Education Limited
4 Crinan Street
London N1 9XW

Companies and representatives throughout the world

Gateway to the World B2 Student's Book ISBN 978-1-380-04311-5
Gateway to the World B2 Student's Book with Student's App and Digital Student's Book
ISBN 978-1-380-04308-5

Designed by EMC Design Ltd
Illustrated by Clive Goodyer (Beehive Illustration) p64; Szilvia Szakall (Beehive Illustration) p148
Cover design by Designers Educational

Cover photographs by Getty Images/Maskot (girl), Alamy Stock Photo/James (landscape)
Picture research by EMC Design Ltd

Author's acknowledgements
David Spencer would like to thank:
– everyone at Macmillan Education ELT who has worked on this project, for all their much-appreciated help, hard work, enthusiasm and dedication.
– all the many teachers from near and afar who have kept me company on the Gateway Facebook page during the whole time I was writing these books.
– all of my great students and colleagues from Colegio Europeo Aristos in Getafe, Spain, especially the 'Class of 2020' who made me smile every day as I was writing this course, and both Luís Ángel Ramírez Angulo and Susana Torres Ramos for their kind help.
– Emily Rosser, for making all of this possible.
– and, last but by no means least, Gemma, Jamie and Becky (and my Mum too, of course!), for all their encouragement, support and love, without which…

The authors and publishers would like to thank the following for permission to reproduce their photographs: 123rf/Vadim Guzhva p46 (br); Alamy/Allstar Picture Library Ltd. p88-89 (c), Alamy/Alpha Historica p24, Alamy/Avpics p39 (cl), Alamy/Mike Bilbao p66 (tl), Alamy/Roman Diachkin p74-75 (tl), Alamy/EThamPhoto p117 (bl), Alamy/eye35 p66 (tr), Alamy/Iurii Golub p135, Alamy/Dimitar Gorgev p2 (bl), Alamy/Jeffrey Isaac Greenberg 16+ p99 (l), Alamy/Lanmas p15 (tl), Alamy/Jacob Lund p78 (tc), Alamy/MBI p146, Alamy/MITO images GmbH p58 (tl), Alamy/Lennette Newell p129 (l), Alamy/PhotoAlto p12 (l), Alamy/Gary Roebuck p150 (br), Alamy/Kumar Sriskandan p150 (bl), Alamy/theatrepix p88-89 (t), Alamy/UPI p92, Alamy/Visions of America, LLC p67 (t), Alamy/Zoonar GmbH p109, Alamy/ZUMA Press, Inc. p7 (tc); Getty Images/aapsky p32 (tr), Getty Images/Tony Anderson p62-63 (c), Getty Images/Emilio Andreoli p53, Getty Images/Yuri_Arcurs p130, Getty Images/Ascent Xmedia p56 (cr), Getty Images/eli_asenova p6 (tl), Getty Images/Oksana Ashurova p114 (bl), Getty Images/AzmanJaka p59 (tc), Getty Images/Bettmann p52 (cl), Getty Images/BRPH p119 (), Getty Images/Peter Cade p13 (r-2), Getty Images/Peter Cade p124, Getty Images/Victor Chavez p87, Getty Images/Petar Chernaev p26, Getty Images/Colin Anderson Productions pty ltd p22-23 (c), Getty Images/Compassionate Eye Foundation/Robert Kent p78 (tl), Getty Images/Cultura p10-11 (t), Getty Images/Dhwee p22-23 (t), Getty Images/DMEPhotography p13 (r-1), Getty Images/Drazen_ p56 (br), Getty Images/duncan1890 p52 (bl), Getty Images/JOHANNES EISELE p3 (tr), Getty Images/JOHANNES EISELE p34, Getty Images/EyeEm p10-11 (c), Getty Images/f00sion p98, Getty Images/FatCamera p45 (tc), Getty Images/FatCamera p78 (t), Getty Images/fizkes p13 (r-4), Getty Images/Guasor p110 (tl), Getty Images/Viktoriia Hnatiuk p70 (bl), Getty Images/Belinda Howell p150 (tr), Getty Images/ivanastar p44 (tr), Getty Images/JanakaMaharageDharmasena p50, Getty Images/jcrosemann p99 (r), Getty Images/john finney photography p100-101 (t), Getty Images/Motoo Fujisawa / EyeEm p112 (l), Getty Images/Kmatta p70 (br), Getty Images/Ishii Koji p13 (r-3), Getty Images/LanaStock p36-37 (b), Getty Images/LightFieldStudios p27 (r), Getty Images/Philippe Lissac p57 (t), Getty Images/Ljupco p70 (tl), Getty Images/Long Feng / EyeEm p71 (tc), Getty Images/Matthias Makarinus p70 (tr), Getty Images/Mark Downey Lucid Images p96 (cr), Getty Images/Darren McCollester p62-63 (t), Getty Images/mediaphotos p96 (tr), Getty Images/monkeybusinessimages p114-115 (bl), Getty Images/monkeybusinessimages p144, Getty Images/Motortion p96 (tl), Getty Images/NASA Photo p38, Getty Images/olaser p6 (tr), Getty Images/Andriy Onufriyenko p65, Getty Images/Correia Patrice / EyeEm p20, Getty Images/Picturenow p77, Getty Images/Spencer Platt p100-101 (c), Getty Images/Niccoló Pontigia / EyeEm p84 (tr), Getty Images/portishead1 p150 (tl), Getty Images/Print Collector p51, Getty Images/Print Collector p59 (tr), Getty Images/Prostock-Studio p84 (tl), Getty Images/Dave Reginek p118, Getty Images/RuslanDashinsky p97 (tl), Getty Images/RONALDO SCHEMIDT p103 (), Getty Images/Steve Schofield p73, Getty Images/skynesher p116, Getty Images/solarisimages p58 (br), Getty Images/South_agency p126-127 (c), Getty Images/stockdevil p117 (tr), Getty Images/Studia72 p102 (r), Getty Images/sturti p39 (tr), Getty Images/Bob Thomas p129 (r), Getty Images/TPN p79 (t-2), Getty Images/KENZO TRIBOUILLARD p3 (tl), Getty Images/KENZO TRIBOUILLARD p35, Getty Images/Underwood Archives p52 (tl-a), Getty Images/Valeriy_G p67 (b), Getty Images/Klaus Vedfelt p31, Getty Images/vgajic p40 (br-A), Getty Images/vicnt p71 (tl), Getty Images/Hector Vivas p96 (bl), Getty Images/vm p83, Getty Images/Chanin Wardkhian p78 (bl), Getty Images/Chris Ware p52 (tl-b), Getty Images/Wavebreakmedia p2 (b – inset), Getty Images/Westend61 p64 (tl-b), Getty Images/Westend61 p108, Getty Images/Witthaya Prasongsin p13 (tl), Getty Images/Yellowdog Productions p105, Getty Images/Topp_Yimgrimm p63 (cr), Getty Images/YinYang p74-75 (c), Getty Images/Yozayo p58 (tr); Macmillan Education Limited© Hello Lovely/Getty Images p13 (r-5), Mars/Cultura p30, Mars/d3sign p3 (cr), Mars/Freeartist/iStockphoto p57 (t-inset), Mars/Stefano Lunardi/Getty Images/p79 (t-4), Mars/mixetto/Getty Images/p44 (tl), Mars/Ariel Skelley/Getty Images/p147, Mars/Mark Thompson/Getty Images/p79 (t-3); Shutterstock/A_Lesik p149 (b), Shutterstock/Kaponia Aliaksei p32 (tl), Shutterstock/architect9 p122 (tr), Shutterstock/Angyalosi Beata p64 (tl-a), Shutterstock/BONNINSTUDIO p111 (tl), Shutterstock/BONNINSTUDIO p111 (tc), Shutterstock/Boyko.Pictures p112 (r), Shutterstock/Marcelo Chello p79 (t-1), Shutterstock/cowardlion p32 (b), Shutterstock/ElenaChaykinaPhotography p85 (tl), Shutterstock/Everett Collection p102 (l), Shutterstock/Nick Fox p145, Shutterstock/garetsworkshop p27 (l), Shutterstock/Gary Roche Photography p15 (tr), Shutterstock/Antonio Guillem p14, Shutterstock/

Halfpoint p18 (tr), Shutterstock/Alan C. Heison p7 (tl), Shutterstock/KPG_Payless p97 (tc), Shutterstock/Ekaphon Maneechot p110 (tr), Shutterstock/metamorworks p33 (tl), Shutterstock/Supagrit Ninkaesorn p18 (tl), Shutterstock/nnattalli p40 (br-B), Shutterstock/Lena Pan p78 (br), Shutterstock/Pixel-Shot p122 (tl), Shutterstock/PR Image Factory p12 (r), Shutterstock/Sashkin p64 (tl-c), Shutterstock/Elena Sherengovskaya p48-49 (c), Shutterstock/Drozdin Vladimir p149 (t).

Commissioned photograph by Pepe Sánchez Moreno p3
Video footage and stills supplied by Digital Learning Associates pp37(t),115(t); Fortemus Films Ltd. p3

The authors and publishers are grateful for permission to reprint the following copyright material:
p85, Alison Flood, 'Short story vending machines to transport London commuters' (2nd April, 2019) The Guardian © Guardian News & Media Limited, https://www.theguardian.com
p85, Esther Addley, 'Free short story vending machines delight commuters' (6th April, 2019), The Guardian © Guardian News & Media Limited, https://www.theguardian.com

Additional sources:
data on p19: Christina Gough, 'Game developer distribution wordwide 2014-2019, by gender' (19th June, 2020) © Statista 2020
data on p19: Laila Shabir, 'How Getting More Girls to Make Video Games Will Change the Gaming Industry' (24th July, 2019), Teen Vogue, https://www.teenvogue.com/
data on p25: 'Turning the ugliest fruit into the loveliest juice', 27th April, 2019, The Week Junior, https://theweekjunior.co.uk/
data on p25: 'How to own and run a sustainable business: Karina's story', https://www.bbc.co.uk/bitesize/articles/zhrgmfr, accessed: 10/12/2020
data on p33: 'World Energy Outlook 2018' (Nov 2018), International Energy Agency © IEA 2018, https://www.iea.org/
data on p33: Mikhail Chester, Andrew Fraser, Juan Matute, Carolyn Flower, and Ram Pendyala, 'Parking Infrastructure: A Constraint on or Opportunity for Urban Redevelopment? A Study of Los Angeles County Parking Supply and Growth', Journal of the American Planning Association, 2015, 81(4), pp. 268-286, doi: 10.1080/01944363.2015.1092879
data on p35: 'Now France's Franky Zapata has flying car on his mind' (5th August 2019), The Connexion, https://www.connexionfrance.com
data on p45: Susan Cain, Quiet Power (Penguin Life, 2016)
data on p45: Susan Cain, 'Revenge of the introverts: It's often assumed extroverts do best in life, but a new book reveals quite the opposite…', adapted by Marianne Power (26 March 2012), Daily Mail, https://www.dailymail.co.uk/femail/article-2120187/Revenge-introverts-Its-assumed-extrovertsbest-life-new-book-claims-quite-opposite-.html
data on p46: 'Effect of Facial Expression on Emotional State Not Replicated in Multilab Study' (27th Oct, 2016), Association for Psychological Science, https://www.psychologicalscience.org/
data on p48: McCrae RR, Terracciano A. Personality profiles of cultures: aggregate personality traits. J Pers Soc Psychol. 2005 Sep;89(3):407-25. doi: 10.1037/0022-3514.89.3.407. PMID: 16248722.
data on p58: Piper Jaffray & Co., 37th Semi-Annual Taking Stock With Teens® Survey (Spring, 2019) © 2019 Piper Sandler Companies
data on p58: '2019 JA Teens & Personal Finance Survey', Junior Achievement USA and Citizens Bank/Citizens One, accessed 19/10/2020
data on p59: Susan Fourtané, 'Sweden: How to Live in the World's First Cashless Society' (24th December, 2020), https://interestingengineering.com/sweden-how-to-live-in-the-worlds-first-cashless-society
data on p59: 'Towards a Cashless Society: Advantages and Disadvantages' (27th April, 2018), https://easycredit.com.sg/towards-a-cashless-society-the-advantages-and-disadvantages/
data on p59: '10 weirdest taxes in history', https://www.historyrevealed.com/eras/general-history/10-weirdest-taxes-in-history/, accessed: 08/01/2021
data on p59: 'The Week Junior' Issue 17 - July 24, 2020
data on p59: Nick Durrant, 'Do I need a TV licence?' (15th July, 2020), https://www.moneysavingexpert.com/utilities/tv-licence/
data on p89: Reagan, A.J., Mitchell, L., Kiley, D. et al. 'The emotional arcs of stories are dominated by six basic shapes', EPJ Data Sci. 5:31 (2016)
data on p91: Sara Bibel, '5 Little-Known Facts About How J.K. Rowling Brought Harry Potter to Life' (13th May, 2020), Biography, https://www.biography.com/
data on pp97: 104, 149: EM-DAT: The Emergency Events Database – Université catholique de Louvain (UCL) – CRED, D. Guha-Sapir – www.emdat.be, Brussels, Belgium
p104, data in audioscript: EM-DAT: The Emergency Events Database – Universite catholique de Louvain (UCL) – CRED, D. Guha-Sapir – www.emdat.be, Brussels, Belgium
data on p98: Aria Bendix and Peter Kotecki, 'Stunning facts reveal how much more devastating wildfire season has become in California and throughout the US' (12th Nov, 2018), Insider, https://www.insider.com/
data on p110: Research conducted by Dr Robbie Love, May-June 2019, from British language corpora
p110, data in audioscript: Research conducted by Dr Robbie Love, May-June 2019, from British language corpora
data on p113: 'The Realtime Generation: Rise of the Digital First Era' Logicalis UK © Logicalis, 2013
data on p113: Przybylski, A. K., & Weinstein, N. (2017), 'A Large-Scale Test of the Goldilocks Hypothesis: Quantifying the Relations Between Digital-Screen Use and the Mental Well-Being of Adolescents', Psychological Science, 28:2, 204–215. https://doi.org/10.1177/0956797616678438
data on p117: Beatrice Christofaro, 'Scientists found that we're spending so much time on our smartphones that it could be changing the shape of our skulls', (14th June, 2019), Insider, https://www.insider.com/
data on p127: Peter Cobus, 'Most Jailed Journalists? China, Turkey, Saudi Arabia, Egypt Again Top Annual CPJ Report', VOA News (2019)
data on p127: 'Democracy at Risk: Threats and Attacks Against Media Freedom in Europe', Council of Europe Annual Report © Council of Europe, February 2019

Printed and bound in Mexico
by Compañía Editorial Ultra, S.A. de C.V.

2022 2021
5 4 3 2